MANAGEMENT STRATEGIES FOR INFORMATION TECHNOLOGY

BUSINESS INFORMATION TECHNOLOGY SERIES

MANAGEMENT STRATEGIES FOR INFORMATION TECHNOLOGY

MICHAEL J. EARL

Director, Oxford Institute of Information Management
Fellow, Templeton College, Oxford

Prentice Hall

New York   London   Toronto   Sydney   Tokyo   Singapore

First published 1989 by
Prentice Hall International (UK) Ltd
Campus 400, Maylands Avenue
Hemel Hempstead
Hertfordshire HP2 7EZ
A division of
Simon & Schuster International Group

© 1989 Prentice Hall International (UK) Ltd

Printed and bound in Great Britain at the
University Press, Cambridge.

Library of Congress Cataloging-in-Publication Data

Earl, Michael J.
Management strategies for information technology/
Michael J. Earl.
p.   cm.
Bibliography: p.
Includes index.
ISBN 0–13–551664–1
1. Information resources management.
2. Information technology.   I. Title
T58.64.E37   1989
658.4′038–dc19   88–28682

British Library Cataloguing in Publication Data

Earl, Michael J.
Management strategies for information technology –
(Business information technology).
1. Great Britain. Business firms.
Management. Information systems.
Applications of computer systems
I. Title II. Series
658.4′038

---

12 13 14 15   98 97 96 95

ISBN 0-13-551664-1
ISBN 0-13-551656-0 PBK

CONTENTS

PREFACE

Computers are about 40 years old. Information technology (IT) is much younger – or it is as generally understood today. IT is the outgrowth of the micro-electronics revolution and comprises, besides all shapes and sizes of computers, automation technologies and communications. The notion that IT is strategic is newer still – at least in academic and professional literature. As we shall see, some companies actually began to exploit computing and related technologies for strategic advantage in the 1970s, if not earlier. However, the strategic opportunities and threats in the late 1980s are much more significant, not only because of the rapid advance of IT but also because of the accompanying economic and social changes that are unfolding. Thus IT has become an important support for many firms' strategies; moreover it has *created* new strategic choices for many companies. These are the themes and rationale of this book.

Accordingly, the approach is not technical. It is managerial. The early chapters suggest both why and how exploitation of IT must be connected to business strategy formulation. Subsequent chapters re-examine some traditional problems of information systems management from this strategic perspective. Throughout, the approach is analytical, the flavour practical and the objective prescriptive. The book draws on research, theory, teaching and practice.

Indeed *Management Strategies for Information Technology* has been heavily influenced by two complementary sets of activities. First, it is born out of the work my colleagues and I have done in the Oxford Institute of Information Management at Templeton College, Oxford. This includes research projects which have taken us into many UK organizations, and management development programmes we have undertaken for several large European business and government organizations. Second, it is grounded in my own advisory work in a number of major companies, where most of the ideas in the book have been applied and tested in some way. This is important for IT and strategy is a new, youthful area of enquiry and at this stage it is valuable to know which frameworks, principles and theories have been found most useful – and in which situations.

ix

In these last few years' work, I have been privileged to know and work with several leading IT directors and practitioners. As IT has become strategic and a source of competitive advantage, it would be insensitive perhaps to name these people and their organizations. However, I am indebted to them, not only for the opportunities they have given me, but also undoubtedly for some of the ideas and material in this book. They have been the business heroes of recent years, carving out quite new directions and ways of managing in their organizations. So, to Bob, Brian, Colin, David, Derek, Dick, Graham, John and Richard, I hope that my book adds something to the value you have given to me!

Much of the research I have done to produce this book was made possible by a grant from ICL UK Ltd, to whom I am grateful. The book never would have materialized without the word-processing skills and determination of Sarah Franklin and Cheryl Carter. Finally, without the support of the Council and Fellows of Templeton College, the Oxford Institute of Management would not have been founded. They saw that information management was going to be a key function and activity in the 1980s and 1990s. I hope that this book will make a contribution to understanding and managing this new era.

Michael J. Earl
Oxford

Chapter 1

THE IT ERA

INTRODUCTION

The concept of an information society where the economy is service-oriented is not new. The key resource is knowledge, and the enabling technology is information technology, especially telecommunications. Nor is it science fiction. Already variously defined and measured, information workers form the largest category of employees in advanced economies, technology accounts for over half of some sectors' capital formation, financial and commodity markets have become electronic, and generation gaps in 'computer literacy' are felt by the middle-aged and beyond. Thus in the late 1980s managers perceive that information technology (IT) is having a significant impact on business, government and organizational life *now*. They increasingly agree that IT has become a strategic resource as it brings about or facilitates major changes in industry sectors, in competitive behaviour and in organizations' own strategy, structure and functioning.

The technological thrust is based on the microelectronics-based convergence of data processing, telecommunications and automation together with the advances made in software, including electronic spreadsheets, fourth-generation languages and the development of knowledge-based systems and artificial intelligence. Equally important, however, this rapid technological advance is happening when many industrial companies arc fighting for survival under global competition, when sectors are changing shape due to liberalization and de-regulation, and when significant social change is emerging, including major new patterns of work, leisure and domestic life.

Thus, the aware chief executive, the advanced IT director, the innovative line manager and the knowledge-based professional sense that a new era in 'computing' has dawned – what might be called the *IT era*. Simultaneously, these same people may be conscious that we still have a legacy from the old era of data processing, which might be called the *DP era*. This includes disappointments with failed computer systems in the past, concern with the cost of computing, outdated concepts of technology, anxieties about human impacts, and very patchy management involvement, commitment and experience of computing across organizations. What becomes clear is that more than ever before IT is a resource that has to be *managed*. It cannot be left to the specialists and its management requires the extra dimension of *leadership*. This is because for many organizations not only has IT become strategic but doing something about it requires strategies for change. The case for strategically managing IT as a resource, and what this requires, is founded on nine statements about the new era.

THE STRATEGIC CASE

The following nine statements about IT suggest what is different in the new era from the past. Some trends are quite new, some represent 30 years' evolution of data processing, and some are seemingly eternal issues about the management of technology. They can be expressed as follows:

1. IT is a high-expenditure activity.
2. IT is critical to many organizations.
3. IT has become a strategic weapon.
4. IT is needed by our economic context.
5. IT is affecting all levels of management.
6. IT may mean a revolution for management information systems.
7. IT involves many stakeholders.
8. IT matters do matter.
9. IT management makes the difference.

Each of these propositions needs fuller discussion and is examined in turn in the rest of this section.

IT: a high-expenditure activity

IT is becoming a high-expenditure activity. It is often claimed that firms spend between 1 and 5 per cent of sales revenue on DP and then suggested that those at the lower end confine DP to a support, back-office role and those at the higher end aggressively exploit IT for strategic advantage. These claims are naïve, for measurement definitions vary, sectors differ, and cause and effect are difficult to measure. For example, some firms make effective use of 1 per cent DP budgets; others in sectors undergoing rapid structural change may be spending 10 per cent or more of sales on IT, and when microcomputing alone is added to mainframe computing, the ratio value may increase by perhaps a third.

> A decentralized conglomerate spent approximately £11.5 million p.a. on mainframe computing and related services. After just over two years of rapid diffusion of microcomputing, expenditure on personal computers totalled a further £4.25 million – which did not include all the hidden costs of user development, support and training, which may add the same cost again. Thus, in this period total computing expenditure was in the order of £15.75 million p.a. The further expenditure on manufacturing and automation technologies was not known.

Nevertheless, cost analysis can be instructive and it is evident that low levels of expenditure produce relatively low benefits whilst *relevant* investment in IT can pay off. The graphs in Figure 1.1 suggest that above-average spending on IT can help secure sector leadership in profitability performance. The detailed argument is not that high expenditure on IT yields higher profits (or that profitability allows high spending on IT!), but that, if appropriate levels of investment are made in IT to complement the strategic, structural and human factors required for sector leadership, IT can yield leverage – or has a multiplier effect. Figure 1.1 is based on US data.[1] However a UK survey found similar evidence: firms leading in the use of IT were more profitable than the laggards.[2]

More interesting than such annualized ratios are the growth figures. Large, leading European organizations' IT budgets are growing at between 20 and 40 per cent p.a. Indeed some firms who believe they must invest in IT for strategic reasons, or who are catching up with their sector, may have growth rates of between 60 and 100 per cent for two to three years or more. It would be difficult to find any other function of business with such budget trends. Indeed, in many UK firms, whereas there are across-the-board headcount restrictions or cut-backs, the IT function is the one exception. In short, IT is a growth function.

> A retail group which had for many years sought to minimize its DP activities, began to invest in electronic point-of-sale, communications networks to suppliers, mail order facilities and office automation. The group had observed similar recent initiatives by its competitors and embarked upon a catch-up, then leapfrog, strategy. In one year its IT expenditure rose by 180 per cent as a result. Three years later the spend was planned to be 235 per cent of the original base.

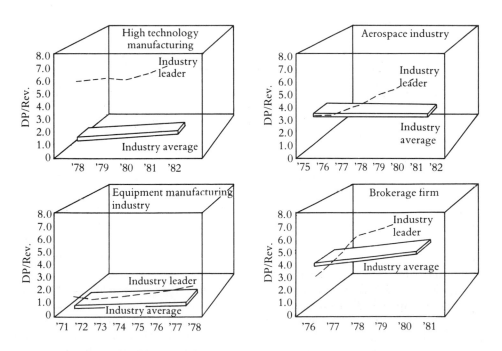

Figure 1.1 IT investment patterns by industry.

The make up of IT budgets is also revealing. Nolan, Norton & Company[1] have predicted that the typical organization will experience a sevenfold growth in its spending on computer-related activities during the 1980s. By 1990 DP spending is expected to have doubled, end-user computing to exceed traditional DP by 50 per cent and functional niche computing (automation, robotics, artificial intelligence etc.) to equal DP investment. In other words, by 1990 most expenditure will be on 'new' technologies – indeed this is already happening in some organizations.

If the IT budgets are then divided into the resource elements of technology and personnel, where technology comprises all hardware, communications and operating or packaged software, and personnel comprises all staff on IT department budgets, another interesting pattern emerges. Typically, in the latter part of the DP era and early stages of the IT era, expenditure on technology was reducing in proportion to personnel – mainly due to the unremitting annual 30 to 40 per cent improvement in hardware cost performance, and to a degree to market-pressured DP salaries. In the mid 1980s, as the pace of new technology adoption accelerates up the S-curves, the balance is changing, as depicted in Figure 1.2.

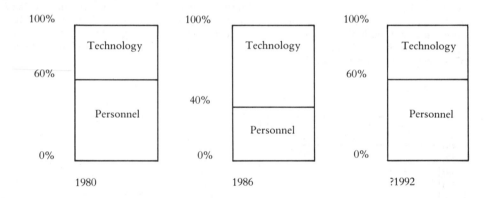

Figure 1.2 Expenditure by IT resource.

Many firms have adopted office or factory automation technologies, implemented communications networks or encouraged the diffusion of end-user computing, but have not fully *exploited* them yet. The technologies are purchased for an obvious early advantage or simple application, and 18 months to three years may elapse before major benefits accrue and more sophisticated applications are recognized and learnt. There is, therefore, both an upfront cost and a lag in capital productivity. Equally, however, the need for specialist personnel and for freeing users and managers to fully exploit these technologies is delayed. Furthermore, recruitment and development of appropriate personnel is slow and difficult because of national skill shortages. Thus, not only is expenditure on technology overtaking that spend on personnel but the benefits of IT may well be delayed until the balance is restored. However, the continued improvements in hardware performance, the lag in fully exploiting the technology, management pressures to deliver benefit, the continuing growth of applications backlog and the limits of application packages all suggest that the resource balance typical of the beginning of the 1980s might be required in the early 1990s. Achieving it may depend on availability of personnel.

> A manufacturing company, which saw and approved the need to invest in computing, communications and automation in order to meet increased customer demands for quality, service and flexibility, had to select a slow build-up IT strategy for one crucial reason. The scarcest resource was IT skills and the firm was located in a region where it was difficult to recruit.

The final cost picture is that of capital expenditure. Up to 50 per cent of firms' total capital expenditure today is often explained by information-related technologies. This applies to firms heavily dependent on IT, and some of them have never had major capital programmes before. For example, many of the institutions in the City of London preparing for the 'Big Bang' and its associated computer revolution in 1986 had to face up to capital funding and approval questions for the first time; their prior experience was confined to property decisions made by incremental or 'obvious' justifications.

The management implications of IT expenditure patterns, therefore, are several. The IT function is significant and growing. Appropriate investment can improve profit performance, and most expenditure will be incurred on the 'new' technologies. Personnel resources will become more crucial than technological resources over the next few years. IT is becoming, and has to be seen as, a capital expenditure item and not an operating expense. IT, therefore, must be properly funded, appropriately evaluated and sensibly controlled.

IT: critical to many organizations

Information processing and IT are becoming critical to many business and government operations. For example, without computing, retail banking would break down. Cheque and account processing volumes demand mainframe computing, the combination of customer service requirements and branch productivity needs demand networks of automatic teller machines (ATMS), and international transactions and settlements demand communications-based systems. In UK government, the Department of Health and Social Security's strategy for social security operations was essentially a strategy for IT, necessitating distributed processing, investments in databases and potential integration with taxation systems. Indeed not only are social security and income tax operations dependent upon computer systems; major policy changes – such as 'negative income tax' – are not feasible until the basic operational systems are automated.

However amidst the 'hype' of IT, managements need to understand whether, why and how IT is critical to their own organization. McFarlan and McKenney have provided a framework – their 'strategic grid' – which helps position a firm appropriately. The grid is shown in Figure 1.3, where the industry examples are mine. Where information systems are seen to be of little impact in the present or future, IT can be seen as a _support_ activity requiring average or below average investment, and only occasional senior management attention. It can be run as a 'don't call us we'll call you' service. Perhaps a cement company would fit this quadrant where some

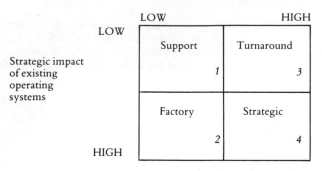

Strategic impact of application
development portfolio

Figure 1.3 IT strategic grid.

administrative systems help improve internal efficiency and islands of specialist technology may be gradually introduced to innovate the manufacturing process.

Where information systems are crucial to current operations and their management, but not at the heart of the company's strategic development, IT may be seen as a *factory* activity. Perhaps a steel works fits this quadrant. Advanced on-line real-time systems were designed in the DP era for planning and controlling iron and steel production. Once these fundamental systems are in place, however, future applications development will not make or break the business. Here IT can be run as 'a tightly managed shop which must not get beyond its station'. The IT budget will always be significant, the systems must operate reliably and efficiently, and the IT executive will have to be a strong, credible departmental manager.

If information systems have always been crucial to the organization and the future is dependent on, or shaped by them, the IT activity may be seen as truly *strategic*. A credit card company may occupy this quadrant. Indeed such a business operation is not feasible without computers, new products and services are computer-based, and possible diversification into banking, insurance, broking and the like – in short, into a financial services conglomerate – is dependent upon computers, telecommunications and integrated, relational databases. Here IT has to be run 'integral to the business' where product-market strategy and IT strategy are the warp and weft of business development. Investment in IT is likely to dominate the firm's capital budget, the IT director will be on or near the main board, and all managers will need to have a sound business understanding of IT.

In their 1981 annual report the American Express company produced a mission statement. One of the three competitive advantages upon which new businesses were to be built was: 'A global data processing and telecommunications network that is the foundation for our delivery systems and a key to keeping us an efficient, low cost producer.'

For many firms, IT is becoming strategic in that the computer systems being planned and developed soon will be critical to the organization's survival or growth. However in the past, IT may have been a lower profile activity. In such *turnaround* firms, IT budgets are jumping up step-curves, leadership is coming from the board, a top IT executive is being appointed, and education programmes on information management are being commissioned for senior executives. A variety chain store retailer exemplifies this quadrant. Computer systems had always underpinned backroom operations, particularly to minimize paperwork and reduce headcount. However as the retailer sought to improve its fashion responsiveness and profile, maximize both sales and stock turnover, and move into financial services it made a major investment in a communications network with its suppliers, in electronic point of sale and in charge card processing with customer databases. The IT activity had to be turned round and elevated in the company's thinking. In turnaround firms, therefore, IT has to be run in a 'let's get on with it' manner.

Three forces drive a firm around the strategic grid. First there is the matching between the potential of IT and the firm's operations and strategy. Next, there are the strategic choices which the executive management make about IT (e.g., whether to exploit IT to improve productivity, move into a new business etc.). Finally there are the changes unfolding in the firm's competitive environment. Thus it is clear that strategic grid positioning can only be done at the level of the strategic business unit, division or product-market entity. Consequently, in a divisionalized or diversified company, different businesses may occupy different quadrants of the grid. Therefore their IT activities will have to be managed differently. Equally the criticality of IT in any business may alter over time and it is important to recognize when a major change in management approach is required. Many businesses who yesterday thought they were in support or factory quadrants are finding that the IT requirements of their business strategies, the actions of their customers, suppliers or competitors, the structural changes in their sectors, or the new opportunities afforded by IT are pushing them rapidly into, and through, the turnaround quadrant.

> An apparel manufacturer found itself in the turnaround quadrant through all these driving forces. It had prided itself on spending 0.4 per cent of sales on DP and maintaining 'a strictly commercial attitude to DP'. Overseas competitors began to reduce costs, improve product quality and produce sophisticated clothing design by factory automation, introduction of production planning and control systems and computer-aided design. Key retail customers began to demand communications links to call off orders more quickly, access stock figures and improve despatch routines in order to back up the use of electronic point of sale information in the pursuit of flexibility and responsiveness. Suddenly the apparel manufacturer required more reliable basic business systems, greater telecommunications capacities, and extra IT skills to keep up with and possibly influence and lead the customers. The firm initiated turnaround management actions. A director for IT was appointed, a strategy study commissioned and a senior management education programme arranged.

The management implications of this analysis are that IT criticality depends on both past and future importance of information systems. This has to be assessed at the level of the strategic business unit reviewed over time as both internal and external forces change. Universal information management principles therefore are dangerous; management practices must fit the quadrant on the strategic grid. This situational approach will be developed in subsequent chapters.

IT: a strategic weapon

IT offers major new business and management opportunities. It has the potential to be a strategic weapon in at least four different ways:

1. To gain competitive advantage.
2. To improve productivity and performance.
3. To enable new ways of managing and organizing.
4. To develop new businesses.

Pursuit of *competitive advantage* implies the use of IT externally to disturb, enhance or limit the competitive forces at work in the firm's sector. This concept is developed further in Chapter 3, but can be demonstrated best by the example of Merrill Lynch's IT-based product, its cash management account (CMA).

> In 1977 Merrill Lynch established the CMA, combining a charge card, checking account and brokerage service into one product. It was one of the initiatives that led to the concept of the 'financial services' industry, because it broke through the traditional boundaries of the banking and securities sectors. Implementation of the CMA required a complex interface of data processing and data communications because Merrill Lynch needed the collaborative services of a selected bank – Bank One of Ohio – to provide the check and credit processing alongside brokerage work. By 1983 more than 915,000 accounts were in place, growing at 5,000 a week, of which 400,000 were new and the managed assets totalled $85bn. The nearest competitor only had 50,000 accounts, Merrill Lynch having 70 per cent market share.

Why were Merrill Lynch so successful? Clearly the CMA was new and satisfied a consumer need. However the infrastructure was complex and difficult to emulate quickly. By being first and IT-based, the CMA became a pre-emptive strike which created a barrier to entry. In the UK, the Nottingham Building Society's pioneering of home-banking using the PRESTEL viewdata network demonstrates similar points. A building society was able to move into banking, developing market share in new market segments and offering related services such as travel booking and portfolio management through its value-added network. This dramatically changed its profile and image.

The kernel of using IT for competitive advantage, therefore, is the use of IT and information processing in either the product or service, or in the channels of distribution and supply, or to change the basis of competition against rivals.

Productivity and performance were often the focus of computing in the DP era. In the IT era, the scope and the potential benefits are greater – and may be built upon for competitive advantage. The focus however is primarily internal. Ford in Europe provides a good example.[3]

Ford at the beginning of this decade were examining the requirements for a viable automobile manufacturing business for the next 20 years. The Japanese attack on export markets, predicted zero or low growth in European companies and over-capacity in the industry combined to paint a difficult scenario. Ford reasoned that survival depended on driving down costs rather than either raising prices or aiming for volume growth. However market share had to be maintained which demanded good and responsive product design, good and reliable product quality and customer satisfaction and loyalty.

The Ford in Europe Systems Office began to plan their IT investment on these assumptions. They developed business visions of CAD/CAM bringing quality products to the market faster, computer-integrated manufacturing driving down costs and raising quality, and telecommunications enabling the company to get closer to the customer. By 1986, 60 per cent of design work was computer-aided, manufacture was planned and controlled by systems built on the just-in-time philosophy – including links to suppliers and between factories – and dealers were using stock control systems, customer query and vehicle locater facilities and point of sale and finance contract routines based on terminals connected into the Ford network. IT had become the foundation of survival in improving productivity and performance. Indeed in 1986, computers and communications were part of Ford's total strategic review.

Exploitation of IT in new ways of managing and organizing has been demonstrated by Rank Xerox.[4] Their networking experiment which was designed around micro-computers, local area networks and mail and document transfer systems, allowed personnel to work from remote locations such as home. The reasons for the experiment were economic as much as social. Increased global competition in Xerography was driving down profits with consequent pressure on funds flow. Thus, research and development, which is vital to the industry, was under threat unless structural cost savings could be made. One way of attacking overheads was to radically change the employment of the firm's creative people, for often they were costly, mobile personnel who required a pleasant work environment. Also their typical job was to produce data, image or text output and they valued work autonomy, self-regulating their work pattern and methods. If they could work away from high cost offices and be fully or semi-autonomous, both economic and social goals might be achieved.

Appropriate output workers were identified and offered the chance to join the networking experiment. They were then asked to leave the company, each starting up as an independent limited liability company through which they would contract to provide their services for Rank Xerox. However never more than 50 per cent of their output was to be for Rank Xerox and contracts were negotiated on price as a means of efficiently allocating the right work to the right networkers. Clearly the volunteers could then work for other firms too and develop both their creative and entrepreneurial skills as well as gain the satisfactions of the self-employed. As of April 1985, 54 networkers existed with one or two joining per month. Two hundred businesses had been created with an aggregate turnover of £13m. The results reported by Rank Xerox were increased productivity, better work allocation and more effective and efficient work by those employees interacting with networkers. The networkers themselves reported sharper work organization, freer lifestyles and high job satisfaction.

This experiment demonstrates much about the potential of IT for changing the ways we manage. It is the telecommunications technology which is significant, breaking space and time constraints of the past. Second, economic and social goals can be achieved together. Finally quite radical accompanying organizational procedures sometimes may be required.

Creating new businesses becomes possible through advances in telecommunications, mass storage and software engineering as well as in computing. The information services which permeate financial markets, the expert system products available to professionals, the data analysis services assisting market research and the videographic tools enhancing media presentations are all examples. Indeed in the UK the Prime Minister's Information Technology Advisory Panel published a report entitled *Making a Business of Information* in 1983. They pointed to the expanding tradable information sector, the new opportunities brought by IT, the key role played by government in collecting and distributing data and in regulating IT access, use and security, and the growth of on-line services in business. They asked that government recognize the information business in policy formulation, that those in information businesses examine how things are changing, and that entrepreneurs look at the opportunities for making a business of information. They might have quoted the emergence of Acorn and Pinpoint market data analysis companies, the widespread adoption of the Lockheed Dialog databases, or the many firms who have opened up new income streams by selling data processing capacity, system operations, software packages, or data analyses as by-products. Above all, they might have quoted the transformation of Reuters from a news agency based on an international cable network which made a loss in 1965 to a financial information services company earning pretax profits of £93.5m in 1985. Reuters created an electronic market place for money out of their Monitor dealing system and 'now have everything they need to look like a bank except a clearing mechanism'.[5]

The management implications of the exemplars are that IT has become a strategic resource offering both opportunities and threats. Therefore strategic planning for IT becomes essential – to seek competitive advantage, to align information systems investment with business needs and perhaps to innovate. Indeed for many firms the business strategy is incomplete if there is no reference to IT.

IT: needed by our economic context

Whilst IT has inherent capabilities of automation and information processing, it is better understood as an *enabling technology*. In general, the dramatic uses and effects of IT are to be found in sectors where there are other major forces for change. In Table 1.1 a distinction is made between 'macro' and 'micro' forces for change. In the macro classification, IT has a leverage effect because it enables and multiplies the other sectoral changes at work. In the micro classification, IT provides new opportunities for those firms which have the vision to harness it creatively.

Today business is undergoing macro changes: we see a transition from an industrial to a service economy, liberalization and deregulation of service sectors, globalization of industrial markets, concentration in certain industries, and the emergence of new economic orders. For the old world and traditional sectors as much as for the new nations and information sectors, IT has found its time and is required in the fight for survival.

The *deregulation* of the US airline industry brought in its wake competitive exploitation of computerized reservation systems. For example American Airlines SABRE system is used by 48 per cent of travel agents across the USA. Providing both flight queries and reservations for American and other subscriber airlines (who had to join such a dominant distribution channel), it displayed its own flights preferentially. As a further spin-off, SABRE was able to collect data on other airlines' custom and collect

— What do you do
— Key tasks
— How much interaction
— Day to day
decision making
How do you get
information

Table 1.1 IT: an enabling technology

	Forces for change	Examples
Macro	Deregulation	Airlines, financial services
	Global survival	Automobiles, textiles
	Structural	Retailing
Micro	Technology	Process innovation, product innovation
	Information	Control, coordination, commodity
	Convergence	Integration, networks, rethinking

the cash float arising from their bookings. The AAdvantage programme offering special privileges and last minute check-ins was built around a customer card and the SABRE customer database. Anti-trust suits followed as other airlines petitioned against American Airlines new-found competitive advantage. This resulted in jurisdiction on flight displays, access to data and cash float. In return the operators of reservation systems were able to charge other carriers for transaction costs. American charged other carriers $1.75 for every reservation made through SABRE on their behalf. Of $400m pretax profits made on $5.3bn sales revenue in 1984, SABRE earned $170m pretax profits on $338m reservation revenues. The President announced: 'We are now in DP as well as in the airline business.' The following case demonstrates still more about IT and deregulation.

> United Airlines has a similar reservation system, APOLLO. When under deregulation United moved into Denver to compete with Frontier Airlines, APOLLO was placed in local agents' offices and before long Frontier who had no comparable system sought to include their flights and reservations in APOLLO. United adopted similar tactics to American whereupon Frontier lost both sales revenue and access to market data. They too filed evidence in the anti-trust cases. By 1986 Frontier were in financial distress. First a merger with People Express had occurred, but People too were in difficulty and both airlines had problems with reservation systems. Then a sale of Frontier to United was discussed, but eventually was aborted through failure to agree post-merger consequences. People subsequently filed for bankruptcy of Frontier Airlines.

In other words, as these cases show, under deregulation the powerful players often are victorious and IT has become a weapon of the powerful to the disadvantage of the small or the laggards.

As many market places become global, but the product-markets themselves fragment and competition focuses on niche markets and quick response, quality-based products with service, traditional firms find their manufacturing and marketing capabilities are outdated. To respond to more, smaller and faster moving markets, IT becomes a vital weapon in transforming products and processes. The required strategy is to move from mass market behaviour of economies of scale and generalized product ranges to niche market behaviour of economies of scope and differentiated service based on flexibility, specialization and quality. The case study of Ford in Europe, quoted earlier, is relevant and can be repeated for British Leyland, General Motors and Chrysler. In sectors supplying the motor industry, the same pressures are observed and, as noted below, the textile industry is another example of a sector fighting for global survival.

Lister-Petter Ltd, the UK diesel engine manufacturer, demonstrates some of these trends. In the 1980s the diesel engine market declined as the oil boom came to an end and aid to Third World countries was reduced due to the world recession. Lister-Petter realized that the market was changing for everybody. 'We were all fighting for a bigger share of a static or declining market – not just because the market was changing, but also because of the long life-span of our product.' The order book was no longer full one or two years ahead and the important requirement for the future was to be able to respond to a rapidly changing, short-horizon order book. Quality, reliability and customer service were identified as 'the three things which actually sell engines for us in the market place'. Quick response to changes in demand and reduced lead times for new products were seen as the strategic aims required to remain competitive.

Lister-Petter then turned to a step-by-step IT programme to achieve these aims. Production control systems were introduced in 1980, computer-aided design in 1981, robotics and numerical control in 1983 and a flexible manufacturing system in 1984. Integration of these automation applications was planned from 1982 onwards and by 1986 plants were linked by data communications with office automation and end-user computing supporting this computer integrated manufacturing (CIM) environment. 'CIM is at the centre of our industrial strategy. In fact, it is fundamental to planning for our company's survival', commented the production director.

As Lister-Petter exemplifies, restructuring production facilities and their management, plus increasing the pace and scope of product development are two key applications of IT for ensuring global survival. To these may be added the external needs of improving market and competitor information and providing the sales force with back office support and field selling tools.

> In March 1976 Yangtsekiang Garment Manufacturing opened their first UK factory on Merseyside. Initiated by one of their customers, the Littlewoods variety chain store group, the new plant was being installed to make apparel not only for Littlewoods but also for other customers in the UK, Europe and the USA. Yangtsekiang were implementing advanced manufacturing technology. Littlewoods' chief executive commented: 'UK firms will have to adopt the same approach if they are to compete.'

The relationship between structural change and IT can be demonstrated by the retail sector. In the UK in the mid-1980s there was a spate of mergers and acquisitions amongst the large food, chain store and department store retailers. Concentration was proceeding rapidly. At the same time new retailing ventures and concepts were being introduced. Often based on specialist niches or fashions and design, these were changing the traditional high street. The 1980s concentration marks: a transition from family dominated concerns to corporate entities; diversification across sector boundaries: rationalization; and the achievement of critical mass and economies of scale. This last motive is particularly based on maximizing purchasing power over suppliers, of affording and developing out-of-town shopping sites or redeveloped city properties, and affording and combining IT networks and systems. The 1980s' new entrants and retailing innovations, however, were often based on revolutionary distribution, design or outlet approaches which were sometimes made possible by technology, such as computer-aided design, electronic point of sale, supplier networks and teleshopping.

On the one hand the required investment for IT is significantly higher than in the past and on the other hand the capability to exploit these new technologies is differentiating the winners from the losers. In the retailing sector, IT therefore is both a cause and an effect of structural change.

The management implications of this analysis are that today's industrial context needs IT; IT is both a cause of sector changes and a requisite response to them. Therefore managements should analyse their sector forces for change and look to IT as a key strategic tool for survival. Whereas for some IT is potentially a source of competitive advantage, for many it is becoming an essential means of competitive parity.

IT: affects all functions and levels of management

Whether we like it or not, IT is becoming pervasive. Schoolchildren are introduced to microcomputers in schools; the gifted can become software millionaires; the computer-fluent can conceive of and design applications which the older generation have not considered; and the average have no fears or inhibitions about computing. Secretaries expect word processing facilities and grow with them, possibly graduating into spreadsheet work, database manipulation and computer graphics – in some cases becoming self-developed information PAs to their bosses. Professionals and specialists demand end-user computing and begin not only to depend on IT but design their work around it. Functional executives are beginning to accept and exploit niche computing because often it comprises packaged solutions, user-friendly interfaces, or stand-alone simplicity or is integrated within other technology; examples include computer-aided design and treasury work stations. Some chief executives call for their own information systems built on personal terminals and corporate databases. Customers become familiar with IT and sometimes expect it, examples being ATMs, viewdata information services and point of sale terminals. In short, more and more people interact with, or are affected by, IT each working day.

Three other characteristics of IT need to be appreciated in order to be aware of both the nature and pace of these changes:

1. IT comprises multiple technologies – whether classified by delivery or use. Accordingly applications, design principles, economics, users, management experience, social implications and even functions responsible for them differ.
2. IT is dispersing. Besides centralized mainframe computing, there are niche technologies serving individual functions, end-user computing meeting personal needs, telecommunications allowing local, national and global data transfer, and customized technologies such as ATMs and external information services. IT is no longer a centralized technology requiring centralized specialisms reinforcing centralization tendencies. There are spatial choices in computing and opportunities for local and personal initiatives.
3. The rate of IT change is accelerating. Basic hardware technology continues to develop rapidly, major software advances are promised over the next few years and the 'functionality' of IT evolves continuously as new applications, techniques and tools are introduced week by week. Indeed the S-curves of diffusion and adoption of new technologies seem to shorten all the time.

A NEDO survey of policy makers and informed sources sought judgements on the long-term social implications of IT. Whilst little consensus emerged on detailed consequences, there was little doubt that IT would have a major and pervasive impact on life over the next 25 years. Most respondents forecast smaller employment units, gradual arrival of office and factory automation, substantial changes in working patterns, and significant use of IT in the home. Opinions divided on whether organizations would be more decentralized or centralized and whether employment levels would decrease, increase or stabilize. The shape of an 'information society' was not clear, but even the most conservative scenarios implied immense social change. The survey team therefore concluded that policies will be required 'that are as innovative as the technologies associated with the changes'. Policies, of course, will not be concerned only with technology supply and use but with the more political matters of access to, possession of, and manipulation of information. We can assume these policies will be required within organizations as well as at the societal level.

The management implications of this analysis are that the rapid adoption, the pervasive impact and the differentiated nature of IT make change a constant for at least 25 years. Technological and social forecasting however have their limits in advising policy makers what to do. Consequently monitoring, understanding, responding to and managing the continuous change and innovation will be equally, or more, important. Management policies then will be required to ensure IT satisfies both economic and social criteria; for without judgements and choices technology will drive people, organizations and society rather than vice versa.

IT: a revolution in management information systems

When James Callaghan was Prime Minister of the United Kingdom he pronounced that IT would bring a revolution in management information. This is not yet proven, but new technologies bring both new possibilities and new pressures for management information systems (MIS). Indeed there are indications that after two decades of applying computers to MIS in largely traditional ways, many innovations are occurring, but are not well documented in the literature.

> A chief accountant of an oil company declared: 'There is no longer a role model for MIS in financial planning and control. All we can do is experiment on our own and I have encouraged my accountants to see what can be done with end-user computing.'

Tricker has noted that the demand for management information continues to grow as organizations become more complex in scale and scope, as the environment becomes more uncertain and as the rate of change of key business influences – not least technology itself – accelerates. There are also two other pressures. First, managers – and thus organizations – spend much of their time in information processing, for example communicating in meetings and by telephone, reading, preparing and analysing reports and gathering intelligence, as both Mintzberg and Stewart have discovered in their studies of managerial work. Thus there should be considerable potential for the application of IT in managerial practice. Second, as new technology is provided for managers and professionals, they often seem to demand more. Simple computer models expand into more sophisticated routines, personal computer users ask for downloading of corporate data, and busy top executives ask for more informative means of presenting data. At the same time Alloway and Quillard have reported that most organizations have many years' backlog in satisfying visible and unknown information system requirements. In principle therefore the market for computer-based MIS seems encouraging.

In Figure 1.4 an opportunities matrix is suggested in order to show the diversity of MIS innovations being spawned by IT. The availability of spreadsheets, typically using Lotus 123 and an IBM personal computer, has brought both efficiency and effectiveness benefits to many financial control routines, for example in cost analysis procedures or simple 'what if' modelling of financial plans. Expert systems look likely to enhance tracking and monitoring procedures as well as automate such activities as credit rating or financial training. Teleconferencing has been adopted by dispersed organizations to facilitate and automate both regular management meetings and irregular crisis consultation. Boardroom presentation systems built around databases, video methods and enquiry facilities are being adopted by an increasing number of UK corporations to communicate planning and control information more effectively and provide data 'on tap'.

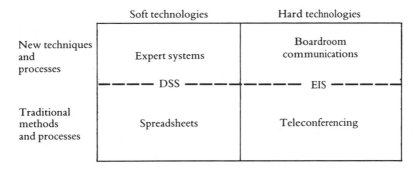

Figure 1.4 MIS and IT opportunities.

Decision support systems (DSS) and executive information systems (EIS) are located in the grey areas. The former usually provide stand alone enquiry, analysis and modelling facilities for individual managers, often designed and driven by themselves. They are classified as 'soft' technologies because the main distinctors between success and failure in DSS seem to be non-technical as Keen and Scott-Morton assert. These include problem orientation, an evolutionary approach, a systems analyst working as a process consultant rather than a provider of solutions, and attention to the man-machine interface. Executive information systems (EIS) are more dependent upon a range of technologies including computer terminals, on-line information services and database architectures. Typically they provide key internal information and a range of external data 'on tap' for a chief executive and his team. The following case quoted by Rockart and Treacy is illustrative.

Northwest Industries, a US $2.9bn conglomerate, developed an EIS, or rather the chief executive did. Comprising 70 reports and trend pictures with the ability to analyse and manipulate 340 data items on 45 databases, the CEO and his team can monitor nine divisions and track environmental trends. This system is now supported by an EIS team, but it grew out of the individual needs of an analytical, IT aware CEO running a business in a volatile environment.

It would seem that DSS and EIS are beginning to provide the analytical and enquiry facilities which hitherto had a background of more traditional monitoring and exception MIS. Alloway and Quillard found that most managers rated analysis and enquiry systems as most suited to their managerial tasks.

IT also brings new pressures on MIS. For example it is increasingly recognized that advanced manufacturing technology is changing the principles of production upon which much financial control and cost accounting were based. Instead of production economies of scale, standard methods, high labour and material costs, optimal inventory control and batch size routines, and significant variable costs, manufacturing firms are moving into a world of production economies of scope, flexible and market responsive manufacturing, high equipment and software costs, just-in-time and MRP 2 systems, and dominant fixed costs. Kaplan has suggested that traditional MIS may well be undermining new production and focusing on quite inappropriate variables in supporting both decision making and control. In other words much management accounting is out of date in the IT era.

Likewise in retailing, the advent of electronic point of sale (EPOS) is posing challenges for MIS. In principle the data collected on sales, prices and stocks, together with the ability to evaluate promotions and alternative displays should allow a more responsive, aggressive and informed approach to retailing. However EPOS requires MIS and buyer/merchandizer information processing skills behind it.

> A major UK retailer was a leader in EPOS. Whereas early cost savings and efficiency gains materialized, the data from EPOS which improve understanding of market needs and apply leverage to relations with suppliers lay untapped. The merchandizers and buyers had no tradition of, or capabilities in, computer-based MIS. The retailer then introduced telecommunications-based supplier links to improve supply chain management and make buying and merchandizing more sales-led, driven by EPOS data. However many of the buyers and merchandizers still resisted technology and would not either load data into the system or change their decision behaviour.

The management implications of this analysis are that IT may well bring both new demands for, and supply of, management information. There is no universal pattern of new MIS emerging, but many innovations seem promising. Organizations clearly need to encourage experimentation in all forms of MIS for planning and control and build decision support systems to back up investment in new retailing and manufacturing technology. At the same time top management needs to create a vision or model of MIS in the future to help ensure developments and experiments are congruent with the organization's preferred strategy, style and structure and to develop manager's capabilities in information processing.

IT: involves many stakeholders

It is perhaps conventional to think that all that is required of IT for success is that elusive factor 'good management'. However, increasingly, it is not only managers who influence, or expect to influence, the development and use of IT. There are many stakeholders involved and if management is to ensure that the exploitation of IT mostly meets its needs, the other stakeholders must be managed. Figure 1.5 suggests who these might be. Business users, particularly managements, have needs of IT and preferences about how it is used. Collective action through trade assocations, computer user groups and corporate lobbying are often required to ensure that business and other large organizations are represented in international, national and sector policy making and implementation.

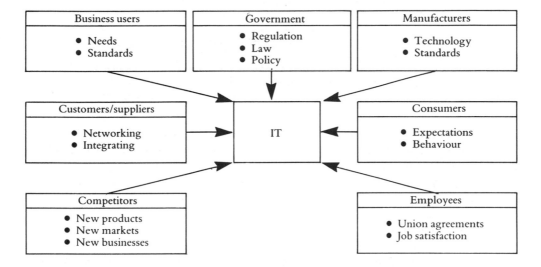

Figure 1.5 IT stakeholders.

Sometimes, however, one set of businesses may not have the same interests as another set. Increasingly, as IT is used as a strategic weapon, businesses are linked up with their customers or suppliers by networking. In some cases collaboration makes sense; in others it does not. For example, getting agreement between suppliers and retailers on article numbering and bar coding has not always been easy – and there can be significant costs at stake.

> General Motors with their SATURN project are investing in IT to integrate and optimize manufacturing, provisioning and distribution. Essential to this is agreement on protocols and standards for communication, data and document transfer etc. Firms in supplier industries are now joining the relevant bodies to ensure that these standards suit all interests.

The remaining five stakeholders can be very influential.

Governments are increasingly involved in IT. In the UK there has been legislation on data protection, regulation of telecommunications through OFTEL and IT policy initiatives including for a period the appointment of a Minister for Information Technology. For effective law and regulation, government needs industry's advice even where industry may feel it is suffering from unnecessary intervention – and, of course, industry may be able to persuade authorities to change controls that are either too lax or too severe. With IT being a plank of industrial policy, firms also may ignore investment, funding, training and advisory opportunities if they do not track and respond to initiatives. The Alvey programme of the UK government and the BRITE programme of the EC are clear examples. Likewise multinationals have to be aware of government policies and actions in other countries, for example in France where central IT planning and control are well known.

> It was not apparent to the government for some time that many multinational corporations in the UK actually wanted data protection legislation. Without it, the governments of countries where they had subsidiaries could prevent storage and processing of personal data of their nationals because the UK was assumed to be a 'data haven'. The long run consequence would be a constraint on the growth and activities of UK-based data processing centres.
> Financial service organizations, especially credit card companies, are seeking to influence GATT so that telecommunications-based services do not become constrained by tariff barriers and other trading controls. Some developing countries, understandably, take the opposite view.

IT manufacturers clearly influence what can be done; they provide the technology and commonly set the standards for its use. Often they have to pioneer both the technology and the standards and will claim that without this leadership role, progress would be slower. Equally, however, it is important that users lobby for their own interests. The debate between advocates of SNA and OSI for communications networks exemplifies the complexities involved, but it is essential that major users have a view. This was thought to be one of the background influences – but not the major factor – in the UK government's decision not to permit the collaboration between British Telecom and IBM on the JOVE value-added network project. Certainly the business community was active in the debate.

Consumers also have a stake in IT. Increasingly as technology enters the home and retail outlets, consumers build up expectations and respond with perhaps unforeseen behaviours. Was it predictable that ATMs would be so popular for example? Will householders expect standards for, and controls on, the supply and use of telecommunications-based information services? It can be predicted that where IT matters, consumer groups will develop. Equally it becomes inconceivable that some developments such as teleshopping would be pursued without consumer participation in system testing.

Employees and, of course, all levels of internal users may expect to be consulted about IT or all participate in systems design. Indeed for some employees IT is a negotiable issue. In Sweden there is national agreement between the employers and organized labour on new technology, suggesting consultation at the earliest stages of IT system development. In the UK, the white collar trade unions have advocated technology agreements in their general support for IT. ASTMS modelled their approach on the Swedish experience and even though their negotiators would prefer to include no-redundancy clauses in agreements, most do not contain this caveat. In central government it has been suggested that exploitation of IT in Whitehall has been retarded by lack of technology agreements. Further, it is not a new belief that employees should have the right to determine their own quality of working life, and some of the pioneering work by Enid Mumford on participative systems design to protect and enhance job satisfaction has achieved economic as well as social benefits in firms. In many ways a system which is good for the user is good for the management.

Earlier it was demonstrated how IT has become a source of competitive advantage. If firms in sectors where IT has become strategic do not monitor competitors' IT investments and initiatives, they may soon be at a competitive disadvantage. Many corporate information technology strategy documents now include analyses of competitors' actions and strengths and weaknesses. More and more one hears of firms' IT personnel attending events to learn of competitors' strategies, but ensuring that they reveal nothing in return. Competitors have become a stakeholder in IT.

The management implications of this analysis are that as IT becomes strategic, firms need to recognize the multiplicity of stakeholders involved and organize themselves to manage stakeholder relationships and influence their IT environment. This may include external activities such as lobbying, intelligence, and collaboration plus internal procedures, such as technology agreements, formulation of standards, and ensuring IT decisions are taken at the appropriate level.

IT: technology matters do matter

It could be said that decisions about technology supply, as opposed to technology use, should be left to the technologists. However, decisions made about hardware, software, data and systems can have major policy repercussions. For example it is reported that two recent building society mergers in the UK fell through partly because the computer systems were incompatible. Hardware and software policies thus could be important criteria in takeover decisions – and a possible defensive ploy to avoid acquisiton.

> A UK company was in the final stages of agreeing a takeover of a subsidiary of a US corporation. The UK chief executive passed the draft agreement to the IT director for perusal because 'it says something about systems'. In fact the agreement said the US business would be acquired without its computer systems (for they were run by a corporate bureau). The IT director pointed out that without systems, there was no business and either this should be remedied in the agreement or the takeover value be renegotiated to reflect the immediate resources which would be required to build new systems.

There are many examples of organizations which have been hindered in reorganization because hardware and systems were incompatible. One chief executive ordered that Data Processing and Data Communications must be so configured that they were not to be a constraint on continuous reorganization. In one decentralized manufacturing firm, an impediment to transporting of systems and diffusion of application innovations has been the proliferation of equipment suppliers. In another electronics firm, the expected commercial benefits of integrating a marketing unit with a manufacturing site into one division were delayed by the inheritance of two different database systems. The basic data definitions as well as the data structures were incompatible.

The DP department of a firm in the service sector decided not to implement a new operating system for its mainframe environment, despite the advantages claimed for it by the supplier. The DP management felt that for user service reasons a period of stability was required and software changes should be avoided. Suddenly top management called for an IT application in order to respond to an innovation by a rival. This could not be done under the operating system that had been retained. Thus implementation of the competitive response application was delayed for some months, to the frustration of top management.

Equally, it is only when security breaks happen that senior management tends to take exposure and recovery seriously. The cost of adequate security can seem excessive until the continued operation of the business is threatened by the loss of data or delays in restoring systems. As one IT director put it: 'I only hear from the Chairman when the system goes down.'

A technology term commonly employed today is *infrastructure*. This comprises the processing power of computers, the highways of telecommunications, the foundations of data, and the fabric of basic business systems. Whilst specialists have the expertise to advise on and recommend infrastructure plans and policies, top management has the strategic responsibility for approving them and accordingly being informed on technology matters.

> A chemical firm approved a major capital investment in an automatic warehouse. It was only subsequently realized that this would be a high technology island because the factory stock control systems were primitive. There were gaps in the systems infrastructure.

Another policy issue in many firms is whether software, systems, computing power, communications capacity or advisory services should be sold to third parties. For example a major airline sold a fare optimization system to help defray the development costs. This was in response to management pressure to reduce the systems budget. Unfortunately one of the airlines which bought the package extracted considerable competitive advantage from it to the discomfort of the airline which developed it. On the other hand, companies increasingly are selling communications network capacity to recoup infrastructure investment and perhaps to move into new businesses. Yet as IT becomes a strategic resource all such decisions cannot be treated solely as technological matters.

The management implications of this analysis are that technology decisions often should be made within a policy framework. Thus major computing, communications, data and systems policies and standards are issues for board deliberation and approval.

IT: management makes the difference

Lack of management attention was identified in the DP era as the primary cause of low adoption of computing and of system failures. Reports by McKinsey and Diebold were typical in their calls for management support and involvement. In surveying the information systems literature of the 1970s, McCosh et al. identified four recurring reasons for disappointment with business computing:

1. Using computers to tackle the wrong problem.
2. Lack of top management support.
3. Poor user involvement.
4. Inadequate attention to behavioural factors.

All these can still be seen today. New information technologies are applied to easy and obvious applications rather than where there is payoff. Top managers can still hope that IT can be dealt with for a few minutes each month. The bridges between users and specialists are still suspect and conflict-ridden. And new technologies such as robotics or office automation are still introduced with scant regard for their human and organizational impact. So it is perhaps not surprising that a report by Kearney for the UK Department of Trade and Industry identified largely management factors which distinguished leaders from laggards in exploiting IT successfully. Distinguishing factors included top management support, degree of IT awareness, level of investment in IT and board level direction of IT activities.

Thus, in many ways, the management principles required in the IT era differ little from those learnt in the DP era; only their importance and context have changed. In particular IT has become an executive management issue.

Management implications here are obvious. IT has to be treated as a resource to be managed like any other. Its exploitation and use, as well as the policy decisions about its supply, are far too important to be left to the technologists.

FROM DP TO IT

The term 'information technology' (IT) can be variously defined. From a *technical* perspective most dictionaries or handbooks take several pages to avoid a definition. In this book IT comprises computing, telecommunications and automation technologies. As an *activity*, IT comprises all the supply, development and use activities in which an organization has to be involved if it wishes to exploit these technologies to its advantage. As a *philosophy*, IT represents a different set of aims, means and responsibilities than was typical in organizations in the first 30 years of computing. The philosophical change can be represented by two contrasting metaphors. The first 30 years may be termed the 'DP era' (data processing) and the new horizons the 'IT era' (information technology).

The nine propositions of the last section can be reformulated into distinctors which differentiate these two eras. Summarized in Table 1.2, they suggest the differences of approach required for information management as organizations move 'from DP to IT'.

Table 1.2 Two eras of information management

Distinctor	DP era	IT era
Financial attitude to IT	A cost	An investment
Business role of IT	Mostly support	Often critical
Applications orientation of IT	Tactical	Strategic
Economic context for IT	Neutral	Welcoming
Social impact of IT	Limited	Pervasive
MIS thinking on IT	Traditional	New
Stakeholders concerned with IT	Few	Many
Technologies involved in IT	Computing	Multiple
Management posture to IT	Delegate abrogate	Leadership involvement

The contrasts in Table 1.2 provide the themes for the rest of this book. Understanding how critical IT is to particular businesses, and the experiences to date, underpins the next chapter which explores in more detail what is meant by information management. The strategic application of IT, its place in our economic context, and the potential for new information systems are examined in Chapter 3. Here the central question is how can IT be exploited for strategic advantage?

The next three chapters then are concerned with putting strategic management into IT. They provide practical, operational guidance on a strategic approach. In Chapter 4, identification of opportunities for strategic advantage and integration of information systems plans with business strategies are the concern. Thus methodologies for formulating an *information systems* strategy are examined. Policy approaches to technology matters are dealt with in Chapter 5 where the formulation of *information technology* strategies is covered. Here the concern is with planning the infrastructure. Chapter 6 then addresses issues to do with the management posture to IT and the management of stakeholders. It proposes a formal framework or *information management* strategy and indicates how this can be formulated.

The final three chapters explore three themes at the heart of IT as a philosophy. Chapter 7 is concerned with controlling IT activities, particularly if IT is perceived as an investment rather than a cost or expense. Issues here include funding, appraising, charging for, and evaluating IT activities. The next chapter suggests how IT **activities** should be organized in the IT era, particularly as the technologies multiply and disperse and their use and impact are pervasive. It is concerned with structuring the IT function, reorganizing IT departments, the job of the IT executive, and board level direction of IT. Chapter 9 examines how the change from the DP era to the IT era can be made and managed. Thus the book concludes on how management can lead, and get involved with, IT and information systems.

NOTES AND REFERENCES

1. Nolan, Norton & Co., 'The economics of computing in the advanced stages', *Stage by Stage*, European issue, Spring 1985.
2. See Kearney A. T. (management consultants), 'The barriers and the opportunities of information technology – a management perspective', report for the Department of Trade and Industry, London, 1984.
3. This data is derived from Gooding G. T., 'Exploiting IT in business development. Ford in Europe' in Earl M. J. (ed.), *Information Management: The Strategic Dimension*, Oxford University Press, 1988.
4. This data is derived from Judkins P., West D. and Drew J., *Networking in Organisations: The Rank Xerox Experiment*, Gower, 1985.
5. Attributed to Walter Wriston, chairman of Citibank for 17 years, in Lawrenson J. and Barber L., 'The price of truth', *Mainstream*, p. 171, 1985.

FURTHER READING

Alloway R. M. and Quillard J. A., 'User managers' systems needs', *MIS Quarterly*, June 1983.

Diebold J., 'Bad decisions on computer use', *Harvard Business Review*, January-February 1969.

Kaplan R., 'Yesterday's accounting undermines production, *Harvard Business Review*, July-August 1984.

Keen P. G. W. and Scott-Morton M. S. *Decision Support Systems: An Organisational Perspective*, Addison-Wesley, 1978.

McCosh A. M., Rahman M. and Earl M.J., *Developing Managerial Information Systems*, Macmillan, 1981.

McFarlan F. W. and McKenney J. L., *Corporate Information Systems Management: The Issues Facing Senior Executives*, Dow Jones Irwin, 1983.

McKinsey & Co., *Unlocking the Computer's Profit Potential*, McKinsey & Co. Inc., 1968.

Mintzberg H., *The Nature of Managerial Work*, Harper and Row, New York, 1973.

Mumford E., *Values, Technology and Work*, Martinus Nijhoff, The Hague, 1981.

NEDO (J. Bessant and others), *IT Futures: What Current Forecasting Literature Says about the Social Impact of Information Technology*, NEDO, 1985.

Rockart J. and Treacy M. E. 'The CEO goes on-line', *Harvard Business Review*, January-February 1982.

Stewart R. *Choices For The Manager: A Guide to Managerial Work and Behaviour*, McGraw-Hill, 1982.

Tricker R. I., *Effective Information Management*, Beaumont Executive Press, Oxford, 1982.

Chapter 2

INFORMATION
MANAGEMENT

INTRODUCTION

Definitions and descriptions of management have become ever more complex as both research and practice have advanced. However, to refine the management of information technology to its essentials, a simple task model is required. Figure 2.1 suggests that information management comprises planning, organization and control of information resources. The diagram also emphasizes that these activities are interdependent. Effective information management requires planning methods, control procedures and organizational arrangements to be congruent with each other. In the main they also must fit the management practices of the firm at large.

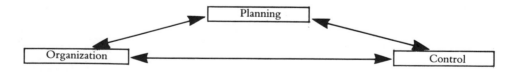

Figure 2.1 A formal model of information management.

Most information management questions asked in any organization today can be classified as problems of planning, organization and control. Table 2.1 lists some of the recurring management questions that originated in the DP era but still recur today. More contemporary questions representative of the IT era are also listed. In addition, of course, there are important questions which are inherently technological. These are not our concern at this stage, but can be thought of as a fourth aspect of information management.

Table 2.1 Information management questions

Activity	Recurring questions	New questions
Planning	What systems should we develop next? Which of our many application needs has priority? What is the next hardware step?	What information systems do our current business strategies demand? What strategic opportunities are presented by IT? Do we need a telecommunications policy?
Organization	Should DP be centralized or not? How do we improve user-specialist relations? How can we secure top management support?	How will IT affect our organization structure? How can we find more IT personnel? Should we have an IT director?
Control	How much should we be spending on DP? Are we getting value for money from DP? Should we charge out all DP services?	How much are we spending on IT? How can you evaluate IT proposals? How can we manage large IT projects?

THE VIEWS OF MANAGERS

In a survey conducted by the author in 1982/83, IT managers from large European organizations were asked to rank the importance of these three management tasks against the purely technological issues. The results, shown in Figure 2.2, indicate that planning was the dominant concern. This covered long-range planning of information systems, linking application of IT to business goals, resource forecasting, exploiting IT for strategic advantage, mapping future infrastructures, and allocating scarce IT resources.

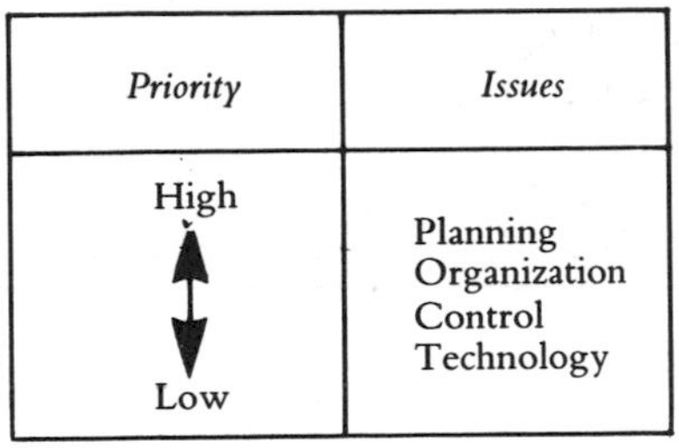

Priority	Issues
High ↑↓ Low	Planning Organization Control Technology

Figure 2.2 Priorities in managing IT.

Close behind the priority of planning were organizational issues. Discussion with respondents indicated two dominant questions. First, how should firms organize for the operation, development and management of multiple, dispersing, accelerating and pervasive information technologies? Second, what are the implications of new technology for the jobs and careers of DP and IT managers?

Control questions were given much lower priority and seemed to reflect the view that management control of information resources was widely in place. New questions were emerging but they were not yet crucial. Chief executives, however, are often less sanguine on this matter and the control questions shown in Table 2.1 are often high on their list of concerns.

Technology issues scored the lowest ranking. This does not suggest that they are trivial or that the management implications are unimportant. Rather, IT managers report that technological issues *per se* are relatively subordinate to management questions in the large at the moment. The nine factor analysis in Chapter 1 probably explains why.

In the same survey, IT managers were asked to rank information management concerns from a list of 17 commonly reported. Table 2.2 presents the top five concerns perceived in 1982/83 and expected over the next five years.

Table 2.2 Concerns of IT managers

1982/83 concerns	*Future concerns*
1. Information systems strategy	1. Information systems strategy
2. User awareness and education	2. Information systems long-range planning
3. Inadequate staff resources	3. Coping with new ITs
4. Information systems long-range planning	4. User awareness and education
5. Coping with new ITs	5. User involvement

For the professionals, therefore, the issues for the 1980s were agreed to be information systems strategy and long-range planning, user relationships and generally coping with new technology. Not unusually, general managers' priorities differed – and often they were responding from the same organization. Table 2.3 presents their views. Here there appear to be two sets of concerns. In the short and long terms, how do we identify the right applications and appropriate objectives and then ensure satisfactory delivery? In the longer term, how do we exploit new technology to advantage and manage the consequences?

Table 2.3 Concerns of general managers

1982/83 concerns	*Future concerns*
1. Relationship with IT/DP department	1. Exploiting new information technologies
2. Defining IS/IT needs	2. Ensuring applications meet needs
3. Agreeing IS/IT priorities	3. Getting projects started
4. Getting projects started	4. Behavioural impact of IT
5. Getting projects finished	5. Managing change

The survey therefore indicates that in 1982/83 the IT community in large organizations were thinking ahead, but their general managers were still concerned about current performance. In 1986, a second survey by Earl *et al.* of the views of IT directors in leading UK firms recorded a convergence of the recurring or short-term concerns with project delivery and the user community and the new or longer-term concerns of IS strategy and exploiting opportunities afforded by new technology. These top five priorities selected from a list of 22 commonly discussed issues are reproduced in Table 2.4.

Table 2.4 Concerns of IT directors

Rank	Concern
1.	Aligning information systems with business strategy
2.	Relations between IS and user departments
3.	User awareness and education
4.	IS project management and implementation
5.	Identifying opportunities for the use of IT

The final view of managers which is instructive is provided by Dickson *et al.* from the USA. In 1984 they surveyed the views of 54 leading IT practitioners plus four academics, using the Delphi technique to achieve a consensus top ten issues of IS management. Table 2.5 reproduces their final list. Again, the dominant concern is improved planning of IS/IT resources. Issues 3 and 4 can be seen as mainly technological. Issues 1, 9, 10 and 10★ can be seen as planning tasks. Issues 2, 6, 7 and 8 are principally organizational. Issue 5 can be seen as a control question.

Table 2.5 The top ten issues of IS management

Final mean rank	Issues
1.	Improved IS planning
2.	Facilitation and management of end-user computing
3.	Integration of DP, office automation and telecommunications
4.	Improved software development and quality
5.	Measuring and improving IS effectiveness/productivity
6.	Facilitation of organizational learnings and use of IT
7.	Aligning the IS organization with that of the enterprise
8.	Specification, recruitment and development of IS human resources
9.	Effective use of the organization's data resources
10.	Development and implementation of decision support systems
10.★	Planning and management of the applications portfolio

The UK and US surveys both recognize that the dominant issue in managing IT is strategic planning. They also seem to agree that besides technology questions *per se*, the priority concerns are planning, organization and control in that order. This was not always the case and it is instructive to see how information management evolved in the DP era, how priorities change and what models can guide managers in the IT era.

EXPERIENCE IN MANAGING IT

In 1974, Gibson and Nolan published a seminal article on managing data processing. They discovered that across different companies both the expenditure on DP and the experiences in managing it were very similar. DP expenditure followed an S-curve over time, but, more important, the curve seemed to represent a path of organizational learning. This path could be described by a four stage model. Each stage, depicted in Figure 2.3, marked a new approach to using and managing computer resources and was often prompted by an organizational crisis in the life of the DP function. Indeed each stage seemed to be a function of the experience and progressive pressures of the previous stage.

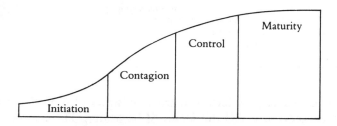

Figure 2.3 Four stages of DP growth.

In the initiation phase, the main objective is to establish whether computing is feasible in the organization's particular business and often those applications which are obvious candidates for automation are developed. These include financial ledgers, payrolls and the like. In the contagion phase, computing expands into other application areas as the organization begins to build confidence, top management exhorts line management to embrace computing, and DP managers follow industry trends. In the next phase, top management anxieties with rising DP expenditure, user management concerns with late delivery of projects and unsatisfied needs, and DP departments' delayed attention to formal management of computing resoures bring about the need for control. This is characterized by moratoria on systems development, a new reporting line for the DP function, appointment of an experienced line manager to head up DP and installation of many management controls. In the maturity phase, the organization begins to be as confident in managing computing as other resources, applications development positively pursues economic benefit again, and the DP manager seeks to manage the balance between short-term delivery and investment for the future. Building on Nolan's subsequent work, Table 2.6 summarizes these application characteristics of the stages 'theory'.

However, it is the management practices over time which are more significant. Each stage depicts a set of formal planning, organizational and control practices which match the abilities and experience of senior management; the awareness of users, the coverage of applications, and the demands of the technology. At the same time important informal processes will be explicating the issues, promoting the crisis and suggesting the solutions which mark the turning point into the next stage. Whilst subsequent research has been equivocal on the validity of these 'benchmarks',[1] the existence of these stages and their general character seem to be agreed. Certainly most managers – in IT and in user areas – identify with them. Table 2.7 depicts an idealized evolution of

Table 2.6 DP stages: applications perspective

Factor/stage	Initiation	Contagion	Control	Maturity
Applications orientation	Cost reduction	New functions	Moratorium	Database: enquiry
Technical specialization	Efficient computing	Applications expertise	Control and effectiveness	Database teleprocessing
Applications portfolio development	Operational control systems	Mainly operational control; some management control	Principally operational control; growing management control	Operational control, management control and some strategic planning
Ratio of development to maintenance	1 : 0	0.75 : 0.25	0.5 : 0.5	0.8 : 0.2

planning, organization and control through the stages. It is based on Gibson and Nolan's original work, Nolan's subsequent development and the author's own experience.

Table 2.7 Planning, organization and control stages

Stage/management	Initiation	Contagion	Control	Maturity
Management orientation	Lax	Selling	Controlling	A resource
Planning	Technology focus Computing plan	Loose budget Applications plan	Budgetary planning Steering committee	Long-range planning Multi-level plans
Organization	DP located where first used Local organization Training is technical Users distant	DP manager promoted Project organization Training on applications Users interested	DP relocated centrally Centralization Training on management Users accountable	DP becomes a function Some decentralization Part of total management training Users involved
Control	Controls lacking Savings justifications No chargeout Any controls technical	Controls lax Informal approvals Costs allocated Informal project controls	Controls proliferate Hard savings sought Full chargeout Financial, project and quality controls	Controls refined Benefits and priorities Selective chargeout Technical standards and management controls

The notion of the S-curve is, of course, significant for it suggests that this model is another expression of the S-curves of technology diffusion and adoption. It seems that each stage lasts three to five years, but that an organization can find itself stuck in one stage – often the third stage – for seven or more years. If organizational learning underpins the curve and this learning is achieved mainly through experience, it would appear that stages cannot be missed out. The management challenge therefore is to anticipate the next stage and avoid either an excessive crisis or undue retardation in the evolution. As Gibson and Nolan concluded, success would be marked not so much in smoothing the expenditure curve, but dampening the organizational traumas and developing applications coverage, management practices, technology profile and user understanding in parallel.

The stage model was born of the DP era. What does it suggest for the era of IT? A significant lesson is emerging. The S-curves of learning seem to be repeated for the new technologies. Certainly, they have been documented by Curley for office automation, by Keen and Mills for telecommunications, and by Henderson and Treacy for end-user computing. Indeed McFarlan and McKenney suggest a generic technology management stage model, along the lines depicted in Table 2.8. The challenge and goals of assimilating technology change through four stages. The growth processes evolve as responsibilities between specialists, users and management change. In managing each stage a different balance of 'tight' for control and 'loose' for innovation is required.

Table 2.8 Technology, assimilation and management

Stage/factor	Technology identification and investment	Technological learning and adaptation	Rationalization/ management control	Maturity/widespread technology transfer
Challenge	Identify technology of potential interest and fund a pilot	Encourage user experimentation on broader base	Develop tools and techniques for efficient use of technology	Adaptation to and adoption of technology
Goals	Technical expertise early applications cut	User insight on application potential User awareness of technology	Value for money reliability and longevity	Diffusion integration
Management	Lax planning and control	Encouragement and observation	Standards, analyses and studies	Organizational processes
Growth processes	Technological advance Application testing	Applications advance User learning	User advance Management learning	Managements advance

Source: McFarlan and McKenney

We can conclude therefore that different management approaches are required according to the stage of adoption of the technology.

Furthermore, given that some of the curves – for example for personal computing and office automation – seem to be much shorter than those for the more complex technologies – say DP and telecommunications – how does an organization digest the variety? This is one of the principal challenges of the IT era! It is a question which is returned to in Chapters 6 to 8.

There now arises a major complication. If, in the late 1980s, most organizations locate themselves in stage three or four of the DP curve, they probably also locate themselves in different stages of the other technology curves. How then can all these information resources be managed efficiently and effectively when the experiences and needs are so different?

One requirement in this scenario is the need to build bridges between the different technologies and their applications. Not only will they have logical and physical dependencies and connections, but also many strategic applications will be based on visionary use of integrated technologies. As Figure 2.4 portrays, the requirement is that of *architecture*, of planning and developing computing, communications, data and systems in a coherent manner. In reality, as we shall see in Chapter 5, 'coherence' involves retreats and rethinks as much as thrusts and blueprints. This is because early exploitation and diffusion of a technology may be better achieved by loose direction, but eventually integration requires tighter reining in.

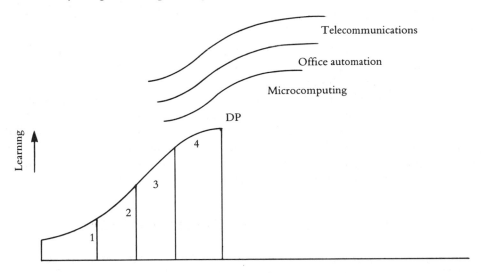

Figure 2.4 Multiple S-curves.

A common experience in the 1980s has been major investment in telecommunications. Often the combination of 'intermediate technology' being available, early payback being achieved by speech rather than data services, and the historical experience and skills being speech-centred has led to the development of networks and support services oriented to speech traffic rather than data transmission. At some point telecommunications planning and implementation are connected back to the planning and development of data and computing in order to be prepared for the explosion in data communications.

This same loose-tight cocktail has a related organizational implication. It is becoming clear that to effectively exploit and spread many of the new technologies, they need to be given to a department separate from DP. For example in microcomputing, the need to experiment, to sell, to provide ancillary services, to learn new techniques and to be flexible in order to build a critical mass of personal computer users has led many firms to set up microcomputing departments separate from DP. The skills required are so different and contemporary DP behaviour too restrictive. In short there is a mismatch of stages. In due course, however, the departments tend to cooperate and even merge, for in the end-user computing environment, users need mainframe access and corporate data as well as local power and personal data. Clearly the successful IT director identifies, anticipates and engineers appropriate management structures for each technology but does not lose sight of his architecture blueprints and how they can be achieved.

A retailing company set up an office automation team separate from the mainframe DP development group. This was done partly to encourage experimentation in office automation, partly to ensure that specialist expertise was developed, and partly to create a unit more responsive to departmental, personal and information analysis needs. After about three years the two groups were brought together again as it was felt that integration between DP applications and office automation was an imminent need. This did not work and so the segregation was restored. The two groups had established different positions and philosophies and agreed on very little. The integration need was not strong enough to force resolution of conflicting approaches. Two years later, combining the groups was again on the agenda as applications requirements were converging – as were the technologies. The time was now right.

Perhaps the stages framework explains why the surveys reported in the previous section discovered a management emphasis on both delivery and strategy, or on both the short and long term. The multiple S-curves of the IT era predict this. The typical firm is still maturing in learning how to manage DP like any other resource; meanwhile new learning on new technologies is occurring across the organization. User managers are concerned about satisfying today's needs and understanding tomorrow's possibilities. IT managers know that without effective systems delivery, they have no credibility; they also have to think strategically, for tomorrow's needs cannot be delivered 'at a stroke'. We return to this balancing act in Chapter 7.

STRATEGIC MANAGEMENT OF IT

The 'strategic grid' of McFarlan *et al.* was introduced in Chapter 1, with the conclusion that different information management emphases will be required according to the position of a firm on the grid. The implications can now be codified within the formal framework of information management developed in this Chapter. For each quadrant of the strategic grid we can deduce the appropriate forms of planning, organizing and controlling information resources – and suggest the likely approach to technology policies. Table 2.9 summarizes the position.

In the support quadrant, planning of IS can be *ad hoc*. The service department reacts to user requests as they occur and as long as the user is satisfied this works well. The IT department thus occupies a 'backroom' position in the organization, not noticed most of the time but appreciated when required. The most important controls relate to project timescales, budgets and goal achievement. The backroom department offers a contractual service and seeks to be as professional as funds allow. One aspect of professionalism that matters is being sufficiently informed about different technologies to be able to respond to new requirements. The IT department offers solutions to *ad hoc* problems and uses whatever approach seems best. Technology policies therefore are eclectic.

In the factory quadrant, it is important to deliver and operate systems efficiently and reliably. The most important aspect of planning therefore is to anticipate resource levels correctly. IT activities have to be tightly managed and accessible to all who rely on them. They are structured therefore into a department, occupying a clear and recognizable position on the organization chart. The budget becomes the main external control because it plans and measures the use of resources. Quality and other operational controls will be important within the department. Since current systems

Table 2.9 Information management by strategic grid

Strategic grid/ information management	Support	Factory	Turnaround	Strategic
Planning	Ad hoc	Resource	Directional	Strategic
Organization	Back room	Department	Function	Complex
Control	Project	Budget	Programme	Mixed
Technology	Eclectic	Conventional	Rethink	Architectural

are important to the running of the business, technology risks and adventures are inappropriate. Technology policies thus are likely to be conventional and follow *de facto* industry standards.

In the turnaround quadrant, IT is seen to be crucial to the firm's future business development. Top management therefore is likely to re-orient information systems in pursuit of strategic advantage. This change is achieved by directional planning of a very focused, emphatic nature. Plans need not be sophisticated, although the prior analysis may be. To revamp IT activities and elevate their status and influence, they are organized as a function and set up on a par with other principal functions of management, such as finance or personnel. External control for a period is very much in the hands of top management who commit new levels of funding on a programme (application initiative) basis and hope that effectiveness is achieved by making correct resource allocation decisions. Since IT is central to supporting or creating new strategic directions, technology policies have to be rethought. New approaches, alternative vendors, different standards, perhaps quick-fix solutions, and new technologies may have to be embraced.

> Coats Viyella the UK textile group saw information technology as an important mechanism for converting the textile industry from a sunset industry to a sunrise industry.[2] IT was applied to design, manufacturing and retailing. Classical turnaround tactics were described by Coats Viyella's Chief executive, Davoud Alliance. 'We can no longer be satisfied with a slow, evolutionary process. We have to leapfrog to emerging new technologies that will give us an edge and position us to continue to provide high quality goods and services competitively in a global market.' This strategy included 'commitment to develop advanced technology from other industries in textiles to give our customers maximum flexibility in innovation and marketing'. It also included hiring a £100,000 a year chief science and technology advisor headhunted from the United States.

In the strategic quadrant, information management is one of the most important responsibilities of the firm. IS planning, by definition, has to be integrated with business planning and is strategic as well as long-term. The two are interdependent.

As IT becomes embedded in business operations and pervasive in business thinking, IT activities now take on more complex organizational forms. Neat and tidy functional responsibility and authority gives way to all sorts of hybrid arrangements as business units and users begin to drive and develop information systems. Control patterns follow suit whereby all managers become information managers with some responsibility for IT usage and perhaps some authority for IT supply. However so important is IT to the business that softer controls and more dispersed organizational structures cannot be allowed to create technological muddle. Thus technology policies become much more architectural and concerned with interfaces, integration, compatibility and manageability.

> An airline placed itself in the strategic quadrant. Its reservation systems, cargo handling systems and operations control systems had become part of the infrastructure of the business. Its future business developments in improving customer service, diversifying into travel-related activities, and creating new marketing programmes were equally dependent on IT. The airline began to examine how information systems planning could be better integrated with business strategic planning instead of being largely project or programme driven. It devolved some of the responsibilities for managing systems development, implementation and operations to divisions, but retained all delivery capability in the centre to protect interfaces and integration. It set up strategy units in the IT division and embarked upon an architecture study to examine where technological coherence was imperative and where it was not. It invested more in a technology assessment unit to explore and experiment with emerging technologies that might yield some competitive advantage to the airline. Initiatives were made to foster greater collaboration and partnership between the IT division and user divisions.

So corporate management not only has to understand what are appropriate information management practices for today's situation, as pictured by the strategic grid. It is also important to anticipate the likely changes, as business units move round the grid, and be able to recognize the turning points.

SECTOR MANAGEMENT OF IT

Senior executives often claim that their business or sector is 'different'. For example, manufacturing managements do not appreciate generalizations made from experience in the financial services sector. They are right to be critical. The work on IT strategy formulation discussed in Chapter 4 suggests that sector differences are significant. The nature and importance of IT use varies from sector to sector and so do their managements' attitudes to, and beliefs in, IT. However sectors have to be distinguished by IT *attributes* not by conventional classifications.

Table 2.10 identifies four sector types on this basis. In some sectors, for example financial services, airlines and, increasingly, retailing, IT has become the means of delivering the goods and services in the sector. Indeed the infrastructure of the sector is often IT itself and so each firm's IT infrastructure is a major plank of its asset base. A poor infrastructure exposes the firm in its daily operations and its future business development. An infrastructure which is inefficient and expensive creates a non-viable, cost structure. This sector is called the *delivery* sector.

In other sectors, for example automobiles or textiles, business and functional strategies are increasingly dependent upon IT for their implementation. Indeed critical success or survival factors in those industries are often reliant upon IT for their achievement. This is the *dependent* sector.

In a third set of sectors, managements believe that IT can yield some strategic advantage and that poor IS may prove to be a strategic disadvantage. However the requirements and imperatives are by no means clear so that managements need faith in IT and IS and have to drive continually for the greatest benefits. Many process and food industries are like this and typify this *drive* sector.

For the final group of sectors, the strategic importance of IT is either not yet apparent or is minimal. IT is never irrelevant but it is unlikely to make or break company performance in these sectors. This sector set is called *delayed* – for technologies or competitive forces may prompt a reappraisal in the future.

Table 2.10 Sector framework for IT

Strategic context	Characteristic	Metaphor
IT is the means of delivering goods and services in the sector	Computer-based transaction systems underpin business operations	Delivery
Business strategies increasingly depend on IT for their implementation	Business and functional strategies require a major automation, information or communications capability and are made possible by these technologies	Dependent
IT potentially provides new strategic opportunities	Specific applications or technologies are exploited for developing business and changing ways of managing	Drive
IT has no strategic impact in the sector	Opportunities or threats from IT are not yet apparent or perceived	Delayed

A major implication of this analysis is that formal information management practices need to vary in emphasis and style with sector. Table 2.11 summarizes the planning, organization and control approaches appropriate to each sector – plus the technology polices. In the 'delivery' sectors planning of goods and services and product-market strategy formulation cannot be done without reference to IT. As one chief executive of a financial services company put it: 'We have no IT strategy, only a product-market strategy.' To him they were the same thing; planning for IT was integral with business planning. The scale and interdependence of information technologies in delivery sectors tend to force a central and corporate organization for IT. Equally, because IT is the business infrastructure it is both extensive and pervasive. Thus investment in IT, plus delivery and application of it, need to be tightly controlled in the main. Discretionary funds and looser controls may, however, be necessary to encourage experimentation, since this is equivalent to research and development of the business. Inevitably the infrastructure quality of IT in delivery sectors makes architecture the central policy concern in supplying IT.

Table 2.11 Sector information management

Sector/ information management	Delivery	Dependent	Drive	Delayed
Planning	Integral	Derived	IT-push	Default
Organization	Corporate	Business unit	Line	IT
Control	Tight-loose	Loose-tight	Loose	Tight
Technology	Architectural	Pragmatic	Enabling	*Ad hoc*

An early example of delivery sector thinking and its infrastructure consequences is provided by the Trustee Savings Banks (TSB) in the UK. Originally these were local savings banks established in the nineteenth century to encourage thrift and self-help among wage-earners. Various Acts of Parliament brought these banks under a statutory umbrella and over time 600 separate TSBs amalgamated into 20 by 1976. However it was only in the early 1970s that the level of cooperation between TSBs developed significantly. They began to share computer facilities, not least as they felt the need to offer their customers a wider range of banking and other financial services. All the TSBs now belong to one group which became a public company in 1986. That is a different story *but* an early push towards creating a group was IT through the recognition that shared infrastructure was necessary for survival and growth in a delivery sector.

In 'dependent' sectors, business analysis and planning begin to highlight the need for technology. Planning for IT therefore is a derivative of business planning. Accordingly responsibility for identifying and perhaps developing IT applications must lie close to where product-market business decisions are made and implemented. IT organization therefore is likely to be based on business units in the main. Indeed their management teams will have both responsibility and authority for exploiting IT. Thus on balance, controls over IT will be loose rather than tight, giving scope to effectiveness before efficiency. In this spirit technology policies can be more pragmatic doing what meets the business need. As one IT Manager put it: 'We analyse the business requirement and then drop the relevant box in.'

In 'drive' sectors, there is an element of taking IT to the users. Planning for IT, therefore, is likely to include some technology-push characteristics, such as subsidizing prototype developments, experimenting with new technologies, and replicating ideas from other businesses. However only line managers can recognize what is relevant and take on the implementation responsibilities. Indeed given an impetus, it is likely to be line managers who drive the organization's application and strategic exploitation of IT. Thus the major criterion in making technology policies is: 'will they enable or facilitate identification and development of business opportunities in IT?'

In 'delayed' sectors the descriptive state of information management is likely to comprise planning of IT by default. IT strategies are what is currently unfolding by request or under pressure. Day-to-day responsibility for IT is handed over to a few IT professionals, but they have to operate under financial constraints. Technology decisions and policies are somewhat random, being influenced by *ad hoc* needs.

Of course, firms can migrate across this sector classification. A firm which embraces IT in support of its business development priorities in a dependent mode may find, in due course, that much of its infrastructure is now IT. Then it takes on the character of a delivery sector firm. Perhaps a manufacturing firm in an advanced CIM (computer-integrated manufacturing) environment would be an example. So once again, managements need not only to adopt information management practices appropriate to their sector, but also recognize when their IT activities have moved them into a new sector metaphor and change their approach accordingly.

Thomson Holidays, the UK leisure travel company selling packaged holidays abroad, introduced an on-line reservation system, TOP, into travel agents' offices in 1982. (Yielding significant competitive advantage, it is described more fully in Chapter 3.) This was an innovative move inspired by the chief executive and backed by the sales director to 'put terminals on travel agents' desks'. By 1986 the system had become the foundation on which volume growth was possible, new products were introduced, and reservation and administration costs had been driven down. TOP had become the infrastructure of the business and its distribution channel. From an inspired application development, characteristic of a company in the 'drive sector' sensing an opportunity in IT, Thomson Holidays had moved into the 'delivery sector' and set the *de facto* standard for delivery of services in the travel trade. Colin Palmer, Thomson's Deputy Managing Director, has commented, 'apart from computer systems, Thomson Holidays owns very little'.

A MANAGEMENT AGENDA

In Chapter 1, nine propositions were advanced for distinguishing the IT era from previous experience. The implications derived in Chapter 1 and the typical positioning of the firms in the frameworks presented in this chapter suggest an information management agenda for most large organizations today. Five major prescriptions emerge.

1. *Normalization:* It is time that management of information, information resources and information technology came of age. The delivery of information systems and running of information technologies will still remain largely a specialist and professional domain. However it now must be seen as a *function* in its own right – a function that is planned, organized and controlled just as are those functions such as finance or personnel, which are responsible for other principal resources. At the same time, IT and information processing comprises a set of *activities* in which most managers and employees are involved. Increasingly every manager is an information manager and should treat information resources as seriously and confidently as he treats manpower, money, materials or machines. In other words, IT has become a mainstream function and a pervasive activity, which together need managing as normally as anything else. Thus information management will come of age when this normalization process has been achieved.

2. *Strategy:* IT has to be seen as a strategic resource which must *support* business strategy and which can *create* strategic opportunities and competitive advantage. Accordingly firms need information systems strategies which link the exploitation of IT to business needs and also identify new business opportunities. Formulation of information systems strategies is thus an urgent priority for most organizations.

3. *Architecture:* Infrastructure, the technological foundation of computers, communications, data and basic systems, has to meet the organization's needs. Connectivity between multiple and varied technologies often is important. The main design parameters of infrastructure must fit the organization structure and management style of the firm. Information technology resources must be planned and provided in an orderly, effective manner in order to implement the information systems strategy. All this means that most IT functions see the definition of IT architecture as an urgent priority if the organization's needs are to be met efficiently and effectively most of the time.

4. *Investment:* Recognizing that IT and information systems are an asset that must be invested in, maintained and managed for benefits is a perspective consistent with the view that the IT is a strategic resource. Executive management then has to consider how much to spend on IT, on what activities, for what return. It has to

consider how to fund IT, charge for it and control it. It has to take a long-term view as well as demand short-term deliverables. In short IT is managed as an investment.

5. *Revamping:* The ratification of IT as a function, the recognition that IT is also a pervasive activity and the conviction that IT is a strategic resource, demand a change in attitudes, skills and management policies. It is likely that IT leadership is essential and this cannot only come from the professionals. Revamping is concerned with change and more than likely management education, organizational development and elevating the profile of IT will be prerequisites for successful transition from the DP era to the IT era.

The remaining chapters develop these prescriptions, beginning first with a detailed examination of the technology-strategy connection.

NOTES AND REFERENCES

1. See, for example, Drury D. H., 'An empirical assessment of the stages of DP growth', *MIS Quarterly,* June 1983, and Lucas H.C. Jr and Sutton J. A., 'The stage hypothesis and S-curve: some contradictory evidence', *Communications of the ACM,* Vol. 20 (No.4), April 1977.
2. Quoted in the *Observer*, London, 22 November 1987.

FURTHER READING

Curley K., 'Word processing: first step to the office of the future? An examination of the evolving technology and its use in organizations', unpublished doctoral thesis, Harvard Business School, 1981.

Dickson G., Leitheiser R. and Wetherbe J., 'Key information systems issues for the 1980s', *MIS Quarterly*, September 1984.

Earl M. J., 'Emerging trends in managing new information technologies', in N. Piercy (ed.), *The Management Implications of New Information Technologies*, Croom Helm, London, 1983.

Earl M. J., Feeny D. F., Hirschheim R. A. and Lockett M., 'Information technology executives' key education and development needs: A field study', research and discussion paper (RDP 86/10), Oxford Institute of Information Management, Templeton College, Oxford, 1986.

Gibson C. F. and Nolan R. L., 'Managing the four stages of EDP Growth', *Harvard Business Review*, January–February 1974.

Henderson, J. C. and Treacy M. E., 'Managing end user computing for competitive advantage, *Sloan Management Review*, Winter 1986.

Keen P. G. W. and Mills R. D., 'Stages in managing telecommunications', in Nolan, Norton & Co., *Managing Telecommunications for Strategic Advantage in Europe*, London, 1984.

McFarlan F. W. and McKenney J. L., *Corporate Information Systems Management: The Issues Facing Senior Executives*, Dow Jones Irwin, 1983.

Nolan R. L., 'Managing the crises in data processing', *Harvard Business Review*, March–April 1979.

Chapter 3

INFORMATION TECHNOLOGY AND STRATEGIC ADVANTAGE

INTRODUCTION

In Chapter 1 it was established that IT is potentially a strategic weapon, capable of achieving strategic advantage in four different ways. Case examples were quoted in detail to support this claim. It also was observed that the combination of the new technologies with certain more macro-forces for change made IT a truly strategic resource in some sectors. Indeed, Michael Porter, a leading scholar of competitive strategy, asserts that 'the power of technology as a competitive variable lies in its ability to alter competition through changing industry structure'. Several writers – as we shall see – have built upon Porter's work on competitive strategy to examine the strategic potential of IT.

Such strategic perspectives are relatively new to the IT and IS communities. Indeed most of the academic literature on information systems had been concerned hitherto with the use of IT to support management planning and control systems, often influenced by the seminal works of Anthony and Simon respectively. In the professional literature, the focus often has been even more basic, namely the design and implementation of transaction-based computer systems to underpin business operations. To distinguish applications which are more strategic in character than these two conventional classes of information systems, the diagrams such as that in Figure 3.1 are beginning to appear.

In this chapter, therefore, we develop 'the technology strategy connection'. The concerns are, simultaneously, how can IT produce strategic advantage and what frameworks or principles are available to guide practitioners in exploiting IT for strategic advantage? Behind these questions lie some traditional and deeper issues familiar to strategists, including the distinction between offensive and defensive moves, the wisdom of being first, second or later movers, and the relative advantages of internal and individual initiatives versus collaboration through networks and alliances. These latter questions can only receive incidental treatment here, as evidence in the IT context is still scant.

By the mid-1980s a number of influential articles had appeared on IT and strategic

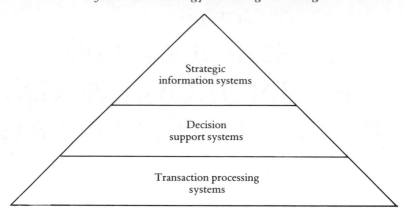

Figure 3.1 The 'new' IS pyramid.

advantage. Most provided a framework for analysis demonstrating the strategic impact of IT or suggesting how strategic advantage might be sought. None of them offers a complete answer; equally most of them are helpful if used appropriately. Accordingly, most of these frameworks are discussed in this chapter, but within a classification that suggests their relative purposes and merits. This analysis is based on experimentation with available models and frameworks in management education, research and consultancy. The classification is portrayed in Table 3.1. Three classes of framework are proposed: awareness, opportunity and positioning, each having its own purpose, scope and use. Experience shows that a selection works best, whether in education or practice but that the right framework must be used for the right purpose in the right context. The next three sections develop these classes in turn.

Table 3.1 A framework of frameworks

Framework/ attribute	Awareness	Opportunity	Positioning
Purpose	Vision	Ends	Means
Scope	Possibility	Probability	Capability
Use	Education	Analysis	Implementation

AWARENESS FRAMEWORKS

The purpose of these frameworks is to demonstrate how IT can be used for strategic advantage, help executives assess, by reference to general models, the potential impact of IT on their business, and open up thinking and discourse on the technology-strategy connection. Thus awareness frameworks are more conceptual and pedagogic than prescriptive and instrumental. They are high level frameworks which will often need detailed, decomposed follow-up investigation. However they are extremely useful in the classroom or workshop. Hinting at strategic possibilities of IT, beginning to point a vision for specific executives, firms or industries, and helping to reorient thinking and delimit the scope. In short, their primary use turns out to be educational.

Three subclasses of awareness framework may be identified:

1. Refocusing frameworks which help change mind-sets.
2. Impact models which suggest the scale of strategic change that may be possible.
3. Scoping models which indicate what might be the overall strategic scope of IT for a business or sector.

These are discussed and evaluated in the following three subsections.

Refocusing frameworks

Several workers have inductively developed refocusing frameworks by rationalizing exemplars of strategic information systems. Benjamin *et al.*'s strategic opportunities matrix is an early, typical example. This is founded on two searching questions which they suggest each senior manager should ask:

1. Can I use IT to make a significant change in the way we are now doing business so my company can gain a competitive advantage?
2. Should we, as a company, concentrate on using IT to improve our approach to the market place? Or should we centre our efforts on internal improvements in the way we currently carry out the activities of the firm?

The four-cell matrix in Table 3.2 reflects these questions and reminds companies that strategic advantage can be gained from traditional systems as much as from revolutionary approaches and whether applied in the market place or internally.

Table 3.2 Strategic opportunities framework

	Competitive market place	*Internal operations*
Significant structural change	Merrill Lynch	Digital Equipment
Traditional products and processes	American Hospital Supply	United Airlines

Source: Benjamin *et al.*

The cases quoted by Benjamin *et al.* demonstrate their refocusing model very effectively. Merrill Lynch's CMA account was discussed in Chapter 1. It clearly had an impact in the competitive market place, redefining the market in a significant way. The other three cases are equally convincing.

American Hospital Supply, the US medical supply company, provided on-line order entry terminals for purchasing executives in hospitals. AHS carried a very broad product range and hospital buyers could use the terminals to enquire on stock availability, price and delivery and then order. So attracted were purchasing executives by the system, that acquisition of an AHS terminal was very acceptable and orders increasingly were placed with AHS. Ordering and distribution costs were reduced for both AHS and their customers. In a market of over 400 rivals and 7,000 major customers, AHS achieved 17 per cent per annum growth in market share in the late 1970s and early 1980s. The system changed the traditional relationship between customer and supplier.

Digital Equipment Corporation (DEC) built an expert system 'XCON' to develop computer configurations for customers, building on the knowledge of design and field service engineers. This reduced costs of rework, reduced installation delays and thus improved both DEC's cash flow and customer satisfaction. The system is also used by sales personnel for specifying alternative configurations in the order generation process. XCON thus represents a radically new approach to internal logistics and their management.

United Airlines adopted teleconferencing for operations management in emergency situations and daily executive briefings. It allowed efficient and effective communication between key personnel located in dispersed airports and controllers at headquarters. Teleconferencing has been used subsequently in labour negotiations across the airline's dispersed network. These are the applications of new technology to traditional processes.

The value of this framework is in raising executive awareness rather than in searching for opportunities. It is thus a powerful pedagogic tool, behind which lie two useful sets of questions. However, it is perhaps too general for firm-specific use. Accordingly, it may require paraphrasing for different sectors and situations.

The framework for the UK building society context was extended and amended. Here the aim was to refocus managers in a sector not only where IT was becoming a delivery mechanism but where liberalization and competition from adjacent sectors were prompting structural change. Implicit in the model shown in Table 3.3 are two sets of questions: the use of new technologies or the extension of traditional ones, and the application of either in the back office for efficiency, the front office for efficiency and service, or beyond the office for service and strategic strikes. Indeed, in this case the cells could represent opportunities for societies or threats from banks, retailers and the like who are moving into the building society market place.

Table 3.3 Refocusing IT in building societies

	Back office	Front office	Beyond the office
Traditional mechanisms	Computerized transaction systems (e.g., account processing)	Enquiry terminals in branches (e.g., passbook updating)	Terminals in value systems (e.g., loan queries in estate agents)
New technologies	Office automation (e.g., mailing)	ATMs (e.g., cash points)	Telebanking and EFTPOS (e.g., home banking)

Impact models

A detailed example of an impact model is the contribution of Parsons. This is based on a recognition and analysis of the competitive environment and strategies of business and focuses on the possible opportunities of firms to exploit IT for strategic advantage. Summarized in Table 3.4, Parsons' model reminds us that IT can be influential at the industry, firm or strategy levels.

At the industry level, Parsons points out that IT can affect the nature of the

Table 3.4 Strategic impact of IT (after Parsons)

Level of impact	Effect of IT
Industry level	Changes fundamental nature of the industry
Firm level	Influences competitive forces facing the firm
Strategy level	Supports the generic strategy of the firm

industry's products and services, the industry markets, and/or the industry's economics of production. For example, electronic publishing, computer graphics and communications have dramatically affected the product life cycle and distribution possibilities in publishing. *USA Today*, the first across the nation newspaper in North America, needed these technologies to overcome the time and space constraints which had previously impeded any such initiative. Business newspapers and journal publishers increasingly look to exploit their data and intelligence by using database and communications technologies to create new information markets: the *Financial Times* in the UK and McGraw Hill in the USA are examples. Eddie Shah's introduction of the *Today* newspaper in the UK sought to be viable through changing the economics of production and distribution by applying electronic newsgathering, typesetting and graphics in printing and communications to speed up and simplify distribution. The power of both the technology and the information of IT has been demonstrated dramatically in this sector.

At the firm level, Parsons draws on Porter's five competitive forces model of competitive strategy. This is discussed under 'Business strategy frameworks' (page 54), but the key message is that IT can be used to limit or enhance the power of rivals, competitors, suppliers, new entrants, or new products in the firm's wider competitive arena.

Parsons also borrows from Porter in his strategy level impact analysis. Here he is concerned with the positioning that successful firms adopt relative to industry structure and competitive forces. Parsons argues that IT can support each of the possible three generic strategies that Porter suggests are available to firms. These are the following:

1. Overall cost leadership – or pursuit of lowest cost production on an industry-wide basis.
2. Differentiation – or differentiating a product or service on an industry-wide basis.
3. Focus – or concentration on a particular market or product niche.

The value of this taxonomy is that it can be used to help align the exploitation of IT with business strategy. We can ask whether IT has any potential for the implementation of the generic strategy the firm has chosen. Alternatively we can ask whether a seemingly strategic information system is consistent with our chosen generic strategy. Finally we can ask whether IT can help us transform our generic strategy to change the basis of competition in the battle with our rivals.

Cost leadership often can be enhanced or made feasible by IT. Examples include substitution of robotics for labour, driving down inventory costs with stock control systems or more advanced MRP II systems, reducing order processing costs by on-line order entry systems, reducing downtime and waste costs by machine sensing, planned maintenance systems or process controls, taking time and high cost effort out of design and testing operations by CAD and CAE, and reducing administration expenses by office automation.

> A packaging company competing with five rivals in Europe aimed to be the lowest cost producer. Relatively late in developing information systems, it had the opportunity to explicitly align investment in IT with the lowest cost strategy. Inventory control systems were introduced to reduce working capital stocks, instrumentation was installed to monitor machine performance in order to improve efficiencies, optimization models were developed in the production process, cost reporting systems monitored the key costs of materials and machine usage, and finally an automated warehouse was constructed not only to reduce stock-holding and space costs but also in order to schedule longer production runs for efficiency gains and maximize sales of each product to increase volumes.

Differentiation is usually concerned with creating uniqueness in the eyes of customers. This may be achieved through product features, customer service, added value services, technological sophistication, brand image, flexibility, quality or customization. Often IT and information systems can create or support such competitive edges. Indeed, whether there is information content in the product or in the production and distribution process, there is scope for providing information-based value which rivals do not offer. On-line ordering, dealer networks, expert system advice, computerized quotation systems, integration of product offerings, communications-based customer hotlines and automated administrative support are examples.

> Friends Provident, the UK Insurance Company, introduced FRENTEL, an on-line quotation service to brokers. Friends Provident's objective was to differentiate in an intensely competitive market place, where the leading market share historically did not exceed 5 per cent. Also, the aim was to thereby increase broker loyalty by allowing brokers through a videotex-based system to obtain quotations and surrender values directly from the insurer's central computer, as well as perform policy maintenance functions. Brokers began to prefer this procedure because service to their clients was enhanced. Being first with on-line quotations, Friends Provident were seen to be different and innovative, resulting in increased market share from 2.4 to 6 per cent.

IT and information systems have become mechanisms for creating, supporting or changing generic strategies. Increasingly we shall see that the implementation of Porter's lowest cost, differentiation and focus strategies depend on appropriate IS for their success. Strategists therefore can no longer analyse and formulate these generic strategies if the IS consequences and potentials are ignored.

Parsons' impact framework therefore becomes a tool of persuasion. It argues that IT truly does have strategic influence. It can be tailored to a particular industry or firm to explore current trends of future potential, but at a preliminary stage of analysis. It can also be used, particularly at his strategic level, to test if current IS investments in a firm are supporting its generic strategy.

Scoping models

Porter and Millar have provided a useful example of a scoping model. It is not always easy to see how information can be developed and exploited for competitive advantage. Information processing concepts can be vague and we still tend to see business and industries as providers of products and occasionally services, where information is but a peripheral concern. Porter and Millar's information intensity matrix brings the information dimension to industry analysis with useful examples, and can be used as a preliminary assessor of overall potential for exploiting IT for strategic advantage in a particular sector. For whilst a general trend in the strategic importance of IT is evident, at the industry level, the direction and pace of change differ. Their matrix in Figure 3.2 can be used to predict the scope, degree and rate of change induced by IT for different industries, and thus also can help position a firm accordingly.

Information content of the product

		LOW	HIGH
Information intensity of the value chain	HIGH	Oil refining	Newspapers Banking Airlines
	LOW	Cement	

Figure 3.2 Porter and Millar's information intensity matrix.

The vertical dimension in Figure 3.2 measures the information intensity of the value chain – discussed later, but briefly defined as the 'Company's technologically and economically distinct activities it performs to do business'. The horizontal axis represents the information content in the product. The publishing industry discussed above rates high on both dimensions.

The same scope can be seen in financial services. In contrast, the oil industry has high information processing in its production and distribution, but little information content in its product. The cement industry is essentially a physical process industry producing bulk, industrial product and is unlikely to be impacted dramatically by IT on either dimension. Thus we see many exemplar cases of strategic information systems in the finance sector, the oil and petrochemical industries striving for competitive advantage and making small but not major gains, and one UK cement company running down much of its DP capability in 1987. However, as the capability of IT increases and the cost decreases, we can expect industries to move towards ever higher information content in both process and product.

So awareness frameworks tend to have high pedagogic value in raising the vision of executives, and IT professionals, for strategic use of information technologies. They show broadly what are the possibilities afforded by IT – but they are generally too high level and too descriptive to guide users to specific opportunities for strategic information systems. That is the purpose of the opportunity frameworks that follow.

OPPORTUNITY FRAMEWORKS

These frameworks are explicitly designed to be analytical tools which lead to firm-specific strategic advantage opportunities and/or clarify business strategies in order to demonstrate options for using IT strategically. They are more instrumental and practical than awareness frameworks, but do have an educational role too. Indeed many of the judgements made in this section are derived from using these opportunity frameworks in workshops during management education programmes at the Oxford Institute of Management. In principle, however, opportunity frameworks aid the process of analytical discovery of ideas for strategic information systems – probabilities to be examined further by feasibility studies.

The following four subclasses may be identified:

1. Systems analysis frameworks – which provide analytical techniques to apply across a business.
2. Applications search tools – which probe the characteristics of specification application areas for good fit with the potentials of IT in general, or of specific technologies.
3. Technology fitting frameworks – which seek to match the attributes of specific technologies to problems or opportunities.
4. Business strategy frameworks – which evaluate the business strategy context of an enterprise and suggest where IT has a payoff.

These are discussed and evaluated in the following four subsections.

Systems analysis frameworks

Techniques for investigating the information flows, impediments, gaps and opportunities in business processes and activities are valuable because they are not confined to any particular application area or technology. They are generic. Thus the traditional methods of systems analysis and more recent methodologies for information requirements analysis may help. However, they rarely have a strategic perspective. Porter and Millar's value chain analysis is more promising as it focuses on *competitiveness* and the role of technology.

Value chain analysis divides a company's activities into the technologically and economically distinct activities it performs to do business. These are called value activities because they should add value for which buyers are willing to pay when they buy the final product or service being supplied. A business is profitable if the value it creates exceeds the cost of performing the value activities. To gain competitive advantage over its rivals, a company must either perform these activities at a lower cost or perform them in a way that leads to differentiation and a premium price.

Figure 3.3 displays the nine typical activities of the value chain, comprising five primary activities involved in the production, marketing, distribution and after sales servicing of the product plus four support activities which provide the inputs and infrastructure that allow the primary activities to take place. A firm's value chain is a system of interdependent activities which are connected by linkages. Linkages exist when one activity affects another in terms of cost or effectiveness and trade-offs and optimization are sought to find the right blend to achieve competitive advantage. Also linkages require coordination. One firm's value chain, of course, is embedded in the collective value chains of both suppliers and customers in the industry. This industry

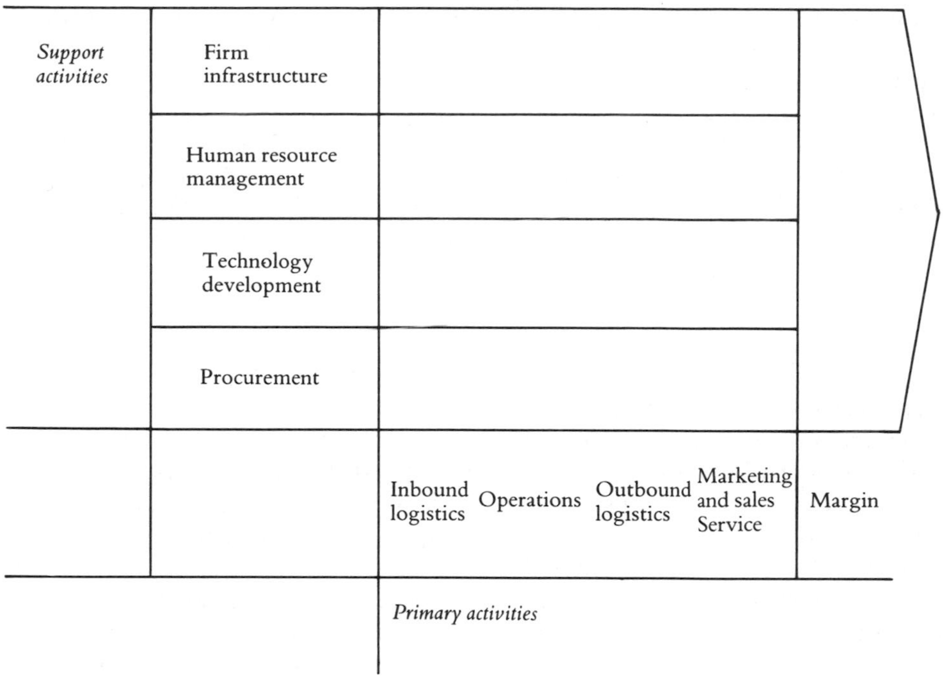

Support activities	Firm infrastructure		
	Human resource management		
	Technology development		
	Procurement		
		Inbound logistics Operations Outbound logistics Marketing and sales Service	Margin

Primary activities

Figure 3.3 The value chain.

stream of activities is termed the 'value system' by Porter and Millar.

The scope for exploitation of IT in the value chain is fourfold, applying either technology directly or its information processing capability to either value activities or their linkages:

1. The technology can physically automate and improve the physical tasks in any activity, e.g., computer controlled machine tools in assembly operations.
2. The technology can physically connect or control activities across linkages, e.g., communications linkages between production and distribution centres.
3. Information systems can help perform, support or manage value activities, e.g., inventory control systems.
4. Information systems can optimize or coordinate activities across linkages, e.g., CAD-CAM systems for computer integrated manufacturing.

Clearly these scopes apply beyond the firm, in the value system interfacing with suppliers and customers, as well as internally. Such external possibilities include telemarketing, remote sensing of equipment breakdowns or stock-outs, and ATMs.

Just mapping the firm's operations and processes by the value chain technique has limited value. It provides no more than a high level checklist and possible prompt for IT applications. Nevertheless one service company which had successfully exploited IT in marketing discovered by value chain analysis that its main cost-base was in procurement and began to shift its focus of IS development activity accordingly. The key is to ascertain the cost of each activity and analyse whether there is opportunity to reduce costs or add value through IT and IS. This may highlight the principal areas for attention. Secondly the linkages then can be analysed to see if there are problems of, or opportunities for, coordination, integration or optimization.

Systems analysis frameworks therefore help in 'homing in' on opportunities. They direct the analyst towards areas of promise. They cannot prescribe what particular technologies have potential and they do not delve into the specific possibilities of highlighted application areas. Thus detailed application ideas may have to be elicited from application users and specialists – or prompted by more specific frameworks such as those in the next subclass.

Applications search tools

These focus on a specific application area (and perhaps also on a specific technology) describing, analysing and evaluating in detail the typical information processing requirements, attributes or gaps. A useful example is the customer resource life-cycle of Ives and Learmonth. This plots the life-cycle of how a customer acquires a product or service and therefore focuses on the linkage between the supplying firm and its customers. The goal is to see where IS and IT can be harnessed to improve customer service, with benefits to each party. The supplier uses IT to solidify its business relationship with its customers, while the customer benefits from the added value of enhanced customer service. Incidentally, Ives and Learmonth claim that the potential value of such activities for building customer loyalty, defending market share, and creating competitive advantage often goes unnoticed. Their customer resource life-cycle, reproduced in Table 3.5 is a development of earlier work by Burnstine. Runge and Earl have taken the framework a small step further, in terms of telecommunications technology.

The major phases of the life-cycle shown in Table 3.5 are the following:

1. Requirements – determining the requirements of the resource.
2. Acquisition – obtaining or developing the resource.
3. Stewardship – managing the resource while in inventory.
4. Retirement – disposing of the resource.

Using Ives and Learmonth's examples, Chevrolet's touch-screen microcomputer system which asks showroom customers about their driving habits and type of vehicle desired, and then recommends several models based on this analysis of needs, is an example of a competitive information system supporting the 'specify requirements' step of the requirements phase of the life-cycle. An estate agency provides brokers with access to an on-line mortgage search service. The system assists prospective home buyers in selecting among mortgage opportunities available through multiple sources. This is an example of a system supporting the 'select a source' step of the acquisition phase. A case of a system supporting the 'maintain' step of the stewardship phase is provided by a consumer appliance manufacturer. They provide toll-free telephone access to trained repair technicians who are backed up by computer-based assistance in trouble-shooting common problems. The 'disposal' step of retirement is exemplified by the hotel chains who now use IT to permit guests to check out of rooms without the time-consuming process of dealing with a desk clerk.

Table 3.5 Customer resource life-cycle

Requirements	
Establish requirements	How much of the resource is required?
Specify requirements	What are the required resource's particular attributes?
Acquire	
Select source	From whom will the customer obtain the resource?
Order	How will the customer order the product?
Authorize and pay for	How will the customer pay for the product?
Acquire	How where and when will be customer take possession of the resource?
Test and accept	How does the customer ensure the resource conforms to specifications?
Stewardship	
Integrate	How is the resource merged with inventory?
Monitor	In what ways can the customer monitor the resource?
Upgrade	How will the resource be enhanced if conditions change?
Maintain	How will the resource be repaired if it becomes necessary?
Retirement	
Dispose of	How will the customer move, return, sell or dispose of the resource when it is no longer needed?
Account for	How much is the customer spending on the resource.

Source: Ives and Learmonth

Applications diagnosis, such as the customer resource life-cycle, is helpful to strategists and systems developers who decide to attack a business activity or application area and assess whether any form of IT usage could yield competitive edge. Here the need is for frameworks which direct the analyst to ask key questions about the activity which will reveal where and how IT might produce competitive advantage. The converse use of such frameworks is to be able to test creative ideas against a sound business and strategic rubric for the activity.

Sales and marketing are typically unsupported by IT and IS. The financial emphasis of the DP era, the limited scope of DP outside the firm, and the hustling and flexible style of marketing managers were often impediments in the exploitation of computing in these areas. In the IT era the strategic focus, the advent of end-user, communications and database technologies and the increasing attention to markets, customers and distribution have changed this picture. Many firms and their managements are actively trying to apply IT to marketing but find it difficult to identify and evaluate opportunities. Furthermore, some IT initiatives seem to make little sense in terms of marketing policy or competitive strategy. This is a special value of Ives and Learmonth's model.

Feeny has developed an opportunities search framework for marketing and this provides a good example of applications diagnosis techniques. Table 3.6 lists six product-market characteristics which Feeny suggests are crucial determinants of the successful application of IT to support marketing. The UK travel industry's use of value added networks as distribution channels provided a laboratory in which Feeny was able to test this model.

Thomson Holidays, the leading leisure travel firm in the UK, have harnessed IT as their distribution channel. Selling packaged holidays and related services through their own and other travel agents, they installed their TOP reservation system. This not only allows agents to enquire about holiday and tour availability, but to make reservations and also interrogate the late or special holiday availability. By building in system advantages over what is possible by telephone ordering, creating a user-friendly system, and eventually withdrawing the telephone service, Thomson built on their market leadership, changed the basis of competition at the agent and customer interface, and reduced costs for both themselves and the agents. On the first booking day for the 1987 season, Thomson made 205,000 reservations. The rivals have spent several years trying to emulate or better the TOP system. Eventually one key rival introduced an almost identical system and explicitly promoted it as similar. Thomson through TOP have been able to differentiate, enhance their market leadership and maintain their quality image all within the low cost economic structure of the industry.

Table 3.6 Marketing opportunity search framework

Perceived product differentiation	*Low*	*Medium*	*High*
	Prime positioning Service provision	Product information System specificiation	Market analysis Benefit selling
Sector channel structure	*Direct*	*Dedicated*	*Shared*
	Sales support Retail alliances	Sales support	Prime positioning Service provision
Relationship between need and product	*Unclear*		*Clear*
	Consumer guidance		
Frequency of purchase decision	*High*	*Low*	
	Fastest source Service provision	Customer tracking	
Frequency of delivery within contract	*High*	*Low*	
	Build partnership Customer relationship status		
Buyers access to IT resources	*Poor*	*Good*	
	Fastest source Consumer guidance Service provision Benefit selling	Build partnership	

Source: Feeny

Feeny suggest that three of the product-market characteristics listed in Table 3.6 helped explain the success of Thomson's reservation system.

1.   TOP was accepted and economically feasible because frequency of purchase in the

agents was high; two earlier movers failed to establish their systems because they had a low market share.

2. Perceived product differentiation was high in one special case. TOP was favoured by late bookers because it provided special information on unsold imminent holidays. Overt competitive advantage accrued to Thomson.
3. Agents have access to IT through VANS suppliers so telebooking is feasible. However, they have to access operator-specific systems to interrogate availability data and thus become somewhat dependent upon Thomson, the market leader.

The value of applications diagnosis techniques is that they are founded on analytical principles of specific applications and ask questions familiar to specialists and managers in the application area. Therefore they help eliminate technological solutions which do not fit the application and suggest the direction that applications development should follow.

Technology fitting frameworks

In the DP era, it was fashionable to match the attributes of computing to the information requirements of different applications. One such framework was the computability profile of McCosh, Rahman and Earl which assessed the capabilities of mainframe computers with the information requirements of management planning and control systems. In the IT era, the need is for more of these frameworks matching each of the multiple information technologies to specific application areas. An early and valuable example of such technology fitting is an opportunities matrix developed by Runge for the exploitation of telecommunications-based information systems (TBIS) linking the firm with its customers to achieve competitive advantage. The framework is a derivative of Ives and Learmonth's Customer Resource Life Cycle.

Runge found in a study of 36 TBISs which linked firms to customers that 12 linkages potentially exist. Each linkage provides opportunities for development of TBIS which either differentiate the supplier from his rivals or create switching costs for the customer. Table 3.7 defines these stages and linkages and the framework is demonstrated in more detail with descriptions of 12 exemplar TBISs in a paper by Runge and Earl.

An example of a TBIS supporting the 'requirements' stage is GTE's provision of portable computer terminals to sales representatives in their commercial lighting division. These access an information system which performs a detailed analysis of prospective customer's lighting requirements and prepares sales proposals on the spot. By helping to establish customer requirements this service has achieved perhaps a 10 per cent increase in sales. Friends Provident's FRENTEL quotation system illustrates a TBIS for the 'acquisition' stage. IBM's PCSS system is an example of a TBIS at work in the 'stewardship' stage. PCSS provides on-line electronic support to IBM's personal computer dealers for handling repair and maintenance queries and distributing product and promotional matter. The hotel check-in service provided by SAS, the Scandinavian airline, is an example of a TBIS for the 'retirement' stage. Here a customer at an SAS hotel can settle his account, book or confirm his flight, check in his luggage and receive his flight boarding pass by one set of interactions in the hotel lobby. The TBIS thus not only closes a sale but opens or continues another; it also exploits SAS's market positioning as both an airline and hotel operator.

Table 3.7 Telecommunications to customers' opportunities

Stage	Linkage			
Requirements	Establish requirements			
	Acquired information			
Acquisition	Specify			
	Select a source			
	Order			
	Authorize and pay for			
	Acquire			
Stewardship	Monitor			
	Manage			
	Support			
Retirement	Terminate use			
	Account for			
		Internal	Link-up	Lock-in

Source: Runge

The horizontal axis of Table 3.7 represents the second dimension of the opportunites search. Runge found that most TBISs for competitive advantage evolved through three forms. The TBISs that achieved a degree of 'lock in' between a customer and a supplier were rarely the result of a revolutionary and strategic strike that was implemented in one move. Rather the systems had evolved gradually, first being 'internal' routines for supporting functional linkages in the customer interaction life-cycle. Subsequently, somebody suggested electronically 'linking up' the suppliers' value chain to those of the customers, but as an extension of the earlier internal routine. Finally, function was added to this 'link up' system to provide more value for the customer and introduce switching costs. The result was customer 'lock in'. In other words most TBISs into customers were extensions across organizational boundaries of existing internal information systems. The TBISs allowed customers direct access to what previously had been a system for internal use only.

Several of the firms studied had extended their customer-oriented systems backwards or forwards through the linkages of the customer interaction life-cycle. Likewise, most had evolved from 'internal' through 'link up' to 'lock in' status. The following suggests how the opportunities matrix can be used:

1. Plot the customer interactions.
2. Ask whether TBIS can simplify, improve or add value to any one interaction.
3. Examine whether the TBIS also can support and add value to any other interaction.

4. Consider whether latent link up or lock in opportunities are available in existing systems.
5. Consider whether new opportunities should strive for lock in immediately or be developed incrementally from internal to lock in due to technical, management or competitive reasons.

Note that Runge's matrix applies only to telecommunications-based information systems in customer relationships.

The complexities of advanced manufacturing technologies (AMT) have been analysed by Meredith and Hill. Their framework, reproduced in Figure 3.4 inevitably is somewhat general. However it informs potential users not only of the differences between in vogue forms of AMT, such as flexible manufacturing systems, MRP II and computer integrated manufacturing, but also of their likely fit with different intentions. The latter are expressed in the form of objectives, benefits, risks and the like. Meredith and Hill classify these degrees of fit as levels of technological integration.

Figure 3.4 is more conceptual than most opportunity frameworks. Its original purpose was to demonstrate the managerial implications of different forms of AMT and it will be developed further in Chapter 7. However, it is valuable in reminding potential users of AMT that some technologies require more fundamental change than others and it warns against 'over-engineering' solutions to manufacturing problems.

The value of technology fitting frameworks therefore is that they allow users to explore the attributes of specific technologies to see if they can be applied to particular problems or opportunities, to understand what they can and cannot do, and to appreciate some of their managerial implications. However, both application search and technology fitting frameworks are given more impetus and focus if they are complemented, or preceded, by the use of business strategy frameworks.

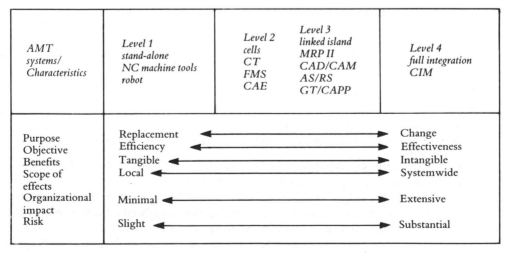

Figure 3.4 AMT framework (*source:* Meredith and Hill).

Business strategy frameworks

These are required to either ascertain or verify the firm's driving strategic assumptions or strategic posture. They also can begin to suggest where IT can bring advantage. Michael Porter's model of five competitive forces has its place here. Reproduced in Figure 3.5 it helps executives at the level of the strategic business unit clarify their business strategy and discuss where IT potentially may yield competitive advantage in terms of defending the firm against these forces or influencing them in its favour.

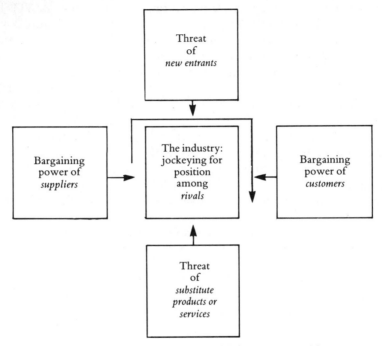

Figure 3.5 Porter's five forces of industry competition.

In its clarification role, Porter's five-forces model helps in the following ways:

1. It focuses on industry and competitive dynamics.
2. It reminds us that competition is not just about the actions or rivals.
3. It provides a simple framework which facilitates discussion and yet is based on sound principles of industrial economics.
4. It usually suggests quickly which are the one or two dominant forces to consider.

However, detailed investigation is usually required subsequently to understand the sources and nature of the significant forces, what strategic actions are possible and what industry reactions are likely. (There are generalizable rules, principles and probabilities governing strategic actions on each force.) Also, one commonly finds some of the forces interact so that in reality iterative analyses are required followed by mixed strategic actions. Nevertheless, Porter's framework has proved useful in helping business managers think strategically and in analysing the competitive context in which IT can be exploited.

Table 3.8 Exploiting IT in the competitive arena

Competitive force	Potential of IT	Mechanism
New entrants	Barriers to entry	1. Erect 2. Demolish
Suppliers	Reduce power	1. Erode 2. Share
Customers	Lock in	1. Switching costs 2. Customer information
Substitute products/services	Innovation	1. New products 2. Add value
Rivalry	Change the basis	1. Compete 2. Collaborate

Porter and Millar, McFarlan, and Cash and Konsynski are amongst those who have built upon Porter's model to suggest how IT can limit and enhance the five competitive forces for a firm. In Table 3.8 their work is built on and simplified to suggest what strategic role IT can play on each dimension and in what possible ways.

An obvious defensive strategic action to limit new entrants in a market is to erect *barriers to entry*. IT can be a powerful weapon here, increasing economies of scale, raising the capital cost of entry, making preemptive strikes in markets or tying up distribution channels. Conversely IT can be exploited offensively to break down or jump over barriers to entry, by changing the cost structure of the industry, creating new distribution channels or changing the traditional economies of scale or scope in the industry through the exploitation of smaller, specialized or more flexible technologies.

> Merrill Lynch's cash management account, described in Chapter 1, represented a pre-emptive strike which others could not easily imitate quickly or cheaply. It erected a barrier to entry in a new service-market. Continued improvement of the cash management account also created an image for Merrill Lynch of being at a leading edge, thereby protecting its market position.

> Citibank exploited automated teller machines (ATMs) to expand its retail banking business in the USA. Providing a high service, low cost route to expansion, ATMs were placed in airports, supermarkets and other high customer-traffic areas. This was an aggressive strategic action which demolished existing barriers to entry such as high property costs, or inter-state banking regulations, by circumventing them. Citibank were not the first bank to exploit ATMs; Chemical Bank adopted the technology earlier but only as an automation move to improve existing retail outlets in New York State.

The potential of IT in managing relationships with *suppliers* is to reduce their power to increase the buyer's control over them. Supplier power tends to be a function of concentration, product choice, actual or potential interdependence or integration and customer importance. One strategic potential of IT is to erode the suppliers' power; another is to share power and responsibility. Examples of the former are: installation of computer-aided design (CAD) links; creation of on-line order placement and call-off systems; and development of on-line scanning or periodic analyses of supplier prices and performance. The strategic intentions here include respectively control of design and specification changes, improvement of responsiveness and reduction of stocks, and selection of lowest cost or best service suppliers. On the other hand, sharing of responsibility and power may be achieved by setting up automatic order and supply chains, for example using just-in-time systems and technologies, perhaps concentrating on one long-term supplier.

> British Home Stores, the UK variety store chain, has set up videotex-based supplier links which call off orders from suppliers overnight, send invoices and labels, enable stock, scheduling and delivery queries to be made and send sales data back in return. The ultimate aim is to reduce the retailers' inventories, improve sales, and improve suppliers' flexibility and responsiveness. BHS plays on its purchasing power and erodes the independence of its suppliers, but shares some of the benefits of the link, by providing suppliers with automation benefits and new information.

> Ford have set up CAD links with their suppliers to reduce design and change costs, reduce the time taken in, and error rate of, design and specification changes and improve parts stock and acquisition procedures. No doubt like the Japanese car firms, such links eventually will be developed with only one or two key suppliers of each product to integrate supplies into their computer integrated manufacturing so that both the car firm and the supplier *share* growth and performance improvements together.

The potential often sought of IT in managing customers is to lock them in. Two principal mechanisms are available. The first is the use of IT to create switching costs for the customer. If an inter-organizational information system linking the firm to the customer can create a dominant distribution channel, provide a special or preferred service, or differentiate the firm from its rivals, the customer may well find it costly, uncomfortable or impractical to switch to another supplier. The second weapon IT provides is to construct customer information systems which inform the firm about customer behaviour, needs, characteristics etc. and facilitate targeted marketing or new forms of distribution and selling.

> The American Hospital Supply application quoted earlier achieved the placement of order entry terminals in 3,000 hospitals. Such was the ease of making stock enquiries and placing orders that hospitals increased their items per order by over three times. AHS achieved lock in by creating *switching costs*; it was inconvenient to change to other systems or terminals. To reinforce this dynamic, AHS also provided stock control software for hospitals to aid their inventory management and encourage customers to regard AHS as the leading supplier in terms of service.

> Sears, the US retailer, have recognized the potential of information to achieve lock in. About 60 per cent of US households possess Sears credit cards. Whenever the Sears card is used for a sales transaction, Sears not only capture sales data but also *customer information*. This is used to target direct mail campaigns, to design and deliver financial services (thereby capturing financial as well as purchasing profiles of customers) and to design and deliver teleshopping. American Airlines' Advantage Card, the Marks and Spencer chargecard and many other customer card programmes are based on this philosophy.

IT has become a source of innovation. IT can be built into new products and information systems can add value to products and services, all thereby constituting *substitutes* in the market place. Examples of new IT-based products include microprocessor control units for white goods or motor cars, computer-based games, software services or data analysis and information presentation products. Ways of *adding value* to products and services include: interactive information systems to design, specify and select products from a supplier; provision of database access to query product specifications; maintenance schedules or part numbers and descriptions; and portable computer or videotex facilities for professional and expert interrogation or support. Often such value-added services help differentiate a product or supplier from the rivals.

> Data Resources Inc, the econometrics subsidiary of McGraw Hill, introduced a *new product* called VISILINK. This allowed personal computer users to access DRI's econometrics database and extract desired information. This service significantly broadened DRI's appeal and allowed it to reach many small companies and individuals who either were unaware of DRI or could not previously afford DRI's econometrics services.[1]

> ICI the UK Chemicals combine have used expert systems to support their agricultural and pharmaceuticals products and sales force. Counsellor is an expert system which advises farmers via viewdata terminals on disease control. It analyses input on wheat varieties grown, soil type, disease history etc. and recommends fungicides. The farmer thereby acquires information on ICI's product range and alternatives from other suppliers. However ICI is perceived to be offering *added value* and a new service and thus indirectly may attract and keep customers.

The potential strategic use of IT in the ongoing battles with *rivals* is to change the basis of competition. Either IT can be used aggressively as a competitive variable or it can become a basis for collaboration to reduce the rivalry. In the former case, IT can be exploited to accentuate the existing basis of competition or to engineer a new battleground. Often this requires IT to be used as a weapon in support of the firm's generic strategy, discussed earlier. On the other hand, collaboration rather than competition may be suggested either by the availability of communications networks where services or their delivery can be shared or by the ever-increasing costs and timescales suffered by organizations whose firm and sector infrastructure is IT-based. Examples here include banks or retailers who exploit telecommunications, computing and automation as distribution channels.

> Thomson Holiday's TOP reservation system quoted earlier helped change the basis of competition in the leisure travel sector. First it was a source of differentiation from rivals in terms of agent support and customer service. Second it allowed Thomson to cut prices and seek volume in an aggressive low cost producer strategy.

> The building societies in the UK have in the 1980s increasingly modernized their services, moved into retail banking operations and enhanced their image. When value-added networks became technologically feasible, several of them saw the possibility of providing nationwide ATM services. They could do this on their own at considerable expense, build alliances with existing cashpoint networks supplied by banks and retailers, perhaps piggybacking into more integrated financial services at the same time, or collaborate amongst themselves. The society with the largest branch network, the Halifax, developed its own ATM network and pioneered a wide range of terminal facilities, thereby building on its dominant physical asset base. Several of the big or medium-sized societies collaborated to share costs and sites, and perhaps enhance their national coverage if their ATM services and their marketing were attractive, through two value-added networks MATRIX and LINK. A few societies also collaborated with bank networks to extend into services they were not permitted to offer and to enter into the worlds of teleshopping and telebanking.

The framework in Table 3.8 and its development above is particularly useful as a pedagogic tool. However it can be used in business strategic analysis in two ways:

1. The framework can be used to identify strategic applications of IT once Porter's initial five forces analysis has been done.
2. Ideas for exploiting IT for competitive advantage, however generated, can be tested against the framework to see if they make sense in terms of competitive strategy.

A more comprehensive, procedural example of a business strategy framework is Wiseman's 'strategic option generator'. He believes that competitive edge results from 'strategic thrusts' founded on the logics of Chandler's growth strategies and Porter's competitive strategy frameworks. Figure 3.6 reproduces his strategic option generator.

The 'strategic target' equates to three of Porter's competitive forces. The 'strategic thrusts' combine Porter's generic strategies with the mechanisms Chandler plotted in his theory of organizational growth. The 'mode' indicates whether the thrust is being used to attack or defend in the competitive arena. 'Direction' describes whether the firm is using the strategic system option itself or providing it for the target's use.

The potential value of the option generator is not only its conflation of previous frameworks of analysis, but the logical list of analytical questions it provides. Like Porter's model, it therefore helps most in clarifying the firm's business strategy and suggesting the direction of the IT-strategy connection. It is less likely to pinpoint specific applications.

All these opportunity frameworks are useful tools for workshops either in management development events or in real-world strategic systems search. The business strategy frameworks provide a necessary context in which to apply the other methods, but their application does need the involvement of general managers or strategy analysts who have already thought about the enterprise in this way. Systems analysis frameworks help confront detail, but additional techniques which bring other

Figure 3.6 Wiseman's strategic option generator.

strategic perpectives besides cost-value analysis would be valuable. We also need more search tools to use in particular application areas and to assess specific technologies.

POSITIONING FRAMEWORKS

Positioning frameworks are best seen as tools to help executives assess the strategic importance, the particular character, and the inherited situation of IT for their enterprise. The aim is to improve executives' understanding of how the information systems function and how IT should be managed in their particular organization. Some positioning frameworks therefore were introduced in the previous chapter. They are concerned with assessing, developing and improving IT capabilities in specific organizations. They are not very useful in searching for opportunities for strategic information systems, but they do indicate the nature of the information management task if strategic advantage is an objective. Therefore positioning frameworks focus more on implementation.

Three subclasses of positioning frameworks can be identified:

1. Scaling frameworks which help indicate the scale of importance of IT to a business and the scale of the management challenges involved.
2. Spatial frameworks which help indicate the character of IT applications and IT management in different business or sectors.
3. Temporal frameworks which help assess the evolutionary position of an organization in using and managing IT.

Scaling frameworks

The McFarlan and McKenney strategic grid reproduced in Figure 3.7 is the most useful scaling framework currently available. Its rationale and implications were introduced in Chapter 1 and developed in Chapter 2. As a framework for analysis it can be used in education, workshop or consulting mode to assess the strategic importance of IT for a business unit. By questioning the past and future importance of IT the framework helps managements understand not only the scale of importance of IT but the likely

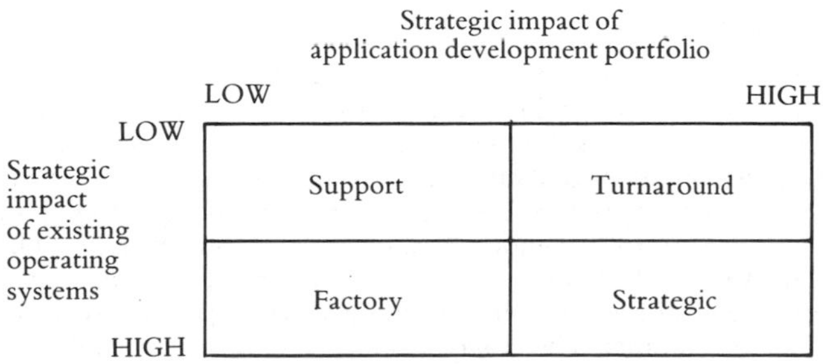

Figure 3.7 Strategic grid (*source:* McFarlan and McKenney).

organizational dynamics involved in managing IT appropriately. It is important not only to look at internal experience and developments, but the effects of other competitive forces' use of IT on the business. At the corporate level, the framework is useful in assessing the differences between business units and identifying appropriate management approaches both by unit and collectively.

So once awareness frameworks have been used to demonstrate the general importance of IT and opportunity frameworks used to point towards particular threats and opportunities for IT, the scaling framework then provides an acid test for concluding how important IT is *now* for a business unit and deciding whether changes in information management policies and practices are required. When combined with spatial and temporal frameworks, some particularly sharp messages can appear.

Spatial frameworks

The Earl sector framework developed in Chapter 2 is valuable in assessing the IT and information management implications for a particular type of business. As argued in that chapter, not all sectors are alike from the information processing perspective and the management impetus required differs as suggested in Table 2.11. When combined with positioning analysis using the scaling strategic grid, the nature of required management actions becomes clearer. For example, many firms position themselves in the turnaround quadrant, but the flavour of information management differs according to whether they are in delivery, dependent or drive sectors.

> A leading merchant bank had for some time operated a sizeable IT department, but mainly in a 'support' role in corporate finance, classical merchant banking, and funds management. It acquired a jobber and broker in readiness for the City of London's 'Big Bang'. With these acquisitions came two 'factory' role DP operations. Corporate management began to see that deregulation of markets coupled with internal notions of developing integrated banking services were forcing the merchant bank into the 'turnaround' quadrant. IT expenditure increased, the need for strategic IS plans was recognized and an IT steering committee was appointed. One year after 'Big Bang' it was clear that much of the new business was being transacted through IT, that good settlement systems were crucial to liquidity and profitability, and that common databases were important in developing integrated financial services. These characteristics of a 'delivery' sector were forcing corporate management to realize that 'turnaround' information management required commitment to architecture, that the increased IT expenditure levels were not a short-term stepped function but likely to continue, and that a strong corporate IT organization was necessary for some years.

> A multi-national electronics company recognized that it was behind in applying advanced manufacturing technology, was being influenced by customers' use of communications-based suppliers links, and was failing to exploit IT in the market place. Classical 'turnaround' information management actions followed: senior management education programmes, introduction of outline strategic systems planning and appointment of new IT directors. Consistent with 'dependent' sector practice, however, the IT function was significantly devolved to business units, IT managers were put into business unit management teams, and strategic systems planning was business-led by the businesses, but aided by corporate consultants. The crucial resource gap turned out to be not technology or technologists but managers who understood enough about technology and much about the business.

Temporal frameworks

The generic assimilation of technology model developed by McFarlan and McKenney is valuable in plotting stage positions in the evolution of information management. It was reproduced in Table 2.8 and can be used to assess relative experience in exploiting specific technologies and relative experience in exploiting most technologies, or a dominant one such as DP. As intended, these frameworks help executive teams assess the current practice of information management and its consequences. They may then either highlight inconsistencies or suggest that a next stage should be anticipated and planned.

However, the stage models are particularly useful when compared with positioning on the scaling strategic grid or spatial sectoral grid. For example stage three 'control' management is fatal in drive sectors, as it tends to *drive out* innovation and experimentation. Stage two management can be potentially dangerous if sustained for too long in delivery sectors, as 'letting one thousand flowers bloom' can subvert any architectural objectives. Even more lethal is a combination of stage three 'control' management with 'turnaround' positioning on the strategic grid. Here the dead hand of cost consciousness and tight resource management constraints precludes major initiatives and leadership by exhortation. The case of Frontier Airlines, quoted earlier illustrates such conflicts – and the possible consequences:

> The US air carrier Frontier Airlines filed for bankruptcy in August 1986. It had been squeezed out of its strong regional presence in the deregulated context of the 1980s. A major cause of Frontier's demise was United Airline's exploitation of its Apollo reservation system around the Denver hub.[2] United used Apollo to tie up the agent distribution channel, bias reservation system information and operation against Frontier and then implement a net ticketing arrangement which favoured the bigger carrier. Previously in 1965 Frontier had 'fired the computers', purchased a reservation system in 1972, and bought reservation services in from Continental Airlines in 1976 – because marketing advantages from owning their own system 'had never happened in Frontier's experience'. In 1978, low cost distributed computing was installed, rather than a mainframe environment typical of the industry, and in 1981 a decision was made never to run a reservation system. Each of these decisions was inspired by concern with costs and lack of faith in benefits – classic stage three thinking. Unfortunately the decisions were made when attempts were being made to turn round the business, but not through IT – and ironically in an exemplar delivery sector where reservation systems were the crucial infrastructure in a deregulated industry.

> A wholesaler and distributor achieved dominant market share in a very competitive sector by locking in principal customers with telecommunications-based inventory ordering systems. The board of the major competitor looked to its IT function to replicate the success and retaliate. Unfortunately the IT manager had just been awarded a significant bonus for reducing his budget by 20 per cent. This stage three management approach was unlikely to motivate or help the IT manager attain competitive parity through information systems!

Individually therefore each of the positioning frameworks is a useful diagnostic tool in assessing the information management task. Used collectively, they bring added value in prognosis and prescription. It is not possible to 'synchronize' positions on all three frameworks since they record overlapping dimensions and different dynamics. However some combinations are clearly dangerous and others suggest a more detailed, sophisticated information management programme than does any one framework alone.

STRATEGY LEVELS AND LINKAGES

Fifteen models or frameworks have been discussed in this chapter so far. The intention has been to evaluate those frameworks which have proved most useful in both practical investigations and classroom presentation. None need be rejected out of hand, for each class of framework and each type within, has a specific purpose. Some may have different appeal for different managers and each may vary in its appropriateness for different firms or sectors. At this stage, robust understanding of the technology-strategy connection and empirical testing of alternative models have yet to develop; the jury is still out on which techniques and frameworks work best. However, managers should be able to select which approaches to use to fit their circumstance and experience. For each framework is useful in the right hands at the right time for the right task.

The many case examples quoted, and their exposition within the frameworks for analysis, also have demonstrated that IT can be exploited for strategic advantage. The technology-strategy connection is seen to exist in two dimensions, namely as follows:

1. IT can support business strategy. For example, IT applications can be aligned with one of Porter's three generic strategies.
2. IT can create strategic options. For example, applications can spearhead quite revolutionary approaches to either the market place or internal operations as Benjamin *et al.* suggest.

    Therefore we can state that no business strategy is complete without reference to IT strategy. Conversely, no IT strategic planning is robust unless it is connected to business strategy. However, the positioning frameworks suggest that scale, sectoral or temporal differences can bring two further dimensions to the technology-strategy connection:
3. IT delivery mechanisms may have to be conceptualized and planned strategically. IT architecture then becomes a strategic concern.
4. Organizational capability in IT and IS may intervene for better or for worse in applying or delivering IT for strategic advantage. Thus management of information resources becomes a strategic matter.

These four concluding statements suggest that 'IT strategy' is not only important for many organizations, but also more complex than it first appears. Three final frameworks are needed to demonstrate that there are three levels of strategy in information technology which have to be formulated. Figure 3.8 introduces the first two levels.

As executives search for IT strategy formulation methodologies which provide a substantive and ongoing procedure for both directing the application of IT and gaining strategic advantage from it, a common confusion can be found. The confusion is between information systems which are the ends and information technology which is the means. This exists partly because of the loose terminology of planning and strategy in discourse and the literature, partly because organizations are still learning how to plan IT, and partly because senior management tends to be concerned about both technology policy issues and business needs and about both planning information resources and controlling them. The delineation in Figure 3.8 between ends and means or between applications and delivery has proved to be valuable in clarifying concepts and practice in strategy formulation. The issue of what should we do with the technology is termed the *Information Systems Strategy*, whilst the question of how do we do it is termed the *Information Technology Strategy*.

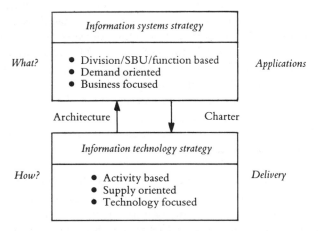

Figure 3.8 Information systems and information technology strategies delineated.

In business it is not unusual to find general managers with inadequate experience and qualifications addressing the delivery strategy and IS executives who cannot know all about business needs trying to drive the applications strategy. It is common to find steering committees quite confused about which of these levels of strategy is their concern. Of course, the two levels are not entirely separable: application needs suggest the charter for the IS function and the technology posture defines the architecture which underpins applications. Nevertheless, the two levels of strategy are distinct in terms of focus, organizational responsibility, methodology and timescale.

The IS strategy is concerned primarily with aligning IS development with business needs and with seeking strategic advantage from IT. Thus, in principle, it is formulated wherever business – especially product-market – strategy is formulated, typically at the level of the strategic business unit. In large and complex organizations, therefore, there may be several IS strategies and they will be the ultimate responsibility of each business unit's executive management. Indeed to borrow from strategic management vocabulary, the IS strategy is formulated at the level of the strategic business unit (SBU), or the level of business where specific customer needs, unique competitors and autonomous resources can be delineated. These strategies may be formulated through a planning methodology and should relate in some way to the business strategy. They will comprise a mix of short-term essential and tactical applications, medium-term business driven needs and long-term visionary investments.

Besides the business unit IS strategies, there is also likely to be a corporate IS strategy which concentrates on group application needs and especially on determining information systems which bring synergy to the whole corporation. For example in financial service companies in the late 1980s the first attempts at formulating corporate IS strategies over and above divisional strategies are being made. A particularly common requirement that is identified is the need for integrated customer database applications for cross-selling etc. Another is the need for risk measurement, capital planning and control, and financial control information systems.

The IT strategy is concerned primarily with technology policies. It tackles questions of architecture, including risk attitudes, vendor policies and technical standards. It is concerned with preferred methods, security levels, mandated systems and the like. This strategy provides the framework within which the specialists provide applications and users use them. It is heavily influenced by the IT professionals, but with top management involvement in order to ensure the technology supply is in line with the organization's needs, style and structure. There are likely to be fewer IT strategies than IS strategies in large and complex organizations, perhaps only one where the information management function has been centralized. The IT strategy may change less frequently than the IS strategy because technology lead–times are longer than many business cycles and because technology trends often are slower to unravel than are business needs.

In Figure 3.9 a third level of strategy is introduced: the *information-management* (IM) strategy. This strategy aims at 'putting the management into IT'. It comprises the policies, procedures, aims and actions likely to be identified from using the positioning frameworks in this chapter. In the late 1970s much 'IS strategy' or 'IT strategy' was in fact concerned with how to manage IT. This question was relegated as concepts such as

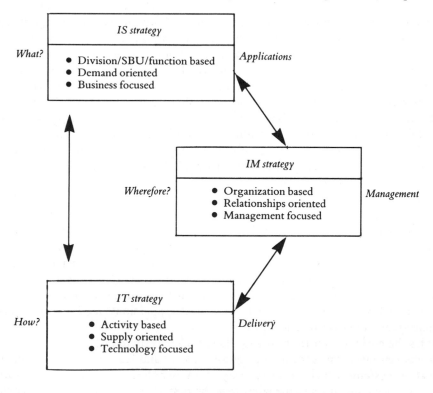

Figure 3.9 Three levels of strategy in IT.

'strategic advantage' and 'architecture' appeared. However in the late 1980s, particularly as the IT function is being revamped and restructured, it is reappearing as a top management concern. Indeed Lucas and Turner contend that 'effective control of information processing' [IM strategy] 'is a prerequisite to the integration of technology with strategy'. The IM strategy accordingly is concerned with the role and structure of IT activities in the organization. It focuses on relationships between the specialists and users and between the centre and divisions or business units. It is concerned with management controls for IT, management responsibilities, performance measurement and management processes. Whereas the IS strategy is about 'what' and the IT strategy about 'how', the IM strategy is about the 'wherefores' - which way?, who does it?, where is it located?, etc.

This delineation of strategies is consistent with strategic management thinking in general. Table 3.9 suggests the correspondence. Corporate strategy, concerned with future directions and performance, which businesses are we in, and what is our structure, is a board responsibility and suggests how IT should be positioned and managed. It is the main influence on the IM strategy. Business strategies are the product–market analyses and plans which each strategic business unit formulates in pursuit of its mission given by the corporate strategy. These are the main influences on IS strategy. Activity strategies are required to implement and support business strategies, examples being finance, manufacturing or human resource strategies. The IT strategy is another and is mainly determined by IT functional management but influenced and approved by business unit and top management.

The next three chapters deal with the formulation of the IS, IT and IM strategies in turn.

Table 3.9 Strategy linkages

Strategy level	Strategic focus	Strategic responsibility	Information linkage
1. Corporate	Global business	Board	IM strategy
2. Business	Product market	SBU management	IS strategy
3. Activity	Delivery	Functional management	IT strategy

NOTES AND REFERENCES

1. Quoted by McFarlan F. W., 'Information technology changes the way you compete', *Harvard Business Review*, May-June 1984.
2. History and quotations taken from 'Frontier Airlines, Inc.', Case study (9–184–041), Harvard Business School.

FURTHER READING

Anthony R. N., *Planning and Control Systems: A Framework for Analysis*, Harvard University Press, 1965.

Benjamin R. I., Rockart, J. F., Scott Morton M. S. and Wyman J., 'Information technology: a strategic opportunity', *Sloan Management Review*, Spring 1984.

Burnside D., *BIATT: An Emerging Engineering Discipline,* BIATT International Inc., 1980.

Cash J. I. and Konsynski B. R., 'IS redraws competitive boundaries'. *Harvard Business Review,* March–April 1985.

Chandler A. D., Jr., *Strategy and Structure: Chapters in the History of American Industrial Enterprise,* Harvard University Press, 1967.

Feeny D., 'Creating and sustaining competitive advantage with IT', in M. J. Earl (ed.), *Information Management: The Strategic Dimension,* Oxford University Press, 1988.

Ives B. and Learmonth G. P., 'The information system as competitive weapon', *Communications of the ACM,* December 1984.

Lucas H. C. and Turner J. A., 'A corporate strategy for the control of information processing', *Sloan Management Review,* Spring 1982.

McCosh, A. M., Rahman, M. and Earl, M. J., *Developing Managerial Information Systems,* Macmillan, 1981.

McFarlan F. W., 'Information technology changes the way you compete', *Harvard Business Review,* May–June 1984.

McFarlan F. W. and McKenney J. L., *Corporate Information Systems Management: The Issues Facing Senior Executives,* Dow Jones Irwin, 1983.

Meredith J. R. and Hill M. M., 'Justifying new manufacturing systems: a managerial approach', *Sloan Management Review,* Summer 1987.

Parsons G. L., 'Information technology: a new competitive weapon', *Sloan Management Review,* Fall 1983.

Porter M. E., *Competitive Strategy,* Free Press, 1980.

Porter, M. E. and Millar V. E., 'How information gives you competitive advantage, *Harvard Business Review,* July–August 1985.

Runge D. A., 'Using telecommunications for competitive advantage', unpublished D.Phil thesis, University of Oxford, 1985.

Runge D. A. and Earl M. J., 'Using telecommunications-based information systems for competitive advantage', in M. J. Earl, (ed.), *Information Management: The Strategic Dimension,* Oxford University Press, 1988.

Simon H. A., *The New Science of Management Decision,* Prentice Hall, Englewood Cliffs, NJ, 1977.

Wiseman C., *Strategy and Computers,* Dow Jones Irwin, 1985.

Chapter 4

FORMULATING INFORMATION SYSTEMS STRATEGY

INTRODUCTION

In the previous chapter, information systems (IS) strategy was defined as the long-term, directional plan which decided what to do with IT. IS strategy was seen to be business-led and demand-oriented and concerned with exploiting IT either to support business strategies or create new strategic options. In Chapter 2, strategic planning for IS was seen to be the top concern of IT managers in the 1980s both in the UK and the USA. Indeed most large organizations today are formulating IS strategies. In a study in the UK Galliers found 84 per cent of companies were formulating IS plans of a strategic or long-term character. This chapter, based on the author's research and advisory work, explores what can be expected of IS strategy formulation, how to do it, and how to manage it.

Most UK companies quote any one or more of four reasons for embarking on IS strategy formulation exercises:

1. Sector exploitation of IT is posing strategic threats and opportunities.
2. The need to align investment in IS and IT with business needs.
3. The desire to gain competitive advantage from IS and IT.
4. The revamping of the IT function and elevation of IT activities.

The first reason is common and is quoted by most firms in 'delivery' sectors and many in 'dependent' sectors. The second reason is dominant and reflects a top management concern for many years that specialists have decided both what systems to develop and how they should be designed. It also reflects a more recent concern that 'the business has not told us what its priorities are'. The third reason is more fragile and is typically stated as 'we have heard all about Merrill Lynch, American Hospital Supply and Thomson Holidays and we want to do something similar'. The final reason can be caricatured as 'DP is dead, long live IT and we will construct a strategy to show we really mean business'.

These four aims are different. They will not be achieved by one simple and universal approach. Nor will they be satisfied necessarily all at once. Furthermore in complex organizations, different business units will have different selections of these reasons – and these may change over time. Yet most manufacturers and advisers have developed their particular methodology for IS strategy formulation assuming universal conditions and often promising relatively quick results. They ignore five important lessons learnt in recent years. These lessons can be expressed as follows and provide the structure to this chapter:

1.   No single IS strategy formulation *methodology* will work.
2.   The preferred *mode* of IS strategy formulation depends on the firm's sector.
3.   Success in IS strategy formulation takes time and is influenced by past *experience*.
4.   IS strategic plans should be managed as *portfolios*.
5.   *Expectations* of IS strategy formulation need to be explicated and managed.

First, what is the outcome of IS strategy formulation? The end result is directional and not detail. Achievement of the four aims listed earlier is largely a matter of giving simple, clear direction to IS development. Too much detail soon loses strategic intent and often gets bogged down in technical debate and short-term resource allocation arguments. Table 4.1 displays the elements of the applications strategic plan, variously called the applications development portfolio, the strategic systems plan or the systems strategy. It is essentially a 'shopping list' of applications and projects. Whilst many consultants have pilloried shopping list approaches, the description is used here because the requirement is for an understandable business-related statement of agreed applications to be developed and projects to be initiated. What is *not* required is pictorial, formalized models of systems, subsystems, dependencies and interfaces. This coherence and level of detail is necessary for formulation of IT strategy, or architecture, the subject of the next chapter. Neither are just words and analyses in a consultant's report enough, because some sharp decisions or choices have to be made and a framework is needed against which challenges, changes or new opportunities can be assessed. However to qualify as a strategy, the shopping list must satisfy three criteria:

1.   The relative spending, or resource allocation, for each area needs to be agreed.
2.   The relative priorities between and within each area need to be agreed.
3.   Each application or project, except mandatory ones, should be strategically justified.

Table 4.1 The applications strategic plan

Mandatory applications	Strategic systems	Traditional developments	Infrastructure investment	System renewals	Maintenance and enhancement	R & D developments	Niche activities

To explain Table 4.1 more fully, mandatory applications are those developments which are essential for legal or similar reasons. For example, UK financial services at the end of 1987 were building new back office systems and management information routines to comply with new securities regulations due to come into force the following April. Strategic systems are those which it is hoped will yield sustainable strategic advantage. There may be very few which are believed to create new strategic options, but many more which support current business strategy. Traditional developments are those applications which are justified on cost-benefit grounds, whether by payback or rate of return or more multidimensional metrics. Infrastructure investment will be recommended by the IT strategy (Chapter 5) and include projects such as database construction development of common basic business systems. System renewals refer to the rewriting of old, out-of-date applications for technical or business reasons. We shall see subsequently that system renewal can be a strategic decision. So can maintenance and enhancement to amend or improve existing systems. Indeed this activity can often create or protect strategic advantage. R & D experiments will be authorized by discretionary funds designed often to assess new technologies and find innovative opportunities. Still more experimentation and innovation may be achieved by approval of niche IT activities outside mainstream IS development, often in the hands of specialist units or line users.

All these elements are the proper concern of IS strategy formulation. The more difficult question is how to derive the applications strategic plan, ensuring it is largely business-oriented, demand-led and supported by management.

A MULTIPLE METHODOLOGY

The first lesson advanced early in this chapter was that 'no single IS strategy formulation will work'. What is argued for here, and proposed, is a multiple methodology or three-pronged attack on the problem. This is derived from both research and experience. However, before developing a multiple methodology, it is useful to position this thinking within past and current work in the area.

Organizations which felt the need to plan IS, together with their most recent desires to align IS development with business plans and exploit IT strategically, have spawned several methodologies for strategy formulation and prompted some evaluative research. Early work borrowed from long-range planning, proposing approaches such as PPBS (Planning, programming and budgeting systems) and arguing the benefits of top-down versus bottom-up philosophies.[1] Later work, for example an early article by King, proposed general frameworks to discover business strategy, interpret it into IS needs and validate the result. Alternatively, procedures were proposed for analysing internal and external environments, strengths and weaknesses and business objectives in order to formulate IS goals, as documented in McLean and Soden's book. Recently, more structured techniques have been developed both by academics and consultants, one example being the 'critical success factors' approach which seeks to logically confirm business goals, derive critical success factors needed to achieve these goals, and indicate IS requirements needed to support or deliver the critical success factors. At the same time computer manufacturers have continued to develop or enhance their planning tools, an example being IBM's 'Business Systems Planning'.

Evaluative work has sought to discover when, how and whether these methods work, for example Shank *et al's* appraisal of 'critical success factors' and McLean's comparison of this method with business systems planning. Useful guidelines are beginning to emerge, but in general the conclusions seem to be that most techniques work in the appropriate context, with skilled analysts and in a supportive environment. Sullivan, however, recently has argued for a contingency approach where he proposes that different methods suit different contexts, the key determinants being how diffused are the organization and its technology and how infused (how well developed and important) are the applications. Pyburn, too, derived a situational approach when he suggested three different approaches to IS strategic planning dependent on factors such as business environment, technological context, management style and organizational structure.

The author's own work suggests that a more complex approach is needed because the challenge is complex.[2] In practice, a firm's management has to tackle three issues:

(a) clarification of the business needs and strategy in information systems terms;
(b) evaluation of current information systems provision and use; and
(c) innovation of new strategic opportunities afforded by IT.

These questions have to be addressed by enterprise management which often has a varied understanding of business strategy, a patchy appreciation of the current IS capability and position, and a low awareness of the technology-strategy connection. Accordingly the multiple methodology depicted in Figure 4.1 is designed to tackle each of the three issues explicitly and by separate means, but in a way that provides a process by which management can learn and overcome the typical impediments to understanding. A three-pronged attack is required to derive the application strategic plan which was depicted in ideal form in Table 4.1. The implication is, therefore, that no single method or technique is likely to satisfy all three concerns or always be preferred. A combination is required where each prong differs in aim, approach and participants. However, as we shall see, each prong interacts with the others; each is necessary but not sufficient and is influenced by the other.

Top-down clarification

The desire and need for a formal attempt to match IS investment with business needs is met by the first leg of the model. It proposes the identification of business plans and goals, followed by deduction of information systems needs using an analytical approach with formal methodology and requiring inputs from a coalition of line, general and IS managers. Essentially 'top-down' it 'puts the business into IS'. Commonly, business plans and goals are not formally available, or are ill-defined, and rarely will be expressed in terms easily translated into IS needs. Thus a formal methodology is required to both elicit business strategy and derive IS needs. Discussions and planning meetings are not enough. The properties required of a methodology are that it is easily understood and used by line and general managers, it can cope with varying robustness of business strategy, it does not consume too much time or resource, it can be repeated as circumstances inevitably change and, as a result of these needs and because it could not achieve anything else, it points to directional IS needs and not detailed specifications.

The 'critical success factors' approach, very much pioneered by Bullen and Rockart, seems to possess some of these qualities. Research by the author[3] suggests that it is particularly valuable when prior strategy analyses have been done, but also provides a workmanlike procedure where strategic understanding is low or business plans absent. Figure 4.2 displays a slightly generalized example of the critical success factors approach by conflating two actual applications of the method.

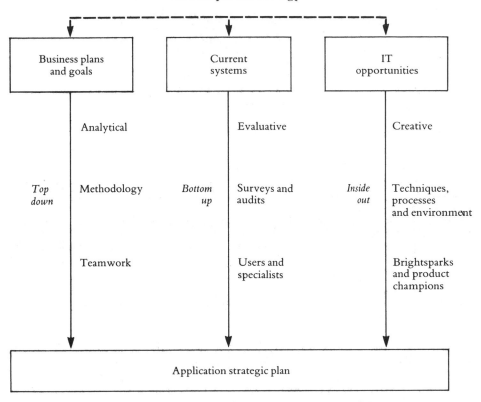

Figure 4.1 IS strategy formulation: a multiple methodology.

The first step involves identification and agreement of business objectives for the SBU. Working from interviews and documents, clear and firm objectives (perhaps goals in planning parlance) are stated. Next the factors critical to success in achieving these goals are explicated. This involves interviews with each member of the executive management team to extract his or her opinions. A crucial phase of alignment follows whereby the whole management team has to resolve different views and conflicts in order to agree the firm's critical success factor set. This can be decomposed into the critical processes or activities upon which the critical success factors depend. Such an intermediate level of analysis (the dotted boxes in Figure 4.2) is sometimes helpful in administrative contexts where broad thrusts are not clear and detailed analysis helps. Finally, the information system supports which these critical success factors require are determined either through the application of technology in products and processes, or the development of information systems for coordination and control of activities and for management decision-making.

Working through the examples in Figure 4.2 should help demonstrate the technique. For example, in one of the case studies, automation of factories and improvement of product quality and responsiveness were thought to be critical to achieving the business objective of improving productivity and increasing market share. This suggested the exploitation of advanced manufacturing technologies, particularly flexible manufacturing systems (FMS). However, no application of FMS in that industry was known, indicating some doubts about feasibility and appropriateness. Thus a pilot project was

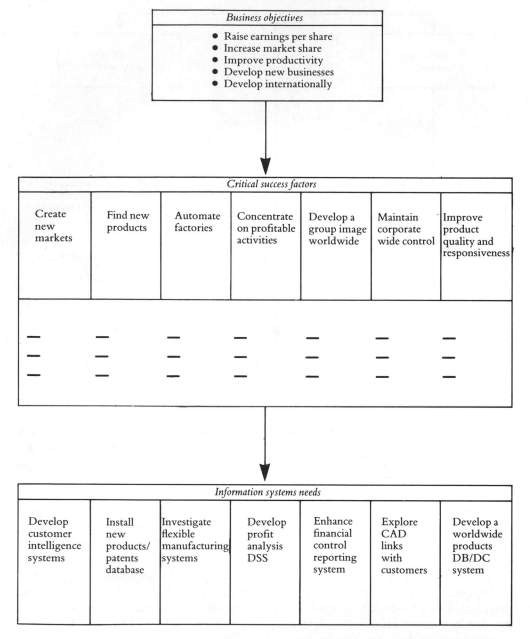

Figure 4.2 A critical success factors approach.

begun to try and customize FMS technology to this particular sector. Indeed, grants were secured for this project, for it was essentially research and development for the industry.

The author's own research indicates that, in the UK, managers have found this approach especially valuable in setting and agreeing objectives and in deriving critical success factors across the business. They often claim that the exercise improved their understanding of current business imperatives and helped them see how their function or activity could improve overall business performance. They also tend to comment that the exercise did not take too long, was a satisfying experience and would not be too troublesome to repeat. These studies commonly take one to three months to complete.

However, the jump to determining information systems needs seems to be more difficult. Senior managers are often not sure what IS recommendations came out of the critical success factor exercise. Meanwhile, the IT specialists find that they had to do much more work on investigations, feasibility studies and experiments to see more precisely how IT can support critical success factors and home in on IS titles and outline specifications. IT managers often claim that they now understand the business better and have established a better working relationship and dialogue with users. Most important, the direction and priorities for IS development do become apparent. Furthermore, if preceded by management education on IS and strategic advantage and followed-up by systems analysis or feasibility studies, often aided by prototyping to test out ideas, more focused identification of IS needs can result. Several of these findings coincide with those of Boynton and Zmud and Shank *et al.* in the USA.

The critical success factor method demonstrates that the essential ingredient of top-down methods is *clarification*. First, business strategies and needs have to be clarified, as much for senior and line management as for IT managers. Then the potential contribution of IT applications can be clarified, suggesting key directions, main priorities and outline needs. To achieve this is well worthwhile for it satisfies one of the objectives of IS strategy formulation, namely alignment of IT and IS investment with business needs.

The critical success factors method, and similar approaches, have one over-riding advantage in this clarification exercise. They end up defining a workmanlike business strategy first without looking as though it was a business strategy exercise *per se*. This is usually important in the politics and psychology of IS strategy formulation. It is fatal if the IT department is thought to be setting the firm's strategy! However the IT director often has to lead the clarification process, but as far as possible from behind!

Bottom-up evaluation

Leg two of the model in Figure 4.1 is more 'bottom-up'. While this may not seem strategic, most organizations when they begin or renew their attempts to plan IS strategically need to understand and evaluate their *current* IS investment. This is for several reasons. It may be important to demonstrate the quality and coverage of IS hitherto in order to gain, retain or regain credibility. Further, top management often is not informed about the current IS position of the business and requires confidence both of understanding IS and of the firm's IT capability before it will approve any major IS investment. Then IS strategies are rarely developed from a greenfield site but have to recognize the strengths and weaknesses of the current applications portfolio. More important perhaps, examination of current systems may suggest either that some could already be better exploited for strategic advantage or be built upon to yield significant added value. Indeed, Runge and Earl show that many applications which have provided competitive advantage were in fact evolutionary add-ons to existing systems, as discussed in the previous chapter.

Thus in leg two an evaluative approach is required, typically satisfied by commissioning an audit or survey of current systems. Several techniques exist and most are effective in experienced hands. Two sets of questions need to be asked. First, what is the existing *coverage* of systems – both basic business systems and management decision and support systems? This seemingly mundane question is significant because, in answering it, gaps by function, by IS type, or of integration may be revealed. For example, it is not unusual to find good coverage in accounting and huge gaps in marketing, or extensive exception reporting facilities for management support but few enquiry or analysis features, or adequate production, engineering and sales systems but poor integration for logistics planning and market-oriented manufacturing. Coverage surveys basically map activities, processes and decisions against functions. 'Business systems planning' and its variant methods are typical mechanisms. However in addition each current application needs to be examined for its business value and for its technical value. Several appraisal methods are available for this, some resembling the grid in Figure 4.3. The systems audit grid represents a high level approach which has proved useful in both teaching and practice.

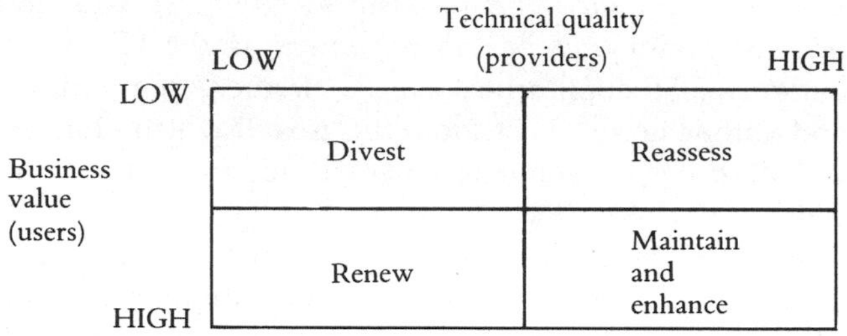

	Technical quality (providers)	
	LOW	HIGH
LOW	Divest	Reassess
HIGH	Renew	Maintain and enhance

Business value (users) — LOW to HIGH on vertical axis

Figure 4.3 Systems audit grid.

The horizontal axis of Figure 4.3 portrays the technical condition of a system. Only the specialists or providers can really evaluate this dimension. Three questions provide an effective metric here:

1. How reliable is the system?
2. How easy is it to maintain the system?
3. How cost-efficient is the system?

Only the users can give a sound view of the business value of a system, which is portrayed on the vertical axis of the grid. Again, they can ask three questions of each system:

1. What is the impact of the system on the business (or what would happen if we took it away)?
2. How easy is it to use the system (or how big a problem is it to make it work)?
3. How often is the system used (which is a proxy of measure of value)?

Each can be answered on a scale from 1 to 3 or 1 to 5 to give a low or high rating. It is important to have both a user perspective and the specialists' view, because they are often not the same. Commonly, the specialists have little idea what the business function of an application is. They only know what it does in 'systems terms'. Equally the users may be happy if the application 'works', being quite ignorant of the technical difficulties that may be involved. More important, they may see future or potential benefits, but they have not been asked before. The resultant evaluation produces four archetypal conditions which suggest four different IS development imperatives.

If the system is poor on both dimensions, it should be eliminated or *divested*. Most firms who have used computing for some time discover one or two of these applications for good or bad reasons. The system may never have been either necessary or appropriate, perhaps initially advocated, driven and designed by the IT professionals. Alternatively the business may have changed, so that the system is outdated and no longer required. Perhaps the system was once appropriate but has been superseded by a replacement application on a newer technology, maybe a departmental minicomputer or a personal computer. In any event, the application inevitably consumes scarce machine, software and support resources from time to time and it should be divested.

> A chief executive of an electronics company sent out a memo to all computer users. This announced that on the following weekend no print-outs would be produced from the weekly batch runs. If any user found on Monday morning that he was inconvenienced by lack of a print-out, he could attend a meeting at 11 a.m. to justify the need to the chief executive. A surprising number of users did not attend the meeting.

If the system is rated highly by users but is unsound technically, it is potentially a business exposure. Were it to collapse, business operations or management capability might suffer. This condition arises for a number of reasons, not least failure to maintain or renew the system over time. Systems have life-cycles and a nine year life represents a 'good innings'. However, because resources are scarce, or because maintenance and renewal have insufficient priority, or because everyone fears the cost and disruption of renewal, systems are kept running beyond their life expectancy. Two stimuli tend to force reconsideration of this abrogation of responsibility: either a crisis occurs when the system collapses and takes time to be remedied or a shock is received when a competitor renews and improves his equivalent system and thereby gains competitive advantage. Thus identification of systems in this condition begins to indicate what proportion of the strategic systems plan should be concerned with application *renewal*.

> A very competitive sector had used networks and point of sale equipment for its distribution channel for some years. One of the rivals improved its telecommunications network and the systems which were communications-driven. In a few weeks its share of transactions jumped as users appreciated the improved service. The other rivals had to follow this enhancement investment in order to regain competitive parity.

If the application is high on technical quality but low on business value, it is in a questionable condition. This situation can arise because the system was always the technician's solution looking for an application, or because the users have failed to support and use the system, or because the system was in advance of the business need or capability. Thus before killing off the system, *reassessment* is necessary. The question to be asked is can it be enhanced in order to add business value? Options include raising user commitment, adding function or re-examining the specification.

An export division of a manufacturing company complained that the sales analysis and order processing system did not meet their needs. The export director spelt out the system inadequacies. This puzzled the home sales division as they found the system satisfactory. The IT manager was then able to point out that the export sales team had always said they were too busy getting business to worry about systems and thus they had not loaded data on the database, tested all the facilities, learnt how to use the system or appointed an export systems officer. The export director pledged that he would remedy these deficiencies forthwith.

Discovering applications which are evaluated highly on both dimensions fulfils three purposes. First, unless they are adequately maintained, they can easily become exposures to the business; thus they should be given priority for any *maintenance or enhancement* and will indicate the minimum size of the maintenance proportion of the strategic systems plan. Second, since many organizations tend to believe that information systems are a disappointment, it is instructive for management and comforting for the IS specialists to discover these successes! Third, several firms who have discovered a competitive advantage application become complacent as their fame increases. Their success often sets a standard for their rivals to match and then beat. In time, without added value enhancement, the originator becomes disadvantaged.

Where an information system is either a crucial element of the firm's infrastructure, a competitive weapon, or a product in the firm's product portfolio, it is quite common for a permanent maintenance and enhancement team to be assigned to it. The same almost certainly would happen if it were a non–IT phenomenon. IT 'stars' and 'cash cows' need similar treatment.

The system's audit grid therefore can help suggest strategic arguments for determining the content and extent of the renewal, maintenance and enhancement components of the strategic systems plan. The coverage survey points to mandatory, infrastructure and possibly some strategic or niche developments.

A third type of survey which can be useful is an audit of technological experience, IS management procedures and user awareness as well as applications coverage and quality – using the benchmarks implied by Gibson and Nolan's stage model of DP management discussed in Chapter 2. This has the merit of informing top management of the current and potential IS capability of the whole organization.

Bottom-up approaches therefore can discover gaps, suggest new departures, and pinpoint exposures. They also provide a map of where an enterprise is now in IS terms. This evaluative leg accordingly helps satisfy another of the aims set for IS strategy formulation. It can be central to revamping the IT function and improving specialist-user relationships.

Inside–out innovation

Leg three of the multiple methodology is of quite different character. Here the objective is to identify opportunities afforded by IT which may yield competitive advantage or create new strategic options. Whilst top-down and bottom-up approaches can give clues to where competitive advantage lies and may suggest opportunities, they are not at all sufficient. Research at the Oxford Institute of Information Management indicates that such opportunities are most likely to be discovered by 'inside-out' approaches. Three strands are involved; the first is based on techniques, the second on processes, the third on technology. In all instances the emphasis is on creativity rather than analysis or evaluation.

Examination of several of the exemplar cases of strategic information systems suggests that whilst the initial, revolutionary idea was inspirational, visionary or wild, it nearly always had to be studied in detail for some time to test its technological, business and organizational viability. So creativity events such as think-tanks, brainstorming groups and Delphi methods may help generate ideas, but they must always be subjected to some sort of feasibility and strategic validation. This is also the place for adoption of the opportunity frameworks discussed in the previous chapter where systems analysis, technology applications and strategic frameworks are commissioned and executed as a one-off exercise. They may be particularly helpful if outside assistance is available, for example advisers with experience elsewhere or consultants who help 'flesh out' an idea and give it credence. However, such techniques do not guarantee success.

The work of Runge, referred to in Chapter 3, is suggestive of the need for investment in deeper processes. In his study of 35 cases of competitive advantage telecommunications-based systems which linked firms with their customers, he found more fundamental patterns of success. He concluded that the rules for success in both spotting *and* implementing strategic advantage IT opportunities more closely resembled the pattern characteristic of industrial innovation than the nostrums of IS administration. Six characteristics emerged:

1. The idea often emanated from a commercial manager operating at the boundaries of the business who saw opportunities to extend IS into supplier or customer businesses.
2. The idea was subsequently backed by one of his or her superiors who became project champion, commissioning resources, giving support and so on.
3. The competitive advantage idea was but a later facility added to an existing system; in other words, many strategic systems are evolutionary not revolutionary.
4. The application generally was prosecuted and developed outside the formal IS administration procedures.
5. The application was developed and implemented with a high degree of customer involvement.
6. The application was designed and launched with high marketing effort, including market research, focused promotion, customer education and synchronization with marketing policies.

In short, innovative use of IT was facilitated by the existence of brightspark commercial managers, backed by product champions who became the system's entrepreneurs, exploiting existing systems often with informal or no support from the IT function, but with high user involvement and marketing effort.

Another colleague, Lockett, followed up Runge's work in one company. He found many of the same factors present in IT innovations which had rendered competitive advantage. Four further enablers were discovered. The first was the existence of a project sponsor where the project champion herself was not able to command the necessary resources. Next was the ability to develop and test a new idea to assess the benefits, discover what worked and gave advantage, and quietly experiment in a way that could be aborted or incremented without public disgrace or excessive justification. It was also helpful if early phases of the systems development life-cycle were managed in a relatively lax way to ensure ideas were given a proper chance and realistic requirements identified. However later phases benefited from tight management to ensure satisfactory installation, effective implementation and good integration with business practices. Finally it was important that the team developing an innovative IT application should ask what knowledge or capability gap existed and seek to bridge it. In particular, users or champions who had some experience of IT and knew who to call for assistance were able to ask the right questions and find appropriate solutions.

The prescriptions which arise from these Oxford studies of innovation therefore are eightfold:

1. Consider recruiting young managers and professionals of brightspark material or who have experience of applying IT in relevant areas.
2. Place brightsparks or creative people in areas where IT may have strategic potential.
3. Ensure managers who have product champion abilities also are located in the same areas so that they will undertake and support the brightsparks' ideas.
4. Develop brightsparks and project champions by management education and development programmes (See Chapters 7 and 9).
5. Examine existing systems for added value potential, much as suggested in the enhancement quadrant of the systems audit grid; there may be as much latent competitive advantage within existing systems as there is potential advantage in new technologies.
6. Accept that some innovative IT applications may have to be permitted or encouraged, even if they have not been approved by the strategic systems planning procedure. This is one reason for strategic funding of niche IT projects.
7. Look to users, particularly suppliers and customers (even their complaints), as generators of innovative application ideas and involve them in systems development.
8. In experimental and strategic applications development, loosen the early stages of the systems development life-cycle and tighten up as implementation approaches.

These prescriptions add up to the second strand of opportunity creation. The need is for organizational investment in processes which foster innovation.

The final segment of the inside-out leg is the fostering and enabling of opportunities by construction of a facilitative technological environment. Our research has uncovered case evidence that by 'taking IT to the people' users may develop strategic or innovative applications themselves. Examples include provision of user-friendly, firm-specific personal computing menus, aids and application generators, investment in professional-specific or industry-specific expert systems shells, or development of viewdata utilities for executives to customize. Often creating such an enabling technological environment needs the creation and dissemination of hardware and software standards so that users can maximize opportunities from supported technologies and techniques.

A UK industrial company commissioned an expert system shell, tailored to its sector's particular products and technology. Within two years of the shell's availability there were over twenty expert systems in operation within the company, some of which produced significant competitive advantage.

American Express in Europe created an applications development team to exploit viewdata when PRESTEL first was launched. The team was led by marketing executives and located outside the systems and data processing departments. An early application which the team developed was 'skyguide', the viewdata system which communicates up-to-data information on flight arrivals and departures at major European airports. Besides earning an award for innovation, the application was part of the American Express marketing strategy to encourage business travellers to use American Express charge cards and travel related services.

This last example makes a point. One way of fostering innovation is to fund and support autonomous niche technology teams in the early stages of a technology's adoption. The prior example demonstrates the benefit of defining discretionary research and development or experimental budgets and projects – the final component of the strategic systems plan.

The third leg of the multiple methodology therefore looks for impetus from inside the organization by use of one-off or *ad hoc* techniques, investment in innovation processes and construction of an enabling technological environment. The general principle of the 'inside-out' leg is designing an organizational and technological environment which enables innovations to happen. It is the leg which most likely will satisfy the fourth objective of IS strategy formulation, namely gaining competitive advantage from IT and IS.

External analysis

Each of the three legs of the model in Figure 4.1 has been described so far from a largely internal perspective. By definition, a strategic approach to planning IS, and in particular the search for competitive advantage from IT, also require an external perspective. Especially in sectors undergoing great change, leg one must address the competitive environment. Inclusion therefore of a threats and opportunities analysis of the firm's competitive forces may suggest other critical IS needs and/or exposures. Porter's five factor framework of new entrants, suppliers, customers, rivals and new products described in Chapter 3 provides a useful structure. Likewise in leg two, it may be important to assess competitors' and potential competitors' IS, using a strengths and weaknesses approach. This may take two or three years before a reliable picture is built and practicable intelligence mechanisms installed. Finally, in leg three, opportunity suggestion may be prompted by collecting and analysing exemplars from other industries and writing scenarios of the future of the firm's particular sector. These external perspectives can be superimposed on the three-legged model of IS strategy formulation as shown in Table 4.2. They are keys to understanding the issues behind the first reason for formulating IS strategy, namely the actual or potential existence of sector threats and opportunities.

This three-legged multiple methodology recognizes that alignment of IS investment with business needs is essential, that innovation and ideation are more a process of fermentation and opportunism than of structured analysis, and that many vital IS developments and much of what is feasible are identified by examining today's

Table 4.2 External perspective in IS formulation

Leg	Top-down	Bottom-up	Inside-out
Technique	Opportunities and threats analysis	Strengths and weaknesses appraisal	Exemplars and scenarios

inherited position. It is for these reasons that no single method works. The three legs are required to tackle each of the challenges specified earlier in the chapter. This is formalized in Table 4.3. However, the emphasis laid on each leg may well vary across firms and over time. These complications are discussed in the next two sections.

Table 4.3 Rationale of multiple methodology

Leg of multiple methodology	Metaphor	Purpose
One	Top-down	Clarification
Two	Bottom-up	Evaluation
Three	Inside-out	Innovation

STRATEGY MODES

In Chapter 2, a descriptive classification of industry sectors was introduced. Table 2.10 posited four sector types – delivery, dependent, drive and delayed – describing the strategic impact and potential of IT in different sectors. In researching large companies' approaches to IS strategy formulation, it was discovered early on that:

(a)   significant differences existed in different firms;
(b)   IS strategy formulation inherently seemed a more complex matter in some firms than others; and
(c)   approaches in practice did not always match either popular prescriptions or the accounts in case documented articles.

The explanation often seemed sectoral and largely suggested the types in Table 2.10.

Modes and sectors

For firms in *delayed* sectors where IT has no strategic impact yet, IS strategy formulation can be disregarded. For the delivery, dependent and drive sectors, however, different strategy modes can be detected, suggesting that the overall approach to IS strategy formulation must be appropriate to a firm's sector. This is summarized in Table 4.4.

In firms in *delivery* sectors – for example, banking and increasingly retailing – rather than work out business needs, strive for strategic clarification, or adopt a top-down approach, much of the thinking behind IS strategy formulation is systems and technology oriented. It is concerned with laying down telecommunications networks.

rationalizing data standards, creating appropriate hardware environments and developing a sound basic business systems foundation. In other words the IS strategy mode is *infrastructure-led*. Sometimes criticized as being non-strategic, uncoupled from business, back office oriented and technologists controlled, this mode does appear more rational on closer analysis.

Often top management in these firms recognized that IT was becoming crucial both to the capability of the firm and the operations of the sector but had less clear views on what was required. The IT function had to second guess where to invest and was safe in ensuring the firm could connect to the emerging sector IT infrastructure, in building transaction databases to support business systems and MIS, and in developing efficient and updatable basic systems upon which new services and products could be quickly built as needs became apparent. Such has been the posture of many UK banks' IT functions. An infrastructure-led approach worked because the sector's infrastructure was becoming IT-based. Infrastructure became the platform for product development. A firm in a delivery sector became exposed if its computer network failed, was inefficient if it did not automate its internal operations, and inflexible in its product development and customer service if it had poor infrastructure. Only later then do more business driven approaches to IS strategy formulation become both more necessary and feasible. At this point, the business is seen as information system and business strategy and IS strategy become the same thing.

The characteristics therefore of the infrastructure-led mode can be summarized as follows:

1. IS strategy both shapes and is shaped by IT strategy.
2. IS strategy cannot be project-led, because integration, interfaces, dependencies and architecture matter.
3. Capital investment in IT never ceases.
4. Choices in IS and IT strategy may be influenced as much by external and sector factors as by internal and firm needs.
5. Infrastructure includes the capability to be responsive to sudden needs.
6. In time the business strategy becomes the IS strategy and *vice versa*.

In firms in the *dependent* sector, for example many manufacturing firms fighting global competition for survival, it is generally discovered that business and functional strategies require major support from IS and/or depend on IT. Once business imperatives are worked out, IT and IS are seen to be obvious enablers for growth or survival. Indeed, in Ford in Europe quoted in Chapter 1, it was the explication of critical survival factors that pinpointed the areas for IT investment: robotics and CIM to improve productivity and quality in manufacturing; CAD-CAM to improve design and market-oriented flexibility; and data communications to improve the effectiveness and efficiency of distribution. In other words, as shown in Table 4.4, in contrast to the infrastructure approach of the delivery sector, firms in the dependent sector can easily adopt a *business-led* IS strategy mode. Here IS strategy can be a derivative of business strategy, whereas for delivery firms IS strategy requires more vision, carries more risk and in some senses due to its infrastructure qualities, is intertwined with, and an inherent part of, business strategy.

In short, in dependent firms the normative prescription of deduce or derive the IS

Table 4.4 IS strategy modes

Strategic condition	Characteristic	Metaphor	Strategy mode
IT is the means of delivering goods and services in the sector	Computer-based transaction systems underpin business operations	Delivery	Infrastructure-led
Business strategies increasingly depend on IT for their implementation	Business and functional strategies require a major automation, information, communications capability and are made possible by these technologies	Dependent	Business-led
IT potentially provides new strategic opportunities	Specific applications or technologies are exploited for developing the business and changing ways of managing	Drive	Opportunity-led

strategy from the business strategy is often applied and can be made to work. Furthermore, general management finds IS strategy formulation not so complex or threatening as in the other two sectors. It should be pointed out, however, that the business-led mode does not imply that infrastructure is unimportant. Indeed, it may turn out to be a major element of the firm's capital investment – but the nature of the infrastructure is more obvious and the financial implications more quantifiable because there is a clearer business case.

A business-led mode thus is likely to have the following characteristics:

1. It may be driven by business strategy.
2. It may be applications-led and thus clearly understood.
3. It may comprise developments with a strong business case.
4. It may be owned by business managers.
5. It may treat IS strategy as more important than IT strategy.

In the *drive* sector, typified by many process and consumer products companies, firms are searching for less obvious strategic gains, although the rewards for success can be high if they outwit the competition. Because there is no sector infrastructure push and there are fewer business dependencies, IS strategy formulation in drive firms is the most difficult. The most likely mode here seems to be *opportunity-led* – a combination of infrastructure investment and business direction, or put another way, a mix of technological push and demand pull.

Indeed in earlier writing, I called this mode 'mixed'. In these firms, the drive for opportunities is seen to require both awareness of IT possibilities and ability to implement them by taking infrastructure to the user community. Such infrastructure includes end-user computing, communications networks, database environments, software tools and IT training. At the same time, so that good opportunities are not thrown away or under-exploited and also to ensure that IT developments which are inconsistent with the firm's strategy do not gain momentum, a framework of business direction and possibilities is often provided. Such frameworks are built by encouraging IS plans to be linked with long-range plans, experimenting with critical success factor exercises or similar, investing in management education on IT and strategic advantage and engaging in opportunity analysis, using methods described in Chapter 3.

In drive firms, while the chief executive may be pushing the IT initiative, it is the IT director or equivalent who has to work out most of the 'how' and lead from behind on much of the 'what'. This is because the IT needs and opportunities are not so obvious and the organization therefore requires much more leadership and help. The case for IT investment is more difficult and the benefits more dispersed and perhaps slower to accrue. Because the IS strategy mode is 'mixed', several methodologies may be attempted over time. Inevitably, however, there has to be some 'up-front' investment in both hard and soft infrastructure.

An opportunity-led mode is the most subtle mode and may be characterized by the following qualities:

1. It may be concerned with innovation and technology transfer.
2. It may be flexible because it creates and adapts to opportunities.
3. It may be hard (technological) and soft (organizational).
4. It may be needing up-front investment which is difficult to cost-justify.
5. It may require any method, including all three legs of the multiple methodology, that may work.

Multiple methods and modes

This sectoral picture of strategy modes has been recognized by many IT directors. The question now arises how does the three-legged multiple methodology fit this classification? The reconciliation is summarized in Table 4.5. For infrastructure-led firms, the obvious clues on what to do are to be found in the current systems of the business and its sector. Thus, a bottom-up emphasis tends to hold sway over time. However, this will be limited unless connected to some vision of the future. Thus every few years a top-down attack will be necessary and from time to time inside-out initiatives may extract unforeseen advantage from the infrastructure investment.

In business-led firms, most of the direction and much of the applications strategic plan can be driven by top-down means. Here the alignment of IS with business needs is the main concern. However, over time the cumulative investment in IS will require a

Table 4.5 Strategy modes and methods

IT strategy mode	Emphasis in strategy formulation
Infrastructure-led	Bottom-up/leg 2
Business-led	Top-down/leg 1
Opportunity-led	Inside-out/leg 3

thorough survey of a bottom-up nature and there may be areas of the business where inside-out approaches may be worthwhile in the hope of finding unique competitive advantage from IT.

In opportunity-led firms, it is clear that the multiple methodology of all three legs will be required over time. It is likely, however, that the propositions of the inside-out leg will have to be adopted continuously, for the mixed or opportunity-led mode is concerned with creating an environment which enables the identification and implementation of IT opportunities.

PLANNING TO PLAN

Most large organizations have been experimenting with IS strategy formulation for two to five years. They often have adopted different approaches over this period and find that the benefits they originally anticipated take four to five years to materialize. Indeed, in my 1982/3 survey of information management trends, those firms who had engaged in either long range planning or strategic planning of information systems, reported that the benefits were somewhat 'soft'. As Table 4.6 shows, they reported improvements in top management support, user communication, resource forecasting, the IT function's understanding of the business and business planning in general, rather than cultivation of IS strategic plans tightly linked to business strategy or any gaining of major competitive advantage.

Table 4.6 Reported benefits of information systems planning

Rank	Benefits experienced
1.	Improved top management support
2.	Improved resource forecasting
3.	Improved business planning
4.	Improved user communication
5.	Better understanding of the organization/business

Later field studies have indicated that this 1982/3 survey was recording the *early* experiences of IS strategy formulation. At that time the planning approaches were experiments and somewhat tentative.

Subsequently, they have been developed and sophisticated in a heuristic and evolutionary manner in the hope of achieving better alignment of IS with business needs and winning some competitive edge from IT. This is one reason why multiple methodologies are required; firms discover, test and modify different approaches according to needs and experience over time. Indeed, firms have to learn how to plan IS strategically in an evolutionary fashion and it may take four to five years before the 'hard', more robust, benefits of strategy formulation materialize. Table 4.7 provides an *ideal* portrayal of this learning process.

Fortunately, as the table suggests, and as the 1982/3 survey indicated, the early 'process' benefits of top management support, better business planning, improved user relationships and sounder understanding of the business are very worthwhile. It just takes time for the 'content' benefits to be released. Thus it seems to be important to manage the firm's expectations of IS strategy formulation and in this sense Table 4.7 suggests how we can plan how to plan.

Planning in stages

Typically, for reasons outlined earlier, most organizations need to understand their current position before they can advance or have the confidence to do so. The first round of IS strategy formulation thus tends to be a bottom-up mapping exercise, including an assessment of technological profile, management capability and resources as well as applications coverage and quality. In the next stage, top management, now more knowledgeable about the enterprise's capability in IT, becomes anxious to ensure that IS development is aligned with business needs and that priorities are clear in allocating scarce IT resources. Here top-down methods become essential but often have to wrestle with poorly defined business plans and needs or business plans which are inadequate for IS strategy formulation. Accordingly there can be one or two 'false starts' in this stage before a more structured methodology, such as the critical success factors approach, is adopted and clarification achieved. The next stage is messy. It involves a mix of detailed planning and investigation. The directions suggested by the second stage need more probing and substance and various trade-offs between immediate and longer-term needs have to be made. Here the enormity of the problem is apparent and the applications strategic plan becomes a set of management compromises between development and maintenance, risks and rewards, infrastructure and applications, and long- and short-term. Also, it has to be recognized that the business by now may have been changing so that some reassessment of fundamentals could be necessary.

The next stage, typically, is marked by a combination of ambition and frustration. Aspirations move towards gaining distinctive competitive advantage from IT. Yet frequently it seems that few opportunities have been highlighted by earlier approaches and perhaps it is felt that some potential strategic systems have been under-exploited. Thus the need is for complementing the evaluation and clarification thrusts of earlier phases with the innovation processes required of the inside-out approach. Users and line managers by now are more aware and competent in IT and can take initiatives.

Eventually the stage is reached when the IT-strategy connection is felt to be fully understood, the linkages between IS strategy and business strategy achieved and the need for multiple IS strategy formulation methodologies accepted. Few companies have reached this stage but some are recognizing that maturity is reached in IS strategy formulation when:

(a) formal business strategies contain within them statements of IS strategy;
(b) IS managers, user managers and general management recognize that IS strategy formulation is their joint concern and responsibility;
(c) the three legs of the multiple methodology are routinely adopted in IS strategy formulation so that top-down, bottom-up and inside-out approaches influence each other (for example, identifying and maximizing strategic opportunities seems most likely when there is clarification of the business strategy, examination of current systems potential and facilitation of innovation);
(d) the firm has adapted IS strategy formulation to fit its own style and structure.

Table 4.7 Planning in stages

Timeframe/ factor	Stage 1	Stage 2	Stage 3	Stage 4	Stage 5
Task	IS/IT mapping	Business direction	Detailed planning	Competitive advantage	IT–strategy connection
Objective	Management understanding	Agreeing priorities	Firming up the IS strategic plan	Finding opportunities	Integrating IS and business strategies
Direction/ involvement	DP/IT lead	Senior management drive	Users and IS mainly involved	Executive management and users	Partnership of users, general management and IS
Methodological emphasis	Bottom-up survey	Top-down analysis	Matching top-down and bottom-up plus investigations and prototypes	Inside out processes	Multiple methods accepted
Planning context	Inexperience/ unawareness	Inadequate business plans for the purpose	Complexity apparent	Impatience	Maturity

Also by this stage, the key actors will have learnt by experience what can be realistically expected and how to manage both expectations and the methods.

For some organizations embarking on IS strategy formulation, this scenario may seem dispiriting. However, there are some comforts available! Typically, different businesses or SBUs in the organization have different IS historiographies. Thus one business or division, through earlier attempts, already may be at the equivalent of stage three or four. Others may be ready to embark on the top-down attack of stage two. Immature or nearly acquired businesses may need the IS mapping approach characteristic of stage one. This is another reason why IS strategy should be formulated at business unit level; experience varies within organizations.

PLANS AS PORTFOLIOS

There are two reasons why applications strategic plans should be thought of as portfolios. This thinking borrows from portfolio ideas in finance and in strategic management respectively. At the level of the SBU, the applications strategic plan should consider the trade-offs and balancing between risk and return – the financial portfolio model. At the corporate level, the allocation of IS resources to SBUs should reflect the priorities of the corporate strategy – the strategic portfolio model.

Risk and return portfolios

At the level of the SBU, not all the contents of the applications strategic plan have equal priority in timescale or for resources. Mandatory applications and maintenance and enhancement (if guided by the systems audit grid) are non-controversial. The other elements of the plan (Figure 4.4) will have different pay-offs, risks and timescales.

Shaping the applications strategic plan into a realistic set of deliverables over time with not too many risks is a necessary task, both rationally and politically. The IT function and its host business need a steady stream of application developments that can be sensibly resourced and properly implemented, enough systems installations over time to be perceived as progressing and to build up cumulative experience, and some breakthroughs and innovations to yield major gains and motivate professional staff. The applications strategic plan therefore must be shaped into a portfolio which yields a smooth flow of deliverables year by year and hedges the many risks in IS development.

Figure 4.4 provides a rubric to aid this shaping process. Various versions of this idea have been proposed by academics and consultants.[4] This format asks two questions:

1. What is the payoff of the system proposal? This can be answered quantitatively or qualitatively, but is a reasonable estimate of returns or benefits.
2. How far away are the goalposts? By this is meant an assessment of the risks, timescales and difficulties amalgamated into one measure. It could include McFarlan's project risk management characteristics of size, structuredness and technology attributes[5] plus an appraisal of duration of, and support for, the project.

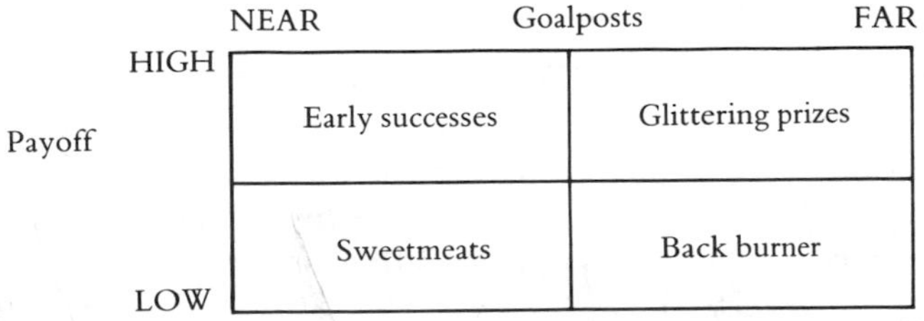

	NEAR Goalposts FAR	
HIGH	Early successes	Glittering prizes
LOW	Sweetmeats	Back burner

Payoff

Figure 4.4 Hedging the applications portfolio.

The metaphors in Figure 4.4, which answers to these questions suggest, are obvious:

1. 'Early successes' are essential for the implementation of any IS strategy. The IT function needs a success to retain or regain credibility and top management is often positively influenced by early gains. So a new applications strategic plan ideally should comprise at least one potential early success.
2. 'Sweetmeats' are also vital. The IT function must be seen to be delivering systems regularly and users tend to respond to steady service. So ideally the IT function needs a store of sweetmeats upon which it can draw at regular intervals. One insurance company called these 'plums', ensuring a continuous flow of system products, none of which took more than one elapsed year to develop.
3. 'Glittering prizes' are rare. However, the concept of the strategic system implies a glittering prize. If an application is truly likely to yield competitive advantage, it is likely in mature or competitive markets that there are difficulties or risks in its implementation. Otherwise, others already may have developed it. Therefore many strategic systems may have potentially high returns but involve considerable

risks. Thus a firm seeking strategic advantage from IT might always be developing at least one glittering prize. However, it would not be pursuing too many, because the collective risks are too high and the relevant skills and management capability likely to be too scarce.

4.   'Back burner' projects perhaps should not be identified by IS strategy formulation procedures. However, after the detailed analysis and design which is necessary to translate directions for systems development into application shopping lists, what was initially a good idea may turn out to be rather modest or overly complex. These projects should be postponed until circumstances change and the risk–return trade-off improves.

The rubric in Figure 4.4 therefore can help SBU management shape an outline applications strategic plan into a practicable development portfolio. However, in most multi-divisional, multi-business companies, not all SBUs will deserve equal IS investment and some may be competing for scarce IT resources at a divisional, regional or corporate level. Furthermore, the corporation may have a different view of SBU priorities and direction than the units themselves. This is where the portfolio models of strategic management have a place.

Strategic management portfolios

In Table 4.8, the elements of the SBU applications strategic plan from Table 4.1 form the rows of the matrix. The columns represent the different SBUs competing for resources or seeking approval for IS investments. The classification at the top of the columns uses the Boston Consulting Group's strategic portfolio terminology (the growth-share matrix).[6] The bottom classification of the columns uses the life-cycle model of business development. These two classifications are alternatives, not equivalents.

What does Table 4.8 suggest? At the corporate level, for example, severe questions would be asked of a dog business (low market share in a low growth market) proposing investment in strategic applications. Likewise, an aged business being run for cash would not be expected to propose large scale infrastructure projects.

> A business unit of a manufacturing company proposed investment in production and process control systems in order to improve its performance and drive down costs. It had been producing marginal results for some time. The proposal was very well argued and had a sound strategic rationale. However, the corporate board was beginning to think that the business might be closed as it was a drain on cash flow. Only when the company chairman was alerted to consider this seemingly good proposal through the perspective of the portfolio model in Table 4.8 were corporate strategy questions asked. The proposal was then frozen; six months later the factory was closed.

Conversely, a mature or cash cow business fighting to preserve market share might well depend on basic business systems (requiring infrastructure development, renewal and maintenance) to maintain competitive parity. It could also justify some strategic systems investment in order to gain some competitive advantage.

Star businesses would expect to receive IS support down all the rows. Question mark businesses, growth businesses and some embryonic businesses exploiting IT, or making a business of information, would merit investment in R & D/experimental

Table 4.8 The corporate IS portfolio

	Stars	Question marks	Cash cows	Dogs
Mandatory				
Strategic				
Traditional				
Infrastructure				
Renewal				
R & D				
Maintenance				
Niche				
	Embryonic	Growth	Mature	Aged

projects and some niche developments as well as more traditional systems support.

In many multi-divisional firms, new or growth businesses are thought to be impaired and impeded by the application of planning and control procedures which have evolved in the mature and aged businesses. Likewise, in the IT era, it can be a mistake to suppose that new and uncertain businesses should wait until they are stable and proven before they invest in IS.

Of course, the portfolio approach of Table 4.8 need not be deterministic. The argument is not that only certain businesses deserve IS or that certain elements of the applications strategic plan only fit a certain strategic condition. Exploitation of IT could change the strategic condition of an SBU. For example, an experimental project or encouragement of niche IT developments could turn a question mark business into a star or regenerate a seemingly aged, dying business. Thus, whilst the portfolio model indicates where the percentages and 80/20 rules lie for IS investment, it must not be used mechanistically thereby killing off sparks of innovation or paths to business recovery.

ACTION AND REVIEW

IS strategy formulation will not be accepted or understood and will not work unless it is practical. This is why the applications strategic plan was described as 'a shopping list'; it must state clearly what systems are to be developed or studied. This is why a multiple methodology is required, for IS strategy formulation is tackling several goals at once and thus different approaches will be needed for different purposes. This is why portfolio planning is recommended in order to convert the strategically directed shopping list into a practicable plan which will have a chance of succeeding most of the time. This is why planning to plan in stages is recommended in order to manage expectations.

However, most organizations have other planning procedures at work at the same time. So that IS strategic plans are accepted and properly considered, it is essential that they are connected with these procedures; in other words, to use the concept of Chapter 2, IS strategy formulation must be 'normalized'. Thus, whereas IS strategy formulation is a complex matter which often has to be tackled as a special exercise, the outputs and consequences must be linked with normal business planning procedures. It is surprising how many businesses have rigorous business planning procedures which do not recognize the planning, resourcing, implementing or exploiting of information systems. The result often is that systems fail because they are not managed seriously.

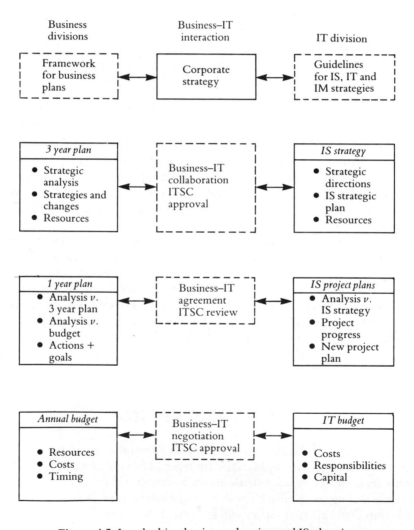

Figure 4.5 Interlocking business planning and IS planning.

Interlocking planning and plans

A financial services group, which was introducing both formal business planning and IS planning for the first time, proposed interlocking these two processes as shown in Figure 4.5. At first it was thought that the corporate planning group would review and oversee business planning and then discuss the outcome with the IT division. It was realized that there were four disadvantages with this:

1. The Planning Group knew little about IT and IS.
2. The business divisions would be distanced from the IT division.
3. It would impede IT and IS opportunities influencing business strategies and plans.
4. IS planning became a late residual of business planning.

Thus the model in Figure 4.5 emphasizes four features for this company:

1. The corporate strategy provides the framework for both IS plans and business plans.
2. IS strategy formulation is a joint business division – IT division activity and responsibility.
3. IS strategy (and long-term business plans) are factored down into project (one year) plans and connect with budgetary planning and control.
4. An IT steering committee (ITSC) of the main board approves the IS strategy, reviews project progress annually, and approves the IT division's budget from a functional perspective.

This is not necessarily a general model. In many organizations it would be important that capital budgeting is connected to IS strategic planning to both capture undeclared IT investments and to test IS consequences. However Figure 4.5 does remind us that IS strategy formulation should not be done in a vacuum and be isolated from the business.

Some organizations, however, prefer more informal management practices. Business planning may be more *ad hoc*, communication mainly personal, and IS strategic decisions opportunistic, and most management decision making more political than rational. In this case, it is unwise to expect the organization to change its behaviour just to suit the needs of the IT department or its strategists! The requirements of IS strategies and their formulation suggested in this chapter still apply; the process has to fit the organizational context. Pyburn recognized the need for such a contingency approach in connecting IS planning to corporate strategy. His research produced the prescription summarized in Table 4.9.

The columns in Table 4.9 represent three IS planning styles that Pyburn discovered. The rows indicate the attributes of organizational context which seemed to generate each style. This matrix can help an organization work out both the appropriate style of the IS strategy process and the preferred nature of the IS strategy outcome. In a study of the IT function in complex organizations, Feeny *et al.* found that in the UK most managements adopted a personal, formal style in organizational decision making. If IS strategy formulation has to adopt this preferred style, Table 4.9 also shows where it is likely to work – in short in average states of each factor of organizational context! In different contexts, the style of IS strategic planning perhaps cannot follow the personal, formal norm.

Table 4.9 Planning style and organizational context

Factors/style	Personal informal	Personal formal	Written formal
Business planning style	Informal	Moderate	Formal
Top management communication	Informal	Moderate	Formal
Volatility of business environment	High	Moderate	Low
Complexity of IS environment	Low	Moderate	High
Status of IS manager	High	Moderate	Low
Proximity of IS manager to top	Close	Distant	Distant

Source: Pyburn

Reaction and review

Finally, not only will the organization's IS strategy formulation capability mature over time, but business pressures will change and surprises happen. All IS strategies should be regarded as evolutionary and not fixed. They are frameworks which can be revised. Thus review points are essential. Annual reviews are normal, but in rapidly changing environments, six-monthly review can make sense. One insurance company reviews its strategy each half year; the business situation is reviewed alternately with the technological environment. In contrast, in a London merchant bank in the mid-1980s, business strategic decisions were being made continuously and often unpresaged. The institution prided itself on being 'responsive, fleet of foot and dynamic'. The need here was for no business strategic decision to be approved before the information systems consequences were considered and agreed. This was an essential mechanism for interlocking a necessary semi-formal IS strategy with a highly informal business strategy. It was also recognized that the IT function had to be adequately resourced if it were to react so flexibly – but that is an issue for the next two chapters.

SUMMARY

In a 1982/3 survey of information management trends by the author, the first five issues listed in Table 4.10 were reported as the most significant problems experienced in IS strategy formulation at that time. Since 1986, a sixth issue often has been brought to the Oxford Institute of Information Management – 'How can we discover competitive advantage opportunities?'

The principles discussed in this chapter seek to address these problems as follows:

1. Top-down clarification methods are vital in the context of inadequate business plans.
2. Portfolio planning helps in agreeing priorities.
3. Planning to plan in stages helps overcome lack of planning experience.
4. Keeping detail out of IS strategic plans, reviewing them periodically, and interlocking them with business planning processes helps cope with business/user change.

Table 4.10 Problems in IS planning

Rank	
1.	Inadequate business plans
2.	Agreeing priorities
3.	Lack of planning experience
4.	Rate of business/user change
5.	Organization structure
6.	Discovering competitive advantage

5. Making divisions or business units responsible for IS strategy formulation and separating IT strategy and IM strategy from IS strategy remove much of the confusion and conflict in complex organization structures.
6. Investing in inside out processes for innovation is key to discovering competitive advantage opportunities. In many ways, strategic ISs are different from IS strategy, which is why a multiple methodology is required.

However, the evidence that underpins the five stage model of IS strategic planning emphasizes that IS strategy formulation is not as easy as it sounds and takes some time to perfect. The problems in Table 4.10 are typical of the early learner in this field and also perhaps show why IS strategy formulation is necessary and important. Above all, these problems coupled with the complexities involved – multiple methods, sector modes, stage learning, portfolio approaches and organizational interlocking – emphasize how important it is to explicate and share the expectations of those involved in IS strategy formulation. There are six useful questions to ask at the outset of an IS strategy exercise which this chapter should help answer:

1. Why are we doing it?
2. What do we want to achieve?
3. Where have we come from?
4. How should our organization approach it?
5. How shall we manage it?
6. How shall we normalize it?

There is also a seventh. What about the IT strategy? This is the subject of the next chapter.

NOTES AND REFERENCES

1. See, for example, McFarlan F. W., Nolan R. L. and Norton D. P., *Information Systems Administration*, Holt, Rinehart and Winston, 1973.
2. See Earl M. J., Information systems strategy formulation', in Boland R. J., Jr and Hirschheim R. (eds), *Critical Issues in Information Systems Research*, J. Wiley, 1987.
3. *Ibid.*
4. See, for example, Cash J. I. and McLeod P. L., 'Managing the introduction of information systems technology in strategically dependent companies', *Journal of Management Information Systems*, Vol. 1 (No. 5), 1985.

5. See McFarlan F. W., 'Portfolio approach to information systems', *Harvard Business Review*, September-October 1981.
6. See Hedley B., 'Strategy and business portfolio', *Long Range Planning*, Vol. 10, February 1977.

FURTHER READING

Boynton A. C. and Zmud R. W., 'An assessment of critical success factors', *Sloan Management Review*, Spring 1984.

Bullen C. V. and Rockart J. F., 'A primer on critical success factors', CISR working paper (No. 69), Sloan School of Management, MIT, June 1984.

Feeny D. F., Edwards B. and Earl M. J., 'Complex organisations and the information systems function – a research study', Oxford Institute of Information Management research and discussion paper (RDP 87/7), Templeton College, Oxford, 1987.

Galliers R., 'IT strategies today: the UK experience', in M. J. Earl (ed.), *Information Management: The Strategic Dimension*, Oxford University Press, 1988.

Gibson C. F. and Nolan R. L., 'Managing the four stages of EDP growth', *Harvard Business Review*, January-February 1974.

King W. R., 'Strategic planning for MIS', *MIS Quarterly*, March 1978.

Lockett M., 'The factors behind successful IT innovation', Oxford Institute of Information Management research and discussion paper (RDP 1987/9), Templeton College, Oxford, 1987.

McLean E. R., 'Strategic planning for MIS: an update', information systems working paper (4–83). Graduate School of Management, UCLA, 1983.

McLean E. R. and Soden J. V., *Strategic Planning for MIS*, J. Wiley, 1977.

Pyburn P. J., 'Linking the MIS plan with corporate strategy: an exploratory study', *MIS Quarterly*, June 1983.

Runge D. A., 'Using telecommunications for competitive advantage', unpublished D.Phil thesis, University of Oxford, 1985.

Runge D. A. and Earl M. J., 'Gaining competitive advantage from telecommunications', in M. J. Earl (ed.), *Information Management: The Strategic Dimension*, Oxford University Press, 1988.

Shank M. E., Boynton A. C. and Zmud, R. W., 'Critical success factor analysis as a methodology for MIS planning', *MIS Quarterly*, June 1985.

Sullivan C. H., Jr., 'Systems planning in the information age', *Sloan Management Review*, Winter 1985.

Chapter 5

FORMULATING IT STRATEGY

INTRODUCTION

In the previous chapter, the problem of formulating an IS strategy – defining the 'what' – was examined. This chapter is concerned with formulating the IT strategy, or the 'how'. IT strategy, as delineated in Figure 3.9, focuses on delivery and thus comprises the organization's technology policies. The IT strategy is best seen as the technology framework or architecture which drives, shapes and controls the IT infrastructure.

The technology framework, hereafter called architecture,[1] comprises four elements:

1. Computing – the information processing hardware and its associated operating system software.
2. Communications – the telecommunications networks and their associated mechanisms for interlinking and interworking.
3. Data – the data assets of the organization and the requirements of use, access, control and storage.
4. Applications – the main application systems of the organization, their functions and relationships, as well as the development methods.

This concept of architecture is depicted in Figure 5.1 and implies that, although each element can be, and has to be, tackled separately, they are interdependent. Not only is architecture seeking to achieve an infrastructure that is greater than the sum of the parts, but each element influences the other. For example the topology of a communications network is influenced by application needs, data transmission requirements and information processing geography as well as by its own capabilities.

The technology framework can contain four levels of guidance. The four levels for each architecture element may be called *frames*. The set of frames makes up the framework. The four levels consist of the following categories:

1. Parameters – the major design parameters of each architecture element. They represent the essential needs, constraints and preferences that over time each element should aim to satisfy.

Formulating IT strategy

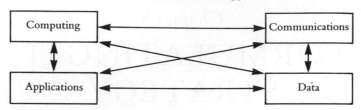

Figure 5.1 IT architecture.

2. Schemas – logical, and perhaps physical, models of what is required of each architectural element and how they should work. Sometimes called models or blueprints they may either be the visual, logical state of the frame as it exists now or an agreed, detailed model of what is being pursued.
3. Policies – concrete, practical statements of how each technological element is to be delivered. Included are technological policies, guidelines, procedures and standards.
4. Plans – firm plans and goals for each element. These may include project plans or performance goals – plus time-phased actions which will move the framework to the next stage of evolution.

By combining the four elements of the architecture framework with four levels of guidance, one view of an IT strategy is presented in Table 5.1. Although shown as a matrix, there are three points to be made about its use:

1. The columns, or levels, represent from left to right increasing degrees of business and technological certainty.
2. At any one time all levels, or columns, may not be capable of completion for each element, or row. Now may they need to be completed if there is no overwhelming business or technological imperative to do so.
3. Each element has to be tackled independently at first, but as they are interdependent, firming up the levels of each element tends to be an iterative process.

These and other methodological points are developed in a later section on deriving the architecture. Whilst the four-by-four matrix may seem daunting, its advantage is that it provides a guiding and realistic structure for formulating an IT strategy.

Table 5.1 A structure for IT strategy

Levels/ elements	Parameters	Schemas	Policies	Plans
Computing				
Communications				
Data				
Applications				

ARCHITECTURE

In the late 1980s several large organizations are engaged in designing and building architectures. Since the task is more difficult than it first appears, it is important to ask why an architecture is necessary. Four reasons stand out:

1. As technology becomes embedded in business operations and sector infrastructure, the need for systems and technology *integration* increases. Architecture provides a framework for, and a mechanism to, consider and design necessary interfaces, compatibilities and integration.
2. As technologies advance so rapidly, organization structures evolve, and business needs change, the IS/IT function is concerned to establish the necessary amount of *order* in information processing. Architecture provides a framework for resolving and reviewing technology choices over time.
3. Once the information systems strategy (the 'what') is formulated, a set of policies and mechanics is required to ensure its effective and efficient *delivery*. Architecture provides a structure for implementing the IS needs of the business.
4. As the relationships between business strategy and capability and IT strategy and capability become closer, a technological *model* of the organization is required. Architecture is already serving this need in companies in the delivery sector where IT infrastructure underpins business and sector activities.

However, despite the increasing attention to architecture in practice, little research-based knowledge exists and few general models are available. Most approaches to architecture are proprietary to IT manufacturers and management consultants. Thus, there is hardly any accepted terminology and no universal definition of architecture. The term is applied to network topologies, software construction, computer structures and so on by manufacturers. Consultants refer to the structure of IT in the business, the conceptual plan for information systems and a process for resolving conflicts and communicating about technology matters. Practitioners often produce diagrams, standards and statements of intent.

Given the reasons, or objectives, for architecture outlined above and based on the overall structure presented in Table 5.1, architecture is here defined as 'the technology framework which guides the organization in satisfying business and management information systems needs'. Because it is broad in technological scope, has to cope with business uncertainty and technological change and will vary in specificity and detail with organizational strategies, structure and IT maturity, it is appropriate to see architecture as a framework. Architecture is a framework for analysis, design and construction of IT infrastructure which guides an organization over time. It is unlikely to be 'set in concrete', to be equally detailed in all its elements, to be neat and tidy at every level and to have a horizon beyond five years. The notion of the framework comprising frames for each element is meant to convey the evolutionary and differentiated nature of the components of architecture.

The concept of architecture has been likened to city planning (Nolan and Mulryan). Faced with many social, economic, political and technological unknowns and complexities, town planners set guidelines on zones, densities, services and so on. They rarely delve into details of mechanics, materials and cases. By planning at this schematic level, towns and cities are able to accommodate new technologies, preserve values, respond to new pressures, and preserve a level and quality of services over time. IT architecture seeks similar goals by similar means. Business needs are to be met, new technologies adopted and exploited, the organization's structure, style and culture respected and yet the technological evolutions and revolutions managed reasonably smoothly.

Elements of architecture

The elements of architecture are those major sets of information technology which require discrete planning and control. The first element, *computing,* is singled out as the principal information processing capability. It comprises therefore not only mainframes, but minicomputers, departmental computers, microcomputers, process control computers, workstations terminals, peripherals etc. One view of the computing element – a schema – is reproduced in Figure 5.2. This was the total set of computer-based information processing that had to be implemented in a manufacturing company. Computing architectural issues therefore are concerned with preferred machines and vendors, configuration planning, and compatibility rules. Operating system software is also included not only because it is integral with computing but also because it influences choices of suppliers, environments and interworking.

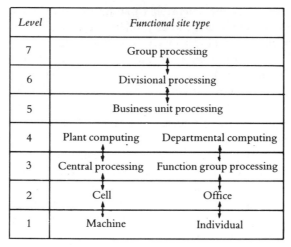

Level	Functional site type	
7	Group processing	
6	Divisional processing	
5	Business unit processing	
4	Plant computing	Departmental computing
3	Central processing	Function group processing
2	Cell	Office
1	Machine	Individual

Figure 5.2 A computing schema.

The element of *communications* has become for many businesses the most challenging aspect of architecture today. Not only do they want to transport voice, data, text and image around their organizations efficiently and reliably but, increasingly, they are communicating with outside organizations such as customers, suppliers and collaborators. These needs involve both interlinking (transportation of data from a source device to a destination device) and interworking (the ability for a source device and destination device to interact with each other). Influenced also by the architecture frame of computing, which normally involves several levels of processing, most large organizations are faced with structuring three levels of networks. Local networks link up local computer configurations, databases and terminals. National networks are often required to link local networks together. International networks may be required to link up national networks.

The problem with deriving the communications frame is that most organizations are still at an immature stage of adopting the technology. They may understand voice communications but are less confident about data or integrated service networks. Indeed, they probably inherit a spaghetti-like communications infrastructure which has evolved to meet *ad hoc* needs. On top of this, national PTTs may be similarly immature in understanding their markets and yet are faced with explosive demands for communications investments. Even worse, progress on international communications standards and integration falls behind most users' expectations.

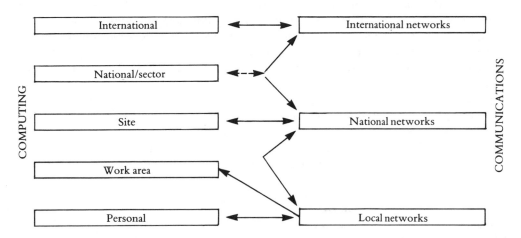

Figure 5.3 A communications schema.

So the architectural issues of communications involve determination of network needs, design of their topologies to fit computing structures and planned traffic, and decisions on whether networks should be publicly or privately supplied. A simple view of one multinational's communications needs – their schema – is presented in Figure 5.3. This firm opted for open systems interconnection (OSI) as the standard for exchange of data around its networks and between different hardware. It followed that X25 was the adopted standard for packet switching of data as this fits the OSI model and is recommended by the CCITT.[2] However, because of the need to couple IBM mainframes, SNA (systems network architecture) also had to be adopted *pro tem*. Such standards questions are typical of communications architecture frames and such compromises typify the current immaturity of the technology.

Data, in principle, is the most important element as it is 'the raw material of information' and thus in a sense both the means and ends of information systems. Indeed, over the years, it has become commonplace to hear of 'precious information resources locked up in inappropriate or inflexible databases and systems'. Nevertheless, data architecture is still intellectually challenging, administratively painful, and practically frustrating – and accordingly often receives a low priority.

Data architecture issues include the determination of data storage location, use and access, the design and administration of databases, and increasingly, the definition and coding of data for Electronic Date Interchange (EDI) between organizations – including article numbering and bar coding. Equally, standards and protocols are required for exchange of data between applications, especially as firms enter the worlds of computer-integrated manufacturing and the like. Concerns about security and privacy also enter the data frame.

Applications become an element of architecture because organizations need a map or blueprint through which to plan development *and* anticipate the requirements of computing, communications and data. Thus, although the IS strategy (the 'what') determines the overall direction, priorities, balances and scope of applications, plans for achieving this strategy are necessary. What is certainly required is a schema of applications, a conceptual framework comprising both existing and planned systems showing their likely interfaces, sequence of development, possible integration and common modules. In this way, long-term goals and visions are explicated and recorded but have to continually reflect and accommodate short-term pressures and incremental moves.

Such a logical schema may benefit from being factored into a more physical representation, separately addressing specific application sets such as transaction processing, management information systems, professional support applications and automation. The concept of applications portfolios[3] depicted in Table 5.2 is helpful as a means of both covering all aspects of IS but ensuring integration needs are considered.

Table 5.2 Applications portfolio

Applications/ management levels	Transaction processing	Decision support	Professional support	Physical automation	External products/ weapons
Strategic planning					
Management control					
Operational control					

Other applications architecture issues comprise applications philosophies, for example, adoption of MRP in manufacturing; system acquisition policies, such as make or buy decisions; system development methodologies, such as the use of information requirements analysis techniques or the encouragement of prototyping; and standards for programming and testing, such as the use of fourth generation languages or quality control techniques.

Levels of architecture

The levels of architecture now should be more apparent. Each element, represents increasing degrees of certainty or mandate. *Parameters,* as the word implies, are the key influence on each frame. They are the factors that must be satisfied by the design and construction of each element of architecture. They are firm, unambiguous, ongoing and agreed criteria for design. They are thus the cornerstone of each frame and for complex uncertain elements, they may be the only necessary and feasible level of guidance that can be completed for the frame. Parameters comprise the needs, constraints and preferences of the organization and are likely therefore to be unique and change only occasionally over time. Their derivation is discussed later. However, many organizations fail in their management of IT and in their architecture endeavours because they have neither identified nor followed these guiding parameters.

Examples of parameters are shown in the completed architecture matrix in Table 5.3. It should be apparent that they are crucial in linking the design and implementation of IT strategy to business imperatives and management preferences. Therefore parameters must be explicit and promulgated to all involved with IS/IT. For the IS function, parameters also become criteria against which future technology choices can be made and reference points for continuing elaboration of the more detailed levels of guidance.

Table 5.3 Architectural examples

Level/ elements	Parameters	Schemas	Policies	Plans
Computing	De facto standards should be adopted	Figure 5.2 (conceptual)	Large commercial mainframe processing will be IBM 370 architecture and associated IBM peripherals	Formulate and promulgate a common standard for office automation across the group by end 1985
Communications	The business should be linked electronically	Figure 5.3 (conceptual)	Any incremental communications requirements must be agreed by group telecommunications	Install new voice network across group by end 1986
Data	Organizational units should control their own data but it should be available to higher levels	Entity-relationship models	Data definitions and structures can be changed only with agreement of the data administrator	Provide security standards and back-up facilities by mid–1985
Applications	Development priorities should be determined by business strategy	Table 5.2 (conceptual)	Application systems should be acquired rather than developed in-house wherever possible	To install common transaction systems by 1987

Schemas are often the mechanism for expressing and interpreting the parameters. Schemas may be logical or physical models of each element. The term is borrowed from database management, where the logical schema represents the user's conceptualization and the physical schema the actual data organization. The schemas in

Figures 5.2 and 5.3 and Table 5.2 are logical; they show the overall requirements of each respective element and suggest logically how everything fits together. Physical versions of these schemas would specify everything more precisely, in terms of systems processors, network routes, protocols, interface mechanisms etc. Schemas are means of prescribing the frames of architecture in a manageable fashion, without losing sight of the aims in too much detail. They suggest the desired state and show the requisite structures and connections. So schemas at any time represent the current views of the future state, but are not sacrosanct.

For some elements, the notion of schemas is established as is the modelling process to develop them. Data modelling is the exemplar case. A classical approach, often known as entity-relationship modelling, is adopted in database studies. Business activities are analysed by function and input-processing-output tables of their information usage are constructed. Entities – objects, people, events – are identified and their attributes specified to become data-items. The logical relationships between entities and data-items are plotted and these drive the logical design of databases and specify the physical requirements. A schema (and subschemas) is then drawn to formally describe the required data organization at the logical level. Figure 5.4, reproduced from McCosh, Rahman and Earl, is an example schema for a production database. (Subschemas are the different application programmers' description of the data they need to use.)

> An airline began an architecture exercise. A previous consultant's report had stressed that key data which was at the heart of operational transaction systems was often not accessible or flexible enough for use in decision support systems and new competitive weapon information systems. The crucial entity was the passenger and his data-item attributes of flight frequency, routes, travel class, associated service use, company and home address etc. were potentially important marketing information assets. Data modelling was thus an obvious priority for the airline's architecture exercise.

Data schemas are essential in identifying databases to be built, relationships and access paths to be designed, the amount and location of data storage required, the nature and extent of data processing and communications needed, the components of database administration that must be installed, and dependencies in the applications architecture frame. However, experience shows that, as for architecture as a whole, data modelling is easier and more successful if it is done around particular functions, activities, or application areas than for the enterprise as a whole – despite the fact that data flows rarely obey such boundaries.

Schemas are also necessary inputs to network planning. Indeed the seven-layer models of telecommunications reproduced in Table 5.4 are high level, universal, logical schemas. At the company level, alternative schemas can be drawn up from the telecommunications parameters and the best fit schema adopted. These might cover both physical topology and the logical blueprint for interlinking and interworking. The firm and agreed portions of the schema will then probably suggest where telecommunications policies need to be formulated.

Policies therefore are, in principle, firm, clear statements about how each architectural element is to be delivered. Only some of these statements may be policies in the sense of the organization's choice on certain key questions. Examples might include a policy to acquire application packages or bespoke software rather than

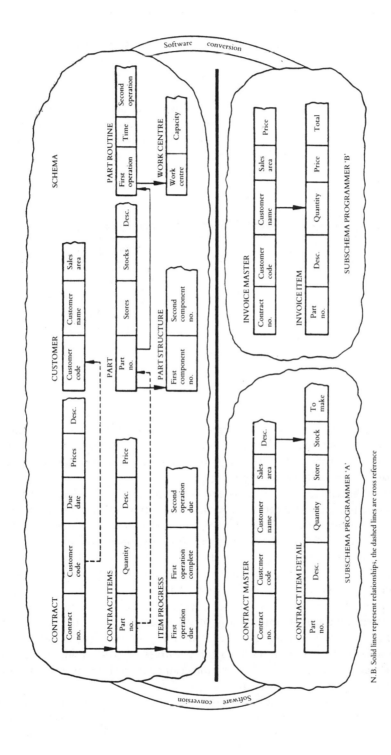

Figure 5.4 Schema and subschema of a production database.

N.B. Solid lines represent relationships; the dashed lines are cross reference

develop systems in house, or the decision to adopt a single vendor for mainframe computing.

Also, there may be 'guidelines' which are softer versions useful in areas of complexity or uncertainty. Through guidelines, the organization says, 'this is our preferred approach to be adopted until a firmer or clearer solution is required or necessary and thus it can be broken only by agreement'. For example, a large, multi-divisional manufacturing company felt uneasy about its proliferation of mainframe suppliers in terms of reliability, compatibility and support. However, with a strong conviction that application needs and software support were more important than hardware rationalization, it formulated a guideline limiting future hardware acquisition to three vendors unless a strong application reason could be made to justify an exception.

Table 5.4 OSI and SNA layers of communications

OSI reference model		IBM's SNA
Application	7	User applications
Presentation	6	Function management
Session	5	Data flow control
Transport	4	Transmission control
Network	3	Path control
Data link	2	Data link control
Physical	1	Physical link

The third type of policy is standards which are rules or mandates instructing IS specialists and users that particular methods must be adopted. For example, standardizing on PC DOS and Lotus 123 for system software and spreadsheet applications is common in end-user computing.

Thus policies are specific, tend towards the concrete, and will refer to suppliers, methods, protocols, products and tools. In architecture, they govern the selection and use of IT. However, because they are restrictive, they should only be developed if they are necessary and proposed if they receive majority support and commitment.

Plans are deliverables or actions. They are the detailed targets, goals and intents for each element. An example of a target would be that of a credit card company aiming to install a worldwide transactions database by 1985. A typical performance goal was the requirement in a commercial company for data centre operations never to be out of action for more than four hours. Intents are very common in the early stages of IT strategy formulation until everyone is agreed on the goal or target. Indeed, once parameters are established, it is often necessary to commission studies which will work out consequent schemas and policies. These actions can be thought of as intents because they are investigating specific areas of concern.

The first IT strategy of a merchant bank comprised little in the way of schemas and policies but tasked different specialists to propose standards in crucial areas through the following year, once parameters were established. The IT strategy thus comprised clear parameters plus a list of intents which would firm up and develop the architecture for next year.

The key to deriving the four frames of the architecture is using an effective methodology. An approach is presented in the next section.

A METHODOLOGY FOR ARCHITECTURE

The matrix in Table 5.1 in some ways provides a methodology for deriving the technology framework for it suggests a logical, analytical structure. However, in deriving architecture, a mechanism is required for interpreting organizational imperatives, building on the current technological position, and linking to IS strategy. The methodology presented below seeks to achieve this and can provide the inputs to the technology framework or IT strategy. Like most methodologies, its effectiveness depends as much on its process as its structure.

Table 5.5 A methodology for architecture

Step	1	2	3	4
Activity	Mapping	Steering	Updating	Shaping
Character	Bottom-up	Top-down	Inside-out	Distillation
Outputs	Inventories	Assumptions	Deliverables	Principles

The methodology for architecture portrayed in Table 5.5 comprises four steps:

1. Mapping – or drawing up current inventories of the four elements of architecture.
2. Steering – or establishing the organizations 'givens' which must guide architecture decisions.
3. Updating – or amending the architecture to reflect changes in the IS strategy or the capabilities of technologies.
4. Shaping – or distillation of the first three steps into principles upon which the architecture will be based.

The first three steps can be pursued sequentially or in parallel. Only when these are completed, can the fourth step begin. Each step is described and specified below.

Mapping

This step is essential in formulating architecture, but it need only be done at the outset of an architecture study and then every few years. In order to understand what may be involved in reaching architectural goals, and perhaps to identify some obvious requirements, it is important to know the current position and capability. Thus, mapping is the straightforward but mundane task of drawing up inventories of all the key elements of architecture, including an assessment of current strengths and weaknesses. It is essentially a bottom–up exercise.

Mapping can be done largely by the IS function (with collaboration of users on some aspects), as the need is to inventory each element of architecture. It need not be exhaustive, unless required for other reasons, but documents the extent, capability and linkages of each element. Figure 5.5 suggests the key questions for architecture. Once the inventories are assembled, they should be simplified by producing three message statements:

1. A sketch map of each element.
2. A summary of strengths and weaknesses.
3. A list of key questions or puzzles.

- What is the current coverage of the element?
- What is the planned coverage of the element?
- What are the major assets of each element?
- What are the major gaps in each element?
- Where are there obvious incompatibilities etc.?
- What important issues have not been addressed hitherto?
- What is the overall impression of the element?

Figure 5.5 Mapping checklist.

These statements can then be discussed and agreed by the architecture study team.

Steering

This step is equally vital because it is concerned with establishing the organization's principal 'steers' for any future architecture. Thus steering is the challenging task of eliciting those goals, policies, values and mandates of the organization which architecture should either facilitate achieving or at least not offend. Because these tend to be a mix of explicit and implicit and of hard and soft, the appropriate term for the output of step 2 is assumptions. Eliciting and validating assumptions is essentially a top-down exercise, conducted every few years.

Steering requires a more open process and demands considerable skill compared with step 1. Often the assistance of consultants is required to both provide experience and bring the necessary process skills. For here, the key assumptions about the organization and its needs are explicated by interviewing senior executives and examining strategy and policy documents. Figure 5.6 is a suggested question checklist, but eliciting answers can only be a semi-structured process requiring experienced, intuitive interpretation as much as analytical, deductive reasoning. When interviewing, it is important to select both those managers who represent the current state of IT awareness in the company and those who have a vision of the business in the future and the contribution of IT. Only interviewing the former set tends to limit the horizons and freeze the IT strategy, but being biased by the second set can produce an architecture in advance of the organization's needs and capability. Both sets must be taken from a corporate, business unit and functional management. It is likely that when principles from step 4 are validated by top management, they also will wish to verify the assumptions from step 2.

- What is the corporate strategy and business mission?
- What are the business strategies and critical success factors?
- What are the estimates for growth and diversification?
- How international is the organization and its management?
- What are the overall goals expected of IT?
- What is the corporate attitude to technological risk?
- Are there any cost/funding constraints on IT?
- What is the favoured organization structure of the firm?
- What is the preferred management style?
- Are there any regulatory factors to recognize?
- How certain is the environment and stable the strategy?
- Who should be accountable for what?
- What is the awareness of, and dependence on, IT?
- Are there any human resource policies to be recognized?
- What is success as regards IT?

Figure 5.6 Steering checklist.

Updating

Step 3 is concerned with updating the architecture and is thus done at least annually and in fast changing environments six-monthly. Here the task is to connect with the IS ('what') strategy and incorporate into architecture planning the latest contents of the strategic systems plan. Also, any important changes in technology (or suppliers) are incorporated into architecture through this step. Because step 3 is continuous and connects with ongoing IS strategy formulation and technology assessment, it can be thought of as inside-out in character.

Thus the updating step provides an important linkage between IS strategy and IT strategy. When the IS strategy is formulated or updated, the contents of the resultant strategic systems plan should then be summarized as:

(a) show what has to be delivered;
(b) suggest how it has to be delivered.

A useful technique here is to draw 'tableaux' which portray both the what and how by major application area, e.g. manufacturing, distribution, administration. Figure 5.7 is a tableau of one firm's vision for quick response supply chain management. Tableaux are pictorial representations of architecture at a conceptual level, kept simple and clean, periodically updated and often made official or public. They are blueprint visions of how IT can achieve business goals by application area. For IT specialists and architects (see later), they provide a graphical method of linking IS strategy to IT strategy, but informed by knowledge of current and emerging technologies. For users and general managers, they are memorable, understandable pictures of technological direction. They therefore must remain high level to provide a consistent picture and fulfil their communication role. The detail which is kept by the IT department may firm up over time and also change.

Such tableaux may be best informed by, or derived from, 'vision statements'. Ives and Vitale found that often project champions behind a competitive advantage IT application had articulated such a vision. Frequently these champions were chief

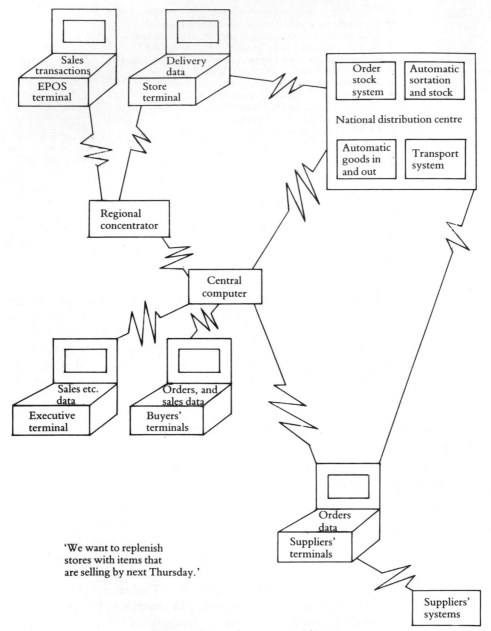

Figure 5.7 Quick response architecture.

executives and some of their vision statements are reproduced below from Ives and Vitale's paper:

Any sales person in the organisation should be able to order an elevator within a single day.

George David, COO, Otis Elevator

As a customer purchases an item off the shelf, an invisible hand replaces it.

Gilbert Wachsman, CEO, Child World

All customers calling the insurance company should be able to accomplish their task with a single call.

Robert McDermott, CEO, USAA

These may be particularly powerful in driving IT innovation. They would seem to be very useful 'terms of reference' or 'clear directions' for drawing tableaux. Equally tableaux may be a necessary technique for translating the vision statement into deliverable systems.

The tableaux technique is illustrated in Figure 5.8. This technique and step 3 as a whole require ongoing evaluation and forecasting of information technologies and their suppliers. This includes development of new products, changes in cost-performance curves, innovations by other user organizations, evolution of industry standards, strategies and performance of suppliers, and outputs of research organizations. A necessary function of architecture and strategy teams tends to be the continuous forecasting and evaluation of information technologies for architecture in general. One company embarking on formulation of architecture decided to visit its major suppliers about current and future technology policies of special relevance to that one company.

Step 3 depends above all, however, on availability of an IS strategy and its continuous review, perhaps aided by vision statements. In organizations where IT infrastructure is crucial, for example firms in the delivery sector, interpreting the IS strategy into architecture design is a key task. Here, drawing tableaux is an effective way of conceptualizing the technological model of the business strategy.

Figure 5.7 is one example. Here a retailing chain[4] is considering how to use IT to achieve quick response supply of goods to meet actual demand. The principle is that electronic point of sale processing captures actual sales and these trigger reordering from suppliers to replenish stores for the following weekend. The vision statement in Figure 5.7 provides the terms of reference. This tableau is but a draft of an ideal systems architecture. However it helps identify architecture questions to be answered. These include the following:

1. The EPOS terminals and system to purchase.
2. Whether to link stores direct to a central computer or through regional concentrators.
3. What terminals to provide for senior executive management information needs – and what applications.
4. What terminals to provide for buyers – and what applications.
5. What central processor to use – and interface protocols with other processors and communications.
6. Whether to recommend or give terminals and software to suppliers.
7. Consideration of interface potential with suppliers systems.
8. What hardware – computers, AGVs, automatic warehousing, laser scanners, etc. – to install at the national distribution centre.
9. What data standards and documents coding will be required to drive the system.

10. Whether to use a private communications network, a public service or a third party value-added network.
11. What approval procedures and controls to install.

It is likely that not all these questions can be answered at once and that there may have to be an evolutionary approach, as much influenced by technology availability as IS development. However the tableau provides a framework for thinking about architecture and a reference point against which progress and variances can be assessed. Over time it will become more detailed and specific as architecture decisions are made. But it is kept as a permanent model to guide all who become involved with this vision.

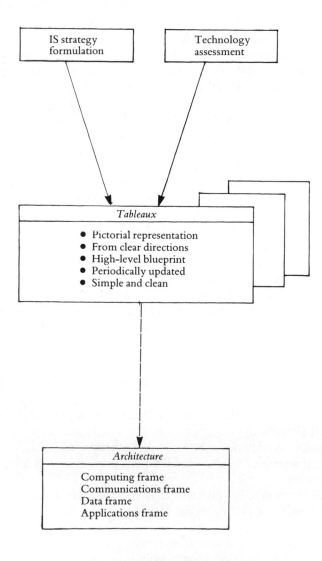

Figure 5.8 Tableaux linking IS and IT strategy.

Shaping

This step is a crucial process when architecture is being formulated for the first time or being subjected to major review. The task is to conflate and distill the outputs from steps 1 to 3 to form a set of guiding principles which henceforth will shape the technology framework. Principles represent the philosophies, objectives, constraints and values of the organization which drive the design and implementation of IT and its management over a period of years. They are high level drivers which apply to all or most elements of the technology framework and which can be factored down into specific parameters for each frame. The step becomes one of distillation of the organization's current and desired mandates for IT.

Shaping is essentially an intuitive, inductive exercise. By comparing, calibrating and cross-examining the inventories from step 1, the assumptions from step 2 and the deliverables from step 3, principles are forged which will shape the design of architecture. Principles provide the means of transition from the methodology to the architecture itself, for they are the drivers of architecture suggested by the mapping, steering and updating steps. In my experience, organizations need high level principles which drive the architecture overall and do not necessarily apply to any one element. From these principles, which become the guidelines of the architecture itself, specific parameters are factored for the relevant elements.

The dominant source of principles are the assumptions from step 2, as these are the organization's 'givens' for the architecture process. They are modified by current feasibility and capability conveyed by the inventories of step 1 and made more immediate by the deliverables identified in step 3. However, steps 1 and 3 are as much concerned with informing the detailed design of the architecture. Principles therefore can be proposed by the architecture study team and normally will require three or four iterations in workshops over several weeks for refinement. However, principles become the mandates for IT strategy. They must be validated by top management and subsequently published as a reference document. They can be usefully debated and recommended to the board by an IT steering or policy committee. Principles become a valuable reference point in subsequent decisions and conflicts about architecture. For the study team's internal verification, for top management's understanding, and for corporate communication, it often helps if each principle is accompanied by a rationale which expands and explains its need and purpose.

There are several important characteristics of principles. They should be limited in number, easily understood and likely to prevail for three to five years. It is quite acceptable if they conflict with one another (objectives and constraints often do) but they must earn the consensus of the study team, the IT community and top management. 'Grand design' statements are acceptable because they are the drivers of architecture; but, they must clearly make sense for the organization in question.

If principles cannot be forged and agreed, architecture design will fail because there is likely to be no need for it, or no support, or no shape to it. Examples of principles are listed in Table 5.6. These are culled from diverse organizations and include complementary rationale statements. Rationale statements are useful in helping management and the IT function understand the basis of each principle. They also remind everybody in the future why each principle was necessary. Once principles are forged and have received the organization's approval, detailed design of architecture into parameters, schemas, standards and plans can be taken over by the IT function and its policy committees.

The following example shows how principle statements help in making architecture decisions.

A corporate IS bureau of a multi-divisional manufacturing company was deciding on which computer to buy for operating a new set of commercial applications. An architecture study had derived a vendor list of three suppliers. IBM was one of them and one of their ranges suited this need. The question was which operating system environment should be adopted: MVS or VM. There was much discussion of the technical merits and demerits of each. Then one of the members of the decision-making team reminded his colleagues of the first principle (Table 5.6) which they had forged – the need for organizational flexibility. Quickly the team then converged on VM as the answer to their question.

Table 5.6 Principles and rationales

Principle	Rationale
IT and systems must not impair flexibility.	We aim to grow organically and by acquisition and we believe in changing the organization structure as needs demand. IT and systems should facilitate flexibility and not impair it.
IT must be developed and managed internationally.	The primary focus of the group is on European and international markets. Computing, communications and data cannot be treated as national issues.
IT is a source and support of competitive edge.	Our markets are becoming electronic and the winners will use IT in a rapid and responsive manner competitively and not just in the back office.
IT requires and involves calculated risks.	To gain competitive advantage, some risky investments are necessary but the security and integrity of the bank must not be exposed.
IT must give value for money.	All government departments are pursuing efficiency and effectiveness targets. Whilst IT can improve operational and management performance, it also has to conform with overall cost-performance goals.
Accountability for IT is in business units not functions.	Each business manager runs an autonomous entity and is responsible for the success and profitability of his business. Any group or corporate function can only be justified if business units require it.

Completing the matrix

Once the four steps above are done, the matrix in Table 5.1 can be completed. How many columns (levels) for each row (element) can be completed depends, of course, on the degrees of business and technological certainty which exist. The starting point is to factor the principles into design parameters for each element. Principles may not always be sufficient for this task and it is a useful pragmatic procedure to see if the detailed conclusions from mapping, steering and updating suggest any more parameters – or any finesses.

Schemas are not mandatory, but as discussed earlier they do help in working out the policies which are necessary to ensure parameters are satisfied. They also become useful documents or representations of architecture.

Policies are the level which 'make architecture happen'. They become the fabric of the architecture or IT strategy. Therefore they are not optional. However they should not be formulated until they are founded on sufficient business and technological certainty and command support. Guidelines may serve as the interim holding version of policies. Alternatively, statements of intent to work out a policy can be included in the plans level.

The plans column generally should be filled in, since at worst there will be intents, more likely there will be goals, and eventually these will be expressed as targets.

When the first attempt at completing the matrix has been made, three final checks should be applied. First, each plan should relate to a policy, schema or principle, each policy to a schema or principle and so on. Second, each principle should be re-examined to see if there are any gaps in the other levels which should or could be completed. Finally, it can be fruitful to apply the same logical checks vertically, that is to see if statements about any element have implications for another element which have not been considered.

Completing the matrix need not be a one-off or annual event. There are many reasons why levels might be worked on continuously. Such practicalities are developed in the next section.

IT STRATEGY IN PRACTICE

The matrix of architecture elements and levels and the four step methodology can convey the impression that IT strategy formulation is both a mechanistic procedure and a periodic exercise. Although clarity, structure and order tend to be the desired result, the means are not so neat and tidy. The architecture process requires creativity and judgement as well as analysis and technical understanding. The four step methodology provides a logical, balanced approach but it requires pragmatism amongst idealism. Experience suggests that certain success factors can be identified in IT strategy formulation, and since architecture studies and development can be slow moving and seemingly an impediment to progress, it is important to appreciate what are the characteristics of a good architecture. The next two subsections address these questions.

Lessons from architecture exercises

Experience suggests that there are seven lessons, or success factors, in formulating an effective IT strategy, particularly in designing and implementing an architecture that works.

Scale and scope
An appropriate horizon for architecture tends to be five years. Beyond that, business and technological uncertainty is too great and within five years, short-term needs can drive out longer-term benefits. However, the scale should not be too big; it is

important to be able to comprehend the architecture, factor it down into modules, and achieve it through short-run actions or goals.

Necessity and speed
In the development of architecture, organizations should only pursue what is necessary. If technical standards have no benefit or will be subverted, do not propose them. If organizational policies and procedures receive no support, do not persevere with them. Particularly for infrastructure development, but often also to make IT and its management visible, quick and partial IT strategies are better than slow and comprehensive ones. Architecture studies which exceed six months are unlikely to help the organization get started and probably will fail through complexity. It often helps to determine what are essential levels and elements and how easy they are to achieve. The matrix in Figure 5.9 can be used to prioritize issues for resolution.

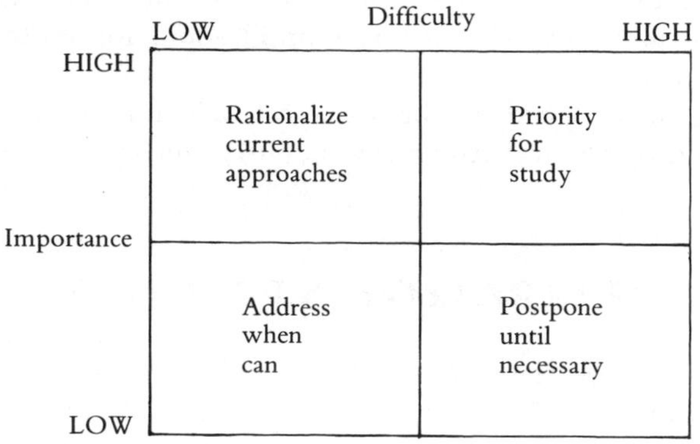

Figure 5.9 Priorities for architecture.

Principles and increments
The cornerstone of the technology framework is explication of principles. This step helps clarify the importance, place and role of IS/IT and connect it to the business. Principles become reference points or criteria for future or *ad hoc* decisions on IT and its management. Thereafter, the strategy can be developed in increments as needs demand and the organization gains experience.

Update and review
IT strategy then is an evolutionary process. Architecture in particular is never completed; it takes shape as demands emerge and issues are resolved. It must be constantly updated to reflect the IS strategy and technological change. Every three to five years it should be reviewed, including retreading steps 1 and 2 in order to check for major changes in the organization and its business and for failure in current infrastructure.

Fit and timing

The requirements and implications of architecture should never be too far in advance of the organization's ability to appreciate the need for the IT strategy and support it. Nor should they be misfits in terms of organization structure, management style and business needs. Timing can therefore be important in IT strategy formulation; a reorganization, a major management change or enquiry, or a change in the pace and direction of business strategy can all prompt the need for, or facilitate the next increment of, IT strategy.

Resources and skills

It is common for exercises in architecture and IT strategy to atrophy due to lack of resources. Specialists' time needs to be freed for the mapping, steering, updating and shaping steps. Management time must be made available to provide inputs to, and validate, the IT strategy. Two mechanisms for propelling the formulation and implementation of IT strategies are to appoint strategists or architects and to employ consultants. Architects and strategists tend to do the 'staff work' and also nurture the strategy; they are both the analysts and the guardians. They cannot do the job without strong, rounded technological knowledge. However, they must also be able to understand the business and connect and converse with key managers. Increasingly as they reorganize for the IT era, IT departments are creating a strategy unit and this is the home for architects. Consultants can help in three areas; setting up architecture studies, working on detailed aspects of architecture, and reviewing the architecture from time to time.

Support and consensus

Many expectations of IT strategy are concerned with managing the IT function better and serving business needs more effectively. Clearly, then, senior management must contribute to, validate, and endorse IT strategies. At the same time, the results also need the consensus of the IT community, which largely designs architecture and implements infrastructure, and of users, who have to accept the consequences. Architecture and IT strategy without consensus and support will not work – and maybe were not required.

Attributes of effective architecture

Architecture development is not easy; it requires sound technological knowledge and a good grasp of the host organization and its business. At the same time, the concept of architecture can seem over-technical, theoretical and obstructive to users and their managers, and in practice somewhat soft, superficial and weak to specialists. So as a conclusion to this chapter, it is useful to consider what are the characteristics of an effective architecture. There are six:

1. The architecture is a framework for developing the company's technology infrastructure and therefore must support and be linked to the IS strategy.
2. The architecture should provide a clear model to all relevant personnel of the

company's information technology infrastructure – equivalent to the chart of accounts or organogram.

3. The architecture is a framework for making technology decisions and therefore must help the company see how elements fit together, understand the place of new elements, and cope with changed needs.

4. The architecture is a framework for resolving technological conflicts and therefore is as much influenced by organizational mandates and business imperatives as technical desirables.

5. The architecture is a technology framework to be used and not archived; thus no cell in the matrix should be completed unless it is usable and enforceable.

6. The architecture is the outcome of IT strategy formulation; it must not be confused with IS strategy the subject of Chapter 4 or IM strategy the subject of the next chapter.

NOTES AND REFERENCES

1. This is not a topic on which there is good research or practical literature. Experience seems to be the most helpful input at this stage. The material in this chapter has been influenced substantially by three sources: (a) the work of the Index Group, information consultants; (b) *the work and various Stage by Stage* publications of Nolan, Norton & Co., DP management consultants; and (*c*) formulation of IT strategies in five major organizations. The resultant output, however, is the author's view and responsibility.

2. CCITT is the Consultative Committee for International Telegraphy and Telephony.

3. For the initial work on applications portfolios, see Nolan, Norton & Co'.s *Stage by Stage*, Vol. 4 (No.3), Fall 1984.

4. A similar example of this IT application is described in a Harvard Business School case study by Earl M.J. and Vitale M.: 'BHS: the supplier link', Ref. 188–094. However, the tableau in Figure 5.7 and the narrative are a hypothetical example which is the responsibility of the authors. It does not imply that the application in the case study was planned in this way.

FURTHER READING

Index Systems Inc., 'Making technology work: strategy and architecture', *Indications,* Vol. 2 (No. 1), November 1984.

Ives B. and Vitale M., 'Competitive information systems: some organisational design considerations, in M. J. Earl (ed.), *The Information Systems Organisation of Tomorrow,* Oxford Institute of Information Management, and PA Computers and Telecommunications, London, 1988.

McCosh A. M., Rahman M. and Earl M. J., *Developing Managerial Information Systems,* Macmillan, 1981.

Nolan R. L. and Mulryan D. W., 'Undertaking an architecture program', *Stage by Stage,* Vol. 7 (No. 2), March-April, 1987.

Chapter 6

FORMULATING IM STRATEGY

INTRODUCTION

Chapter 3 concluded by distinguishing between IS, IT and IM strategies. In Figure 3.9 the information management (IM) strategy was seen to be concerned with the 'wherefores'. In other words, neither the IS strategy nor IT strategy can be implemented (or indeed formulated) unless IT activities are *managed*. Thus the IM strategy is the management framework which guides how the organization should run IS/IT activities. It is organization-based, relationships-oriented and management focused.

IM strategy implies substantial formalization of information management practices, processes and procedures. Accordingly, the concept dates back to the 1970s when companies were either sophisticating their management of DP in a classical control stage manner or seeking to adjust organizational relationships as they moved into the fourth integration stage of managing DP. In the early 1970s the IM strategy, if it existed at all, was probably manifested in the form of a management standards manual. By the late 1970s the notion of an activity or functional strategy for what was then commonly known as IS was gaining attention. Indeed the concept is strongly present in McLean's and Soden's early, influential text on strategic planning for MIS.

These notions however were soon taken over by the twin realizations that information systems could be a competitive force and information technology was becoming an array of multiple technologies posing complex policy questions. Thus IS strategy and IT strategy backgrounded IM strategy. However, as argued earlier, these distinctions were rarely made and both terminology and thinking became confused.

In the UK, 1987 seemed to be the year when concerns about IM strategy returned. This reflected perhaps the wider involvement of managers and users in IT, the increasing desire to be clear about corporate and divisional responsibilities for IS and IT, the recognition that revamping information management might need reformalization of practices in some areas, and the realization that formulating IS and IT strategies was necessary but not sufficient – unless 'management was put into IT', action and progress could be disappointing. This last point often arises in one particular context.

117

Architecture studies frequently discover that a necessary prior step to validating principles and factoring them into parameters, schemas, policies and plans is to restructure the way IT is managed in the organization. Hence architectural exercises are often accompanied by changes in the corporate management of information resources. In short, a management framework is needed to complement the technology framework.

> One large consumer products company recently published corporate guidelines for IS, informing user managers what was recommended practice in dealing with all aspects of IT and IS. 'If the finance function issues a manual, why shouldn't IS?' was the corporate rationale behind this initiative, in the belief that most managers did not know what their IT responsibilities were, when to exercise them and how.

THE MANAGEMENT FRAMEWORK

The 1987 trends reported above are re-expressions of some of the arguments for information management presented in Chapter 1. In principle, six reasons for formulating IM strategy can be identified:

1. Information and IT are resources which need to be managed as efficiently and effectively as other resources.
2. The organizational, business and management impact of IT require IT/IS to be managed as an integral part of the business.
3. As business strategies increasingly are dependent upon, or created by, IT, the IT function is too important to be managed without some formalization.
4. In the past lack of top management support and involvement has impeded the successful exploitation of IT.
5. As technologies advance and choices have to be made, technology matters do matter.
6. As IT becomes embedded in business and organizational life and pervasive in use, many stakeholders are involved, so that managements need to take strategic views.

The elements and attributes of an IM strategy can now be examined.

The elements of IM strategy

It is clear from the above analysis that the management framework is concerned mainly with the relationship between the IS/IT function and the rest of the business (and beyond). The issues at stake, which again may be called *elements,* were presented in Chapter 2. Four tasks of information management were specified: planning, organization, control and technology.

Planning has been covered in the previous two chapters. It is concerned with deciding the 'what' and the 'how' and integrating this decision-making with other planning processes in the business.

Organization is often discovered to be a key element during architectural studies. For example, the structure of the IT function is found not to fit the host organization, user perceptions of IS needs and progress are discovered to be quite different from those o. the specialists, and human resource skills and abilities turn out to be the major constraint on progress. So, the organizational element comprises questions like centralization or decentralization of the IS function, the role, structure and working of steering committees, management education and development in IS/IT, the internal organization of the IS department and the role of the IS executive. These are complex matters undergoing rapid change that are discussed in detail in the next chapter.

Control is concerned with questions of investing in, funding, charging for and evaluating IT and its applications. Controls are often the dominant aspect of formal management of IT and commonly are dysfunctional. They can impair the organization's exploitation of IT when they do not keep up with the demands of technological, business and organization changes. Often faulty models of IT and the organization drive the control process, yet resolution of some of the control issues is far from easy. Thus, detailed discussion is postponed until Chapter 8.

Technology covers inherently technical questions which are at the core of IT strategy or architecture. However Chapter 2 added technology as a *management* factor to planning, organization and control because there are specialist management practices required. Examples include systems development methodologies, security practices, or data management techniques. Because of the overlap with the previous chapter, they need not be discussed further.

The IM strategy therefore is a summary of the choices made from all the analysis of planning, organization, control and technology analysis described in the rest of this book. Thus this chapter can only provide a framework for IM strategy, the attributes of an effective strategy, and a methodology for completing and presenting it.

The attributes of IM strategy

IM strategy is usually an attempt to raise the visibility and profile of IT and IS in managers' thinking. It also specifies the wherefores of the four tasks of information management. Five attributes seem to be required if this degree of formalization is to work. Vancil expressed similar thoughts for development of corporate strategies.

Writing down. IM strategies benefit from being written down. This helps explicate issues, make the resultant framework, visible and influential, and emphasizes formalization. In some corporations, the IM strategy is codified as a corporate manual or a chapter of the corporate strategy.

Operational guidance. The IM strategy should contain operational guidance. This includes how it is to be implemented, the procedures to be followed, and actions and goals to be pursued.

Managerial commitment. The IM strategy requires managerial commitment. Top management understanding, validation, support and commitment are necessary if strategies are to be accepted and implemented. Often therefore final approval is required from the board. The proposer and prefect of IM strategy can be the corporate IT steering or policy committee (see Chapter 7).

Strategy, structure and style. The management framework must fit the host organization's strategy, structure and style. IM strategies which assume or demand practices the organization has never experienced, or will be countered by vigorous and discordant informal and unofficial behaviours will not work. In some IT-dependent businesses, however, the IT function may have to help move the organization into formalizing certain aspects of management in order to manage IT effectively.

Capacity for change. The IM strategy must be capable of change. Because technologies, business needs and organizational contexts change and because managements learn by experience how to manage IT, the management framework − like the architecture − must be reviewed over time and become more or less formal as demands dictate.

A structure and method which helps satisfy these conditions is presented in the next section.

A STRUCTURE AND METHOD

McLean and Soden proposed a structure for MIS strategic planning in 1977. This fits the needs of IM strategy rather well. Parsons in 1983 wrote about 'the linking strategy'. This helps recognize and delineate the alternative philosophies which can drive IM strategy. Each is developed in turn.

A methodology

The structure shown in Figure 6.1 was prompted by McLean and Soden and the literature of corporate strategy. It has been applied successfully in several organizations. It is a useful approach to formulating IM strategy because it adopts conventional management terminology and strategy concepts.

The four boxes in Figure 6.1 can be seen as the *levels* of the management framework and together they help formalize and normalize the management of IT.

Many organizations have recently developed *mission* statements for the IT function, feeling the need to establish the importance of IT, write a charter for the IT function, delimit the function's activities and responsibilities, and specify its relationships with the rest of the organization. So, just as firms find it necessary to define what business they are in or are not in to give strategic clarity, the same applies to the IT function in terms of applications, technologies and organizational scope. For example, in a chemical company, a key decision was whether the IT function should incorporate automation and engineering technologies. In a corporate IS division, it was important to state what was being provided and controlled corporately and what was not. In a government department, the very rationale of the department and its information processing had to be established in a political climate of cost-cutting, rationalization and privatization. Three examples of mission statements are provided in Figure 6.2.

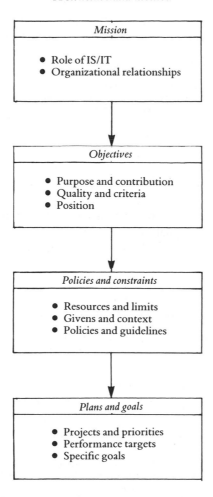

Figure 6.1 Management framework or IM strategy.

Objectives state the purpose and contribution of the IT function, the performance objectives or criteria by which it will be measured, and the relative position or posture against peers or competitors. The aim clearly is to define what is success for the IT function and, in some organizations, to set goals just as for any other business or function. Thus, timeless, directional and future intents have their place as do tighter financial and performance goals. Objectives both give direction to the IT function and specify key results. Examples are shown in Figure 6.3. Principles derived in architecture studies can be incorporated here.

Policies and constraints comprise resource and other limits imposed by the host organization, givens and mandates of the business, and policies and guidelines for information management. Policies and parameters from architecture studies can be

- Defining corporate-wide architecture and infrastructure of information systems and automation ... and maintaining and enhancing in-house expertise and professional skills (electronics company corporate IS)
- To optimize the investment across the group in systems, information management, computing and technology while supporting the individual needs of group companies/business sectors in pursuance of business objectives (bank's group IS)
- To assist industry and commerce through the provision of information services uniquely available to government (Government Department's IS division)

Figure 6.2 Mission statements.

incorporated here. This box really comprises the detailed management framework within which the IT function and IS activity work. Examples are shown in Figure 6.4.

Plans and goals comprise the concrete actions required of the IT function, such as projects and priorities, specific goals and performance targets. These can include all the plans from architecture studies as well as management actions agreed for the function. Examples are shown in Figure 6.5.

- To ensure excellence of service to customers (credit card company)
- To automate where we can (automobile company)
- To achieve an ROI of 18 per cent and be self-funding (information services business)
- To match the information services provided by our competitors (government agency)
- To effectively manage and lead the exploitation of information systems and resources in an ever-changing technological environment (financial services company)

Figure 6.3 Statements of objectives.

- To spend up to 3 per cent of turnover on IT (consumer products company)
- To spend 5 per cent of IT budget on R & D projects (automobile company)
- To invest in projects earning 20 per cent IRR or better (automobile company)
- To preserve divisional and regional independence (insurance company)
- To use IBM or IBM-compatible computers (financial services company)
- Never to sell software outside the company (chemical company)
- To buy applications software rather than develop it where we can (consumer products company)
- Not to be a leading edge user of technology (manufacturing company)

Figure 6.4 Policies and constraints.

- To install common transaction systems by 1987 (financial services company)
- To achieve 10 per cent reduction in DP budget in one year (industrial supplies company)
- Each DP staff member to receive 10 days' technical training p.a. (financial services company)
- Develop a common standard and protocol for data, text, image, and voice interworking across the group by end of 1985 (chemical company)
- Install basic business systems by mid–1987 (chemical company)

Figure 6.5 Plans and goals.

Using this structure as a methodology, it is not essential to begin by fashioning a mission statement. Working through the four levels becomes an iterative process. For example, the senior management team of a government agency focused on policies and constraints, mindful of the political and regulatory givens it had to recognize. Out of this discussion, it became clear that a mission was required. Objectives then helped the team think how the mission could be achieved. Conversely, a corporate IS division of a decentralized company felt it necessary to clarify its mission before pursuing an IT strategy any further; it needed a charter in order to survive in a decentralized environment. Other companies have adopted their own management terminology when using this structure. For one firm, goals were objectives and vice versa, and for another objectives were principles, which were then exploded into policy objectives and specific objectives. Such company-specific translations are sensible; they are a sign that IT is being managed as normally as other activities in the organization.

The iterative approach can provide a check on the IM strategy. The objectives can be assessed to see if they fit the mission, the policies and constraints checked to see if they relate to the objectives etc. A reverse check also helps to see if each box has been sufficiently 'exploded' at the next level down. Finally, as in IT strategy, some companies have found it helpful to write an expanded, explanatory rationale for each statement. Rationales narrate the strategy.

The mandate

Parsons developed the concept of a *linking strategy* to 'provide the broad management framework to guide IT into and within the business'. He identified six generic linking strategies which represent different approaches to managing IT resources. These are summarized below and perhaps are best seen as alternative philosophies – or even political economies – for information management. They are not alternative IM strategies *per se,* but they are useful in showing that different sets of policies, practices and procedures fit different situations and bring about different results. Thus we can regard each linking strategy as a *mandate* for IT and use it to:

(a) test a draft IM strategy to see if it is consistent with our intentions; and
(b) help think through the organizational dynamics of each box or level in Figure 6.1.

Parsons' six generic linking strategies are as follows:

1. Centrally planned – a central decision-making unit integrates business needs with IT capabilities by understanding the competitive opportunities and requirements of the firm and the potential of IT for creating or furthering competitive advantage.
2. Leading edge – state of the art IT is developed to create business opportunities.
3. Free market – users determine their own needs and how to satisfy them; IT specialists compete against outside vendors for users' custom.
4. Monopoly – an internal IT group is set up as the sole source to meet IS/IT demand within reasonable costs.
5. Scarce resource – IT resources and expenditure are constrained and their use determined by resource allocation procedures, such as ROI criteria.
6. Necessary evil – IT is not used unless there is no alternative.

These six generic strategies or mandates are caricatured in Table 6.1 matching them with the McFarlan and McKenney strategic grid and the strategic terminology of this book. Each mandate tends to be determined as much by past experience of IM as by future hopes of IT. The main implications of Table 6.1 are that in strategic or turnaround contexts only centrally planned or leading edge mandates are a good fit. The former is generally preferred because it seeks to achieve a good link between the IS and IT strategies and the business. The planning unit is not necessarily corporate; it is central within a corporation, division or business unit depending on the host organization's structure, style and strategy. However it does require business as well as technological competence, top management involvement and effective, integrative planning processes within the business.

Leading edge mandates suit turnaround contexts and perhaps some enterprises finding themselves in the early stages of being in a delivery sector. It is expensive and involves risks. The company backs technological initiatives and pushes down new business directions. To paraphrase: 'some you win and some you lose'. This also may be a workable mandate for a corporate IT department charged with providing what the more business-led IT dependents in the organization cannot do and with seeking corporate synergies from IT.

Free market mandates have all the merits and demerits of free market economics. In good hands, the 'customer is King' and 'only efficient and effective suppliers survive and prosper' policies can work. When there are market failures, however, central intervention is inevitable – or the business may also suffer.

Other mandates have a risk of being non-strategic in outlook and bear the character of the DP era. This emphasizes, of course, how important it is to assess each *de jure* or *de facto* IM policy, procedure and practice to see which mandate it seems to represent. In this way, amendments can be made to the actual or potential IM strategy to achieve consistency and orientation towards the desired result. The next subsection develops this role of Parsons' mandates in IM strategy formulation.

A management matrix

The tasks of information management-planning, organization, control and technology – have been defined as elements of IM strategy. The boxes of Figure 6.1 – mission, objectives, policies and constraints, and plans and goals have been described as the levels. This repeats the terminology used in architecture development in Chapter 5 and a similar matrix can be constructed, as in Table 6.2. This provides a cross-checking, cross-impact instrument for completing and checking the IM framework proposed in Figure 6.1.

It is not a methodology! Figure 6.1 is a better guide and an iterative use of it was proposed earlier. The matrix provides a final checklist. Not every cell in the matrix should be completed. The mission covers *all* elements and the mandate represents a philosophy running through *all* levels. The objectives column may be expressed in terms common to all elements, but there are likely to be policies and constraints and plans and goals for each element. As with architecture, intentions to work out new or better objectives or policies in the future may be expressed as interim plans and goals. Also architecture statements in the IT strategy which have clear or direct relevance for

Table 6.1 IT mandates (after Parsons)

	Centrally planned	Leading edge	Free market	Monopoly	Scarce resource	Necessary evil
IS strategy	Central planning unit responsible	Infrastructure-led	Business-led	Resource planning	Resource allocation mechanisms	*Ad hoc*
IT strategy	Central planning unit responsible	State of the art	Reactive or interactive	Resource planning	Rationalization approaches	Conservative thinking
IM strategy	Centrally planned economy	Supply side economics	Market economics	Contractual economy	Monetary economy	Pre-information economy
Strategic grid	Strategic or turnaround	Turnaround or strategic	Turnaround or support	Factory or support	Support or factory	Low level support
Management logic	Central administration knows best	Technology will create opportunities	Market knows best	Information is a corporate good	Information is a limited resource	Information is unimportant
Critical success factors	Business competence Senior management involvement Linkages at all business levels	Abundant resources Management drive Technological competence	Knowledgeable users, market-oriented providers Market beliefs	Policies and procedures, service orientation Resource forecasts	Agreed rubrics good information and controls	Strict management Stable context

Table 6.2 Matrix for IM strategy

Levels/elements	Mission	Objectives	Policies and constraints	Plans and goals
Planning				
Organization				
Control				
Technology				
Desired mandate				

management may be included in the levels of IM strategy in order to make them visible in the management domain.

MANAGING THE IT BUSINESS

Behind development of management approaches and techniques in the DP era often lay a concept of managing DP as a business within a business. This notion can be applied equally well in the IT era. Indeed it makes the case for an IM strategy and provides a model for deciding what needs to be included and what does not.

A business model

McKenney and McFarlan have used the business within a business perspective to synthesize the requirements of information management. In particular they have exploited the concept of the marketing mix to analyse what is required of IT business to satisfy its customers, the analogy of the board of directors to understand the key tasks of general management in IT, and the notion of the Chief Executive Officer to explore what is required of the head of the IT function.

Since these particular issues are developed in the next three chapters, the concept of a business within a business is exploited here in more general terms. The model in Figure 6.6 is valuable in helping general managers see why an IM strategy is necessary, why certain policies are their responsibility and cannot be left to the specialists, and what are the key, current issues for their organization.

In Figure 6.6 the relationship between the IT function and the board can be explored in terms of the ownership and control paradigm. If IT is to be funded as capital investment it needs capital injections from its owners. In return the shareholders or board need information to assess the stewardship and return of their investment. Thus funding mechanisms and performance evaluation reporting have to be put in place. An alternative is to fund IT out of revenue, in which case the users or customers have to pay. Chargeout then becomes an issue of more importance than usual. In return, there need to be mechanisms in place for determining customer needs (or wants), for example IS strategy methods and request procedures.

The IT function may not be made responsible for supply of all IS or IT. Third parties

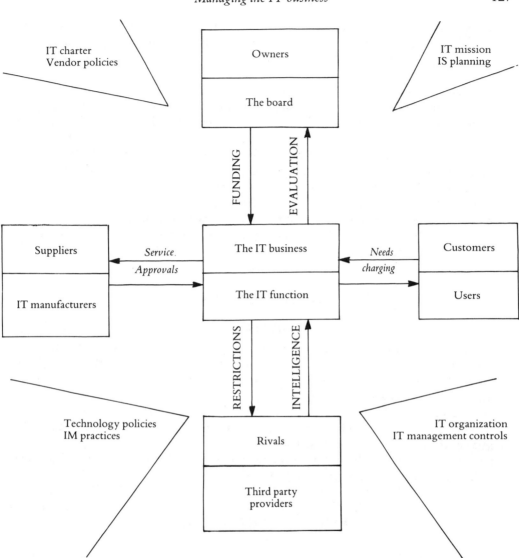

IT charter
Vendor policies

IT mission
IS planning

Owners

The board

FUNDING

EVALUATION

Suppliers

IT manufacturers

Service
Approvals

The IT business

The IT function

Needs
charging

Customers

Users

RESTRICTIONS

INTELLIGENCE

Technology policies
IM practices

IT organization
IT management controls

Rivals

Third party
providers

Figure 6.6 The IT business.

(rivals) – including end-users – may have a role, so that responsibility boundaries need to be drawn. Equally it is important to monitor the development of new products and services so that any monopoly or near monopoly IT function does not stagnate; thus market intelligence and forecasting are required. Indeed the concept of monopoly for the IT function, or indeed monopsony for the supplier, can be argued against oligopolistic or free market regimes. This will lead to different regulatory mechanisms and management controls.

It may be important to regulate the list of suppliers and to devise service agreements. In other words, an IT supplier might be treated as a strategic supplier and purchase decisions not made on technical grounds alone. Equally preferred and standard information management practices might be laid down for the supply of all services whether supplied internally or externally. Indeed the merits of making or buying information systems is another potential policy decision.

Thus the arrows in Figure 6.6 demonstrate some of the interactions of the IT business within a business. The boxes are the dominant stakeholders, the upper label as seen through business eyes, the lower label as seen by technologists. The vectors contain the principal policy issues – the contents – that an IM strategy needs to address to govern these interactions. Indeed govern is an appropriate word. If we add the stakeholders listed in Chapter 1 – government, regulators, consumers, employees etc. – it becomes clear that the IT business may need running as much from a wider governance perspective, as much as from a management control viewpoint.

In other words, Figure 6.6 can be extended to represent any situation – once we wish to understand that wherefores (IM strategy) are as important as the what (IS strategy) and the how (IT strategy).

CONCLUSION

IM strategy is simple in concept. It is the formal expression of the wherefores of the four tasks of information management. This chapter has suggested a structure and methodology which have been found useful in practice. In many ways, these have been no more than application of textbook, formal management thinking to an area of the business which is not always thought of in business terms.

The IM strategy is likely to change quite often. Organizations learn to manage IT by experience and their demands change quite frequently. It is thus worth checking the validity of the current strategy annually.

The detail is complex. It took two chapters to explore the planning task. The next two chapters examine organization and control.

FURTHER READING

McFarlan F. W. and McKenney J. L., *Corporate Information Systems Management: The Issues Facing Senior Executives,* Dow Jones Irwin, 1983.
McLean E. R. and Soden J. V., *Strategic Planning for MIS,* J. Wiley, 1977.
Parsons G. L., 'Fitting information systems technology to the corporate needs: the linking strategy', Harvard Business School teaching note (9–183–176), Harvard Business School, 1983.
Vancil R. F., 'Strategy formulation in complex organisations', *Sloan Management Review,* Winter 1976.

Chapter 7
ORGANIZING IT ACTIVITIES

INTRODUCTION

In Chapter 2, organization was seen as one of the three tasks of information management at the corporate level. Indeed, surveys suggest that senior managers currently regard organizational questions as second only to the strategic issues of IT in their information management priorities. Furthermore, when formulating information technology or information management strategies, as discussed in the previous two chapters, it is usual to find that some organizational issues require early resolution. Typical managerial concerns about organizing IT activities include the following:

1. Are we structuring IT activities correctly both to meet business needs and to fit the current organization structure?
2. Is our IT department organized to cope effectively with multiple technologies?
3. What sort of IT director do we need and at what level should he operate?
4. Do we need an IT steering committee and, if so, how can we ensure it will work?

These questions are representative of the four topics examined in this chapter.

THE IT FUNCTION

One characteristic of the IT era is that IT or IS is regarded as a management function alongside finance, production, marketing and the like. Unfortunately, the function suffers from many descriptors – information technology, information systems, information management, information services, management services, technology, management systems and MIS being common examples. In this chapter, it will be referred to as the IT function and in this section the question addressed is how to structure it, especially in complex organizations. This is an important question since in most businesses the IT function has undergone recent structural change, or alternatively some restructuring is imminent. Indeed, in some corporations, structural change is constant. Yet, there is often an apparent lack of confidence in what is the appropriate way to structure the IT function. This perhaps arises from the many observable alternative patterns that exist, not least in similar sectors.

> General Motors acquired EDS, the IT service company, in 1984. Different reasons were reported for this bold move including diversification strategy, the need to bolster internal IT resources, and the injection of innovative forces as IT was becoming more and more strategic to the automobile industry. Meanwhile, British Leyland had earlier formed its major IS department into a profit-responsible division, subsequently allowing it to become a semi-autonomous business venture known as ISTEL and competing in the market place. In 1987, ISTEL, by then a well known IT company, was privatized through a management buy-out, but with responsibilities to provide IT services to BL as one of its clients.

This apparent paradox, from the automobile sector, is indicative of puzzles that exist and of the change that is occurring. The forces for change tend to be the following:

1. Changes in the structure or character of the host organization itself.
2. Technological change, especially the increasingly distributed nature of computing, the network implications of telecommunications, and the boundary problems raised by automation technologies.
3. IT-related pressures, not least the recognition that IT has become a strategic resource for many businesses.
4. Management anxiety about the efficiency, effectiveness, or responsiveness of the IT function.

These forces for change have brought about two seemingly contradictory organizational trends. The tendency to break up large organizations into more profit responsible reporting businesses and strategic business units, combined with the felt need to make IT/IS more responsive to business needs, has led to considerable devolution of IT activities from often quite centralized or corporate structures. In contrast, the convergence of computing, automation and communications technologies has emphasized the need for coordinating mechanisms and perhaps for an overall corporate IT department or division. Second, the technology developments that have put computers in the personal hands of managers, publishing on desk tops and workstations in offices have given information processing power to users. Yet, the bewildering variety of technological solutions and consequent interfacing problems has meant that specialist expertise and advice are still valued. These directions are manifestations of the two tensions that drive the structuring of the IT function over time.

The first tension has been traditionally labelled the centralization versus decentralization problem. Classically, it originated in the days when the economics of computing pointed towards a centralized DP function, even in relatively decentralized organizations. But, there are many more factors involved in this debate. The second, related but different, tension is that between specialists and users. Again, it is a long-standing issue, but is brought into sharper relief today as information technologies have become more user-focused and user managements have become more confident about technology.

Each of these tensions is now examined, and frameworks for analysing them presented. Subsequently, policy guidelines are offered based on recent research by the author and his colleagues.

Centralization *v.* decentralization

The following two cases depict some of the issues and choices behind this tension.

> Volvo, the Swedish automobile corporation, was reorganized in 1972 into separate business divisions with a substantial reduction of central services. Computer systems and operations were structured as a subsidiary, Volvo Data, serving the host organization as a cost centre. In addition, several divisions and subsidiaries organized their own IT departments. Today, Volvo Data provides about 40 per cent of the total IT services consumed by the Volvo Group and competes for business both inside and outside the group.[1]

> One of the UK's leading consumer products groups is organized domestically into four large product divisions. For many years, the IT function was centrally organized as a profit centre. In the late 1970s, divisions appointed systems managers to direct their IS development and one division grew a small development and operations department. In mid–1987, the central data centre, development team and ancillary services were abandoned. Each division was to be responsible for its own IT activities. Almost overnight, the data centre was handed over to two divisions, the development team was re-allocated across divisions, the ancillary services were sold to a management buy-out and the corporate IT director took a divisional position.

There are many arguments for both centralization and decentralization of IT activities. Hardware economies of scale, communication needs, common-systems, core transaction processing infrastructure, scarce human resources and critical mass, synergies from integration, hard control over resource allocation and, above all, a centralized host organization can point to centralization of some or all IT resources. Serving different business needs, giving resource allocation control to business managements, the dispersion of the technologies, communication and coordination costs, IS responsiveness, availability of IT services in the market place, ease of adding and spinning off business units, and, above all, a decentralized host organization can point to devolving IT activities. However, not only do all these – and more – factors have to be weighed up, but the IT function, or IT resources, are not a homogeneous activity. At the infrastructure level, there are computing, communications, data, and core transaction systems. At another level, there is the crucial activity of development – analysing, designing and implementing IT applications. There is also the matter of overall direction – strategy formulation and policy-setting, involving questions of planning and control. As IT advances and information management understanding matures, there are organizational choices at all these levels.

Table 7.1 summarizes the most important factors to be considered and which way they point in the centralization versus decentralization argument. The contents have been influenced by McFarlan and McKenney, Tricker, and Feeny *et al.* respectively. Three levels of analysis are proposed: operations, development and direction. It can be readily appreciated that, with this variety of factors to consider, the choice between centralization and decentralization will vary from organization to organization and over time. Furthermore, extreme positions will be the rarest, many organizations looking for the right balance at the right time.

Increasingly, however, dispersion of technology, decentralization of corporations, and the desire to identify and deliver business-led IT applications are moving organizations to devolve at least some of their IT activities. When this happens, it is important to ask what should nevertheless remain centralized. In other words, what

Table 7.1 Structuring IT activities

Level of analysis	Towards centralizing	Towards decentralizing
Direction	Giving funding boosts Tight or directional resource allocation Pushing initiatives Optimizing suppliers and costs Formulating and policing technical policies Attending to group and corporate needs Centralized host organization	Removing bureaucratic controls Autonomous or business-led resource allocation Facilitating innovation and responsiveness Recognizing diverse needs and preferences Formulating and implementing IS strategies Decentralized host organization
Development	Serving group, corporate functional needs Attending to architecture needs Attracting and keeping staff Needs for common systems or data Specialist teams required Centralized host organization	Responding to local needs Dissatisfied with centralized service Integrating user and specialist staff Simplifying IS approaches and delivery Exploiting specific technologies Decentralized host organization
Operations	Manageable geographical spread Professional service levels Scale economies of some technologies Attracting and keeping technical staff Availability of corporate or common data Integrated or common systems Centralized host organization	Dispersed geographical spread User control and local responsiveness Reduced communications costs and easier computing Opening up career paths Local data needs Local system needs Decentralized host organization

reserved powers should be vested in a central or corporate body? Interpreting the literature referenced at the end of this chapter and building on recent experiences of European corporations, the following set comprises likely candidates:

1. Formulation of group IT strategy and architecture.
2. Derivation of clear standards and policies.
3. Guiding hardware, software and consulting acquisition.
4. Monitoring group standards and policies.
5. Providing group communications requirements.
6. Meeting corporate IS needs.
7. Coordinating human resource development.

The following set of facilitating activities might also be provided centrally:

1. Providing IT assistance for small units.
2. Providing technical support for large units.
3. Taking inventories of planned and installed hardware, software and liveware.
4. Providing system audit and review services.
5. Facilitating technology transfer.
6. Facilities managing shared services.
7. Providing consultancy services, especially on IS strategy.
8. Initiating and providing education courses.
9. Initiating and doing IT experiments.

When Manufacturers Hanover Corporation set out in 1985 to clarify the role of a centralized IT department in a decentralized environment, they identified all the IT management functions which had to be organized. These are listed in Table 7.2. At the same time a mission for the central IT group was clarified, namely 'to ensure the competitive use of technology and to provide cost-effective utilities, while minimizing operational and technical risks and facilitating organizational flexibility'. Every function that supported this mission then became the responsibility of the central group, to varying degrees. A transition team was appointed to handle the reorganization. Four executives spent three months full-time on this task.[2]

With devolution of any significant IT activities, however, decentralized units also take on key responsibilities, particularly aspects of direction. In other words, acts of devolving IT give elements of control to decentralized units and their managements cannot opt out of those responsibilities. This begins to fuse with the second balance that has to be struck, namely that between the specialists and the users.

Table 7.2 IT management functions in Manufacturers Hanover

Level	Function
Strategic	1. Strategic planning and control 2. Market place intelligence and technological research 3. Architecture planning
Tactical	1. Resource planning and acquisition 2. Systems development 3. Computer and telecommunications operations
Infrastructure	1. Policy standards and management 2. Human resource management 3. Risk management

Users *v*. specialists

At every level of the decentralization-centralization argument and whatever the extent of IT devolution, the question still remains: for what should users be responsible and what is best left to the specialists? Even in an autonomous product division of a large holding company with its own IT department, this boundary has to be examined. However, much information management research shows that users and specialists do not have either the same views of the world (Hedberg and Mumford) or their managers share the same priorities (Earl). The following two cases illustrate the pressures for user power and the perils of user inexperience:

A management development department of a large multi-divisional corporation required a personnel information system. The group management services division were unaware of this need, were slow to respond to a request for proposal, and eventually recommended a seemingly high cost, unfriendly solution. The management development department located an external software house who offered to provide a cheaper, friendlier, quicker solution. This was about to be accepted until another consultant brought in to arbitrate pointed out that there was no system specification, no credit check on the supplier, no record of a really similar application having been installed by the supplier elsewhere, and that the hardware and software were abnormal in the industry and could not be easily supported in-house.

A garment manufacturer decided to install a strategically important system by circumventing the DP department and using an external agency. This was an act of little confidence in the internal IT function, a desire to strike a new hardware policy and a motivation to do the job quickly. After weeks of overtime working in the testing phase, the system seemed destined to fail. Management asked the DP department to resurrect the old system, the external agency went bankrupt and the user manager driving the project resigned.

The arguments for giving users the responsibility for directing, developing and implementing IT usually include cost efficiencies (especially avoidance of technical overheads), system effectiveness (meeting user needs), the end-user nature of many of the new technologies, responsiveness (more immediate reaction by users themselves to their needs), innovation through users being close to market forces and business needs, the ultimate form of decentralization, greater availability of IT products and systems in the market place, and concern with results and benefits rather than means and costs. In contrast, specialists often respond to these apparent advantages with concerns that users do not understand the complexities of IT and IS and thus frequently rely on specialist help to 'bale them out'. Other concerns include the need to develop a critical mass of technological competence, the necessity for overall coordination, the importance of systems reliability and quality, the need for professionalism, the contribution of specialists' initiatives, the avoidance of duplication, the responsibility for long run objectives and costs (as opposed to suboptimizing through continuous quick-fix solutions), and the possible requirement to centralize some control in one group.

Buchanan and Linowes, prompted by the trends of distributed processing, proposed a generic set of wide-ranging and separable IT activities. These, they suggested, could be distributed between users and specialists in a spectrum of patterns, the choice of which would be largely dependent on the characteristics of the host organization. Their list is reproduced in Table 7.3. The important point is that there are many choices and that at any time the pattern of distribution between users and specialists will be quite a mix.

Table 7.3 IT activities to be distributed

Function	Activities
Operations	Hardware operation
	Communications
	Systems programming
	Applications maintenance
Development	Database administration
	Applications programming
	Systems analysis
	Systems documentation
	User training
Control	Providing security
	Setting priorities
	Standardization
	Accessing data
	Scheduling tasks
	Personnel planning
	Budgeting
	Evaluating products

For the foreseeable future, however, the likely balance, as discussed later, will be a delegation of direction and of some development of IT to users, whilst requiring the specialists to provide the staff functions and much of the operations. Indeed, reserved powers are likely to be given to the specialists in the areas of standards, monitoring and audit, IS human resource development, technology research, utility services, vendor relations and overall IT architecture. These are areas requiring continuous technological expertise, a technological overview of these and knowledge of the IT function itself. Increasingly this scenario has the specialists in a service role; the consequent responsibilities falling on users therefore are real and inescapable, for users and their managers become the drivers of IT.

A contingency model

A framework for structuring the IT function and resolving the two tensions has been developed by Feeny, Earl and Edwards. Their research study examined the structure and effectiveness of the IT function in thirteen large European organizations. Drawing on the contingency theory of organizations,[3] they concluded that there is no universal best way for structuring the IT function. Rather, each organization must work out what is the most effective structure for itself over time *contingent* upon a number of situational factors. Feeny *et al*, preferred the term, *arrangements*, to structure. This term emphasizes the total set of structures, processes and accommodations that evolve for organizing IT in large organizations and avoids the narrow debates about alternative structural forms. Thus, arrangements might comprise the structure of the IT function, the organization of IT within IT departments, the mechanisms for user-specialist cooperation, the leadership for IT and the organizational mandates given to IT.

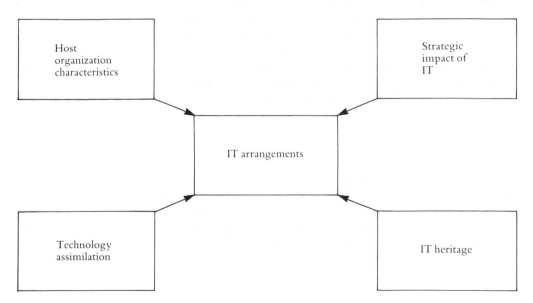

Figure 7.1 A contingency model of IT organization.

Feeny *et al.* isolated four independent variables which generally influence the design of these arrangements. Figure 7.1 portrays this relationship. *Host organization characteristics* mean organization structure, management control systems and organizational culture. *Strategic impact of IT* can be measured by positioning the organization on the McFarlan and McKenney strategic grid, that is, assessing past and future strategic dependence on IS. *Technology assimilation* refers to the stage of adoption and managing the multiple technologies in use, based on Gibson and Nolan's stages of EDP growth and McFarlan and McKenney's more generic version. *IT heritage* describes the existing, inherited IT structure and the past successes and failures in IT, given that tomorrow's arrangements are much influenced by today's and yesterday's experiences. This historical factor appears particularly important, as Edwards earlier suggested that organizations move in and out of alternative ideal structural forms in certain patterns as they learn how to manage IT.

The particular disposition of IT arrangements that an organization chooses, then, is contingent upon these four variables. Depending on the state of these variables, the disposition can follow one of Edwards' five ideal types:

1. *Centralized:* A unified IT function reporting to corporate management.
2. *Business unit:* IT is unified but set up as a business within a business, but primarily serving the host business.
3. *Business venture:* IT is a business unit but set up to serve external as well as internal clients.
4. *Decentralized:* IT is distributed to each business unit and under its own control.
5. *Federal:* Decentralized IT units exist alongside a centralized IT unit which is responsible for overall policy and architecture.

In practice, however, Feeny *et al.* found that most large, complex organizations end up with a mix of these ideal types, but basically within the federal arrangement. This arises because, at the operations, development and directional levels of IT, various accommodations are worked out balancing the tensions between centralization and decentralization and between specialists and users. The classical federal evolution, then, begins with much or all of the operational services being provided centrally, followed by appointment of IS managers and perhaps user support resources in the business units. Subsequently, development may be devolved to business units but with significant operations responsibilities retained at the centre because the central service facility is well regarded for its delivery capability. More than likely, a strong development team is also retained at the centre to work on common and group applications; often, however, this team is not so well regarded, being perceived to be out of touch with the business, pursuing irrelevant goals and taking too long to develop systems. Nevertheless, this federal arrangement appears to be the most stable of the ideal forms because it can be aligned with multi-divisional companies, be adopted to a number of hybrid host organization designs and fits the matrix structure of many complex organizations.

However, the contingent model does not say this solution is always the most effective. Certain contingent relationships were apparent from the Feeny *et al.* study. The guidelines which relate to the characteristics of the host organization include the following:

1. Centralized IT arrangements are fast disappearing but can work in a heavily centralized organizational context or in functional organizations.
2. Decentralized IT arrangements work in decentralized organizational contexts and in holding companies.
3. Business unit and business venture arrangements rarely work because internal customers do not like relying on heavily market-oriented IT units. Also, the IT units tend to lose touch with their host organization. More seriously, they can become more innovative for the competition and competitive forces than for their owners.

The strategic impact of IT variable bears more on the user–specialist tension, namely:

4. In support contexts, specialist dominance is quite likely and generally works.
5. In factory contexts, specialists can concentrate on delivery but need a user-service mentality.
6. In turnaround contexts, users need to direct the IS strategy but specialists may well be best able to direct and implement the IT strategy.
7. In strategic contexts, user dominance is most appropriate as IT and IS become integrated into the business.

The technology assimilation variable (or stage model of information management) suggests the following:

8. When technologies are new and in the early stages of adoption, it pays to put them in the hands of uses and/or individual businesses in order to learn what applications are possible and how to exploit the technology.
9. As technologies mature, the specialists (and perhaps a central/corporate functional body) need to take responsibility in order to routinize delivery performance and integrate the technologies where necessary.

The IT heritage variable suggests the following guidelines:

10. The current structure for IT will be influenced by the outcomes of the last structure.
11. Over time, specialists may increase their responsibility for IT operations and users increase their involvement in development and direction.

Structural policies

The conclusions that can be inferred about structuring the IT function are now clear. There are two over-riding tensions to resolve: centralization versus decentralization and users versus specialists. The consequent prescription is therefore to think of arrangements rather than structure, for an effective IT organization is likely to comprise a mix of the ideal types and dispositions, including some ambiguity much of the time. Extreme approaches will rarely work; evolutionary patterns are more likely to be effective. In particular, the solution should not be driven by the apparent needs of the technology. The crucial determinants are:

(a) the characteristics of the host organization and the IT heritage which mostly influence the centralization versus decentralization balance; and

(b) the technology assimilation process and the strategic impact of IT which largely influence the user versus specialist balance.

It is not wise to arrange IT activities in contradiction to the host organization characteristics. In general, however, two driving questions should be asked. First, why should not IT activities be decentralized? Second, why should not users have responsibility for IT activities? There may be several reasons why these two patterns should not be followed, but the questions should be asked this way round, for decentralization of, and user responsibility for, IT activities seems often to be effective.

> A merchant bank had a centralized IT group serving four divisions plus corporate needs. When the IT strategy was subsequently formulated, it was decided that IT should remain centralized:
> (a) to ensure IS and IT supported an increasingly integrated financial services strategy;
> (b) to serve emerging corporate needs on risk measurement, capital adequacy monitoring and regulatory reporting;
> (c) to attract and retain scarce IT specialists; and
> (d) to avoid short-term costs of business stream/user learning about IT until needs and supply were more stable.

Whatever arrangement is worked out, the critical requirement is that there is good integration between the IT function and the business. (The four contingent variables represent this in many ways.) This takes time to develop, requires a number of approaches, and is discussed in the last chapter. Drastic and rapid changes in structuring the IT organization are therefore unlikely to succeed.

THE IT DEPARTMENT

Whatever IT organizational arrangement is adopted, managers still have to structure their specialist departments. This 'internal' structure seems to change at least as frequently as the 'external' structure discussed in the last section. Confidence in the outcome of these departmental level changes is probably more limited still. There are three sets of issues to resolve:

1. *Performance:* Departmental structures will follow, but must also support, the overall organizational arrangement for IT if they are to be effective. Also, because IT departments can be large, often the largest organizational unit in some information-dependent businesses, they must be structured with efficiency goals in mind.

2. *Challenges:* IT departments in the late 1980s are often grappling with four new challenges. They are being asked to be customer-oriented. They are having to cope with multiple technologies. They inherit a backlog of development and maintenance. Finally, size, technological variety and strategic importance have highlighted that information management requires more than technological competence; also needed are managerial capability, organizational sensitivity and business understanding.

3. *Resources:* IT departments face quality and quantity shortages in all levels of human resource, but particularly in managers, systems analysts and new technology specialists.

Each of these issue sets is examined in turn.

Effectiveness and efficiency

The principal determinant of departmental structure should be the overall organizational arrangement for IT. The objectives, tasks and relationships of the department will depend on which responsibilities are devolved to business units and users and which are retained centrally or with the specialists. In any event, the Feeny *et al.* study showed that the IT department must have structures and mechanisms which closely integrate it into the business and do not create an island of technologists. The second deteminant arises from the scale of activity and the multiplicity of technologies, specialisms and business relationships with which IT departments have to cope. In short, IT departments have to be manageable. This implies simple structures which factor the problems down to size so that efficiency and responsiveness are not impaired.

The IT department of 1990 therefore is somewhat different from the DP department of 1970. The contrast is presented in Table 7.4. What are the implications?

Table 7.4 Departments in the DP and IT eras

DP department c.1970	IT department c.1990
Technology focused	Service focused
DP oriented	Multiple technologies
Specialists only	Specialists and support units
Hierarchical structure	Flat structure
Within the department	Within and without the department
Change infrequent	Change frequent
Departmental size	Divisional size

1. The classical DP department was organized around the technology. Operations and development would be separated. Operations would be organized around the tasks of computing: data preparation, machine room and operations control. Development would comprise technical support, programming and systems analysis, the last perhaps project-organized into application areas. The modern IT department is structured more like a service company. Data centres (computing), communication networks, and information centres (end–user computing) are run as bureaux or utilities planned and controlled according to customer demand. Development is likely to comprise integrated programming, systems and maintenance teams organized to deliver applications but within divisional, functional or business unit nomenclatures, i.e., as customer account centres.

2. The DP department was concerned principally with DP. Any new or adjunct technology – telecommunications or timesharing for example – was either handled as a subservient part of DP or left to another 'inferior' department in the organization. The IT department today is normally responsible for data

processing, office automation, CAD, end-user computing, telecommunications, expert systems and perhaps factory automation and robotics. As discussed later, it has to work out the degree to which these technologies should be managed independently within IT and yet brought together when necessary.

3.   In 1970, DP departments were inhabited by specialists with specialist career paths and specialist career histories. In 1990, IT Departments still will be populated by specialists. However, they are already supported by other staff in support units – for example, accountants to administer and audit IT activities, marketing staff to build up and improve customer relations, personnel officers to recruit, train and develop IT human resources, and planners to plan both tactics and strategy. Increasingly, therefore, some inhabitants of IT departments will be non-specialists on tours of duty from other line and staff functions.

4.   The mature DP department was characterized by perhaps five or six levels of management in classical chain of command structures. It was easy to see a career route through development or operations. The IT department of 1990 is likely to be much flatter, with many subunits managed by very capable senior managers but fewer levels of command below. Why is this? The proliferation of technologies, the customer account orientation, and the new support units lead to the creation of many departmental subunits. Many rather than fewer subunits allows specialization around technologies, responsiveness to user groups, ability to change to meet new demands, and creates cleaner more efficient structures – as long as the IT director can manage a wide chain of command.

5.   In the DP era, capability was located almost entirely within the DP department. In the IT era, direction, development and operations may be located also in both business units and the hands of users. Thus, the IT department does not have a monopoly, may have agents within the businesses, and probably has personnel devoted to building partnership between the specialists and the users.

6.   Changes to departmental structure in the DP era were infrequent and usually prompted by internal failings. Changes in IT departments are frequent and are prompted by changes in the host organization structure, business needs and the technologies. Change is not necessarily a sign of indecision; it is more likely to be an indicator that the IT department is responding to its environment.

7.   There were always large and small DP departments. Today, however, some IT departments are huge – perhaps the size of divisions. Indeed, in many information-dependent businesses, such as banks and airlines, they are divisions. This tends to change the status and visibility of IT; its importance is recognized and its failures cannot be hidden! However, specialist departments are not often one of the biggest units in a business; this unusual pressure therefore can lead management to demand that IT is run as a business within a business. This concept, developed in the last chapter, is useful for identifying the need for an IM strategy and for defining its contents. However, it was concluded in the previous section that running the IT function as a business unit or business venture is rarely effective.

A typical structure for an IT department is shown in Figure 7.2. This is a late 1980s structure for an IT department serving a centralized, functionally organized informa-

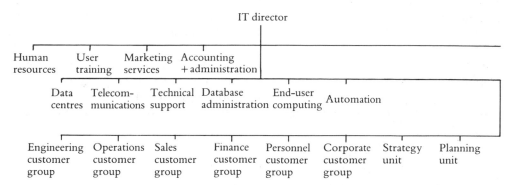

Figure 7.2 IT department structure.

tion-dependent business. In other words, it is the extreme case of a large IT department. Such a department consists of certain key features including the following:

1. Units for each major technology: computing, telecommunications, databases, automation etc.
2. Development and service organized around major customer accounts.
3. Support units for marketing services, personnel, user education and administration.
4. A strategy unit to guide and coordinate IS strategy and formulate and control IT strategy (architecture).
5. A planning unit to plan and programme resources such as manpower, mainframe capacity and buildings.

Challenges

The customer orientation challenge can sound like public relations or semantics. What it really means is embracing the marketing concept rather than adopting a production mentality. The emphasis is on seeing users as customers and accordingly identifying customer needs, working closely with customers, putting a premium on customer service, and marketing and selling systems and services. Although this may mean that 'the customer is king', it is perhaps more appropriate to adopt models of industrial rather than consumer marketing. Thus, a critical aspect is building a partnership between IT specialists and users so that each can learn from the other to determine needs and service levels.

Customer orientation therefore requires customer-focused development and service teams (as in Figure 7.2), account executives finding and minding critical customers, marketing plans to identify, develop and deliver information services, customer feedback, suggestion and complaint mechanisms, and skills in marketing and selling services. All this might be supported by a small, professional marketing services unit designing and providing promotion materials, marketing research methods etc.

The challenge of coping with multiple technologies is now clearer than it was in the early 1980s. Research studies are reasonably consistent in their prescriptions.[4] When bringing in a new technology – for example personal computing, viewdata or office automation – create a separate unit to exploit it, test it and experiment. This unit should be uncoupled from the mainstream IT department so that energy is focused on the new technology, innovative and suggested ideas can be worked on quickly, early development and application is not hamstrung by standards and constraints, a critical mass of visible expertise is built up, and new skills can be learnt or bought quickly. As the technology matures and the organization learns how relevant the technology is and what it can do, the unit may be brought back into the mainstream IT department. This may be necessary:

(a)   to acquaint all IT personnel with it;
(b)   as the technology coverges with others;
(c)   as architectural concerns become more important.

The following two cases illustrate this two stage responsibility.

> American Express in the UK believed in 1978 that PRESTEL viewdata might have commercial relevance for them as it was a technology that could interact with agents, offices and homes. It created a niche team separate from its DP and systems department to exploit viewdata. The main skills brought into the team were marketing experience and business knowledge, so that any innovative use was both consistent with marketing strategies and consumer focused.

> A manufacturing company set up a separate personal computing group to test, sell and apply personal computers across the business. This was very effective for three years until demands came to develop systems more suited to departmental and mainframe computers and until requirements arose to transmit data from mainframes to micros and to have interworking. The pc group was re-integrated with the IT department whereupon it was found that the mainstream IT personnel knew little about personal computing, often ridiculed micros and wanted to program in COBOL rather than BASIC or micro-software.

There are three complications to this pattern of adopting new technologies. The first is the problem of what are really old but rejuvenated technologies. Classic examples are telecommunications or process control. Telecommunications has long been the responsibility of office management or the telephone exchange. As data communications (and image and text) became important, it was necessary to *move* the responsibility for telecommunications to the IT function. Systems integration and interfaces forced this as did the need for data and computing knowledge as well as cabling and communications expertise. The pattern hereafter is as above, a separate telecommunications group within the IT department becomes the only viable organizational design for some time. The catch up timetable, the specialist skills, the different suppliers, the utility nature, and the desire often to centralize responsibility are the drivers towards this solution. In time, however, coordination is required between telecommunications and the other operational and development units and subsequently most of the units in Figure 7.2 would also have their telecommunications personnel.

The second complication was discovered in the Feeny *et al.* study. Early experimentation and R & D with new technologies seems to be more successful if it is done within appropriate user/application areas rather than under the loose wing of the IT department. Ideas flow and are captured more quickly, local threats and opportunities stimulate ideas, and users react to, and adopt, the technology more positively. So, creation of the early adoption unit of a new technology might be on a dotted line relationship to the IT director, but within a customer account area. Some examples amplify this point.

> An automobile manufacturer set up a new technology experimental unit within the centralized business venture IT department. Not one commercial idea emanated from this investment. In contrast, a chemical company encouraged development of expert systems in business units. Several competitive advantage products emerged (for which the central IT department claimed some credit!)

> A bank pioneered the use of ATMs through its IT group. It was one of the first banks to place ATMs in public places. However, the services offered were primitive and limited. When the operations function and their branches were brought in to develop the next step, a number of customer needs were suggested and relatively 'advanced' services then developed.

> A textile company bought a sophisticated CAD system to enhance design, colour and pattern opportunities. It was bought by and placed in the design group and achieved early productivity gains. However, nothing really innovative was tried until some IT specialists demonstrated to the designers and others what might be possible.

The last example, of course, makes the point that technological *expertise* must be placed in application areas if most users are to respond to the technology and experiment fully.

The final complication of the multiple technologies challenge is technology tracking. How do organizations go about information technology forecasting? This is not well understood. However, current practice indicates that IT departments believe that tracking, monitoring and assessing new technologies is their responsibility. This task is typically done by the strategy group (see Figure 7.2) and is the stage before the technology is placed in the business units. However, it would seem sensible to encourage users to take on the same work, particularly those with technology experience such as engineers or scientists. Indeed, Feeny *et al.* found that the scientific and engineering functions in companies were often early adopters of IT and became relatively mature users and providers without too much help from the 'IT professionals'.

The third challenge is the development and maintenance backlog. There are many available ways of tackling this problem. All have to be utilized – planning, productivity tools, subcontracting etc. – but the problem will rarely be solved completely. Nevertheless, there are three organizational mechanisms available:

1. In tackling the development backlog – often thought to be three times the current capacity and perhaps nine times as much if the invisible backlog is included[5] – a common policy is to buy application packages where possible and to subcontract development to software houses. Such policies were discussed in Chapter 5. The subcontracting route makes good sense where the application is well understood, the software consultants have a track record, the analysis and implementation of the application can be handled in-house, and there is no desire to develop any special technology expertise.
2. The maintenance backlog can sometimes be reduced by creating a special maintenance unit. By focusing energies, bringing in experienced analysts and programmers for a fixed term, and attacking maintenance lists aggressively more

can be achieved and possibly with less risks. In input and output subsystems, some work can be devolved to users, if changes are local.

3. Users can help reduce the development backlog. The growth of end-user computing has meant that some applications formerly dependent upon mainframe computing can be developed by end users for end users. This goes beyond one-off analysis routines and personal models and spreadsheets. It can include personal, office and departmental systems; however, for this scale of development, users may well require, and benefit from, specialist help, support and troubleshooting.

The concept of the *information centre* is one important organizational response to the end-user computing phenomenon. It involves the creation of a separate end-user computing unit within the IT umbrella to encourage, train and support end users who use computers directly to generate reports and create applications. The information centre manages the end-user computing environment and provides database tools, query, languages, modelling systems, application packages, preferred pcs, user training, help lines, newsletters and networks, support and consultancy, and new product advice.

The fourth challenge is the information managers themselves. The flat organization structure of the IT department demands managerial horsepower to lead and manage the subunits. The sophistication of IT departments – not least housing their own support functions – demands general management capability. The multiple technologies demand new technological competences, and the customer and service orientation require business knowledge.

This means that IT managers must be developed as thoroughly as any other line or functional managers. Yet, curiously, management education and development activities seem to pass by the IT function; the IT department is an island. Thus the business and management demands may require importation of managers from line departments who know little of technology. The technology challenges may require injection of external and young managers in some positions.

In short, whereas in the DP era, DP departments survived by self-taught, minimalist management, in the IT era IT departments need real managers in key positions. However, they must be able to cope with the specialist environment. Such roles are notoriously difficult!

Resources

The manager gap highlighted in the previous section exemplifies the human resource shortage. In many ways, this gap is the easiest to tackle in that each organization can mobilize education and development programmes around a few key positions and begin to grow successors. However, companies who lead in this can soon be denuded of their newly developed talent by opportunistic poachers, unless the jobs and conditions match the new expectations.

The systems analyst gap is more pervasive. There appears to be a lost generation of analysts. The 1950s and 1960s spawned them as DP applications expanded and the excitement of exploiting a then new technology attracted bright, impatient and pro-active graduates. In the 1970s and early 1980s they appear to have been replaced by system designers who knew how to redesign applications, perfect the technology, and adhere to standards and structured methodologies. In the late 1980s, it is difficult to find systems personnel who know how to analyse business requirements, understand new management techniques, see the scope for the new technologies, and apply system development methodologies which can explore and test ideas. It seems likely that the response must be to:

(a) start a new breed of 'hustling analysts' again;
(b) use consulting and software houses to inject and apply new applications and technology skills; and
(c) embrace any end users who have the necessary attributes.

The new technologists gap is slightly more complex than it seems. A new generation of personal computing specialists is emerging. Telecommunications experts are being trained and can be bought at a price. Engineers do know about factory automation and process control. What is scarce is people who are competent in computing *and* telecommunications, automation *and* information systems etc. As many of the business pressures ('quick response') and 'flexibility'), new management philosophies ('just in time' and 'supply chain management') and modern technologies ('value-added networks' and 'desk top publishing') need multiple and integrated bodies of knowledge, these multidisciplinary personnel will be required. It is here that IT education must improve; higher education cannot continue just to sophisticate computer science courses by taking formal methods into mathematics and vice versa. Also required are programmes that mix computer science, engineering, business and management and so on.

A final caveat is necessary. In tackling the new challenges and plugging the resource gaps, the importance of the ongoing IT business and existing skills must not be overlooked. The development and operation of 'mainstream' DP systems is just as important as ever. Particularly in organizations for whom IT is strategic, 'delivery' is a key result area.

THE IT DIRECTOR

Analysing the organization of IT at the functional and departmental levels raises an important question. What sort of executive is required at the head of IT? This issue can be posed in terms of the IT director. Common questions include the following:

1. Do we need an IT director?
2. At what level should he be appointed?
3. What would he actually do?
4. What skills and attributes should an IT director possess?
5. Where can we find one?

These questions about rationale, job description and specification, performance measurement, and management development are discussed below.

Rationale

The implications of the earlier analysis of structuring the IT function are threefold. First, since the most likely arrangement is some devolution of direction, development and operations to business units and some retention of technology policy and delivery centrally, there may be two sorts of directors required in organizations where IT is important. Besides a corporate IT director, local IS directors may be required to direct the use of IT, ensure IS strategies are formulated and perhaps manage some IS development. Second, given the tensions and ambiguities which characterize IT arrangements in organizations, the overall IT director is likely to require considerable social and political skills. Third, the local IS directors who are expected to connect IT with business needs must possess credible business knowledge.

Two implications arise from the departmental level of analysis. In the ideal, extreme departmental structure (Figure 7.2), the many subunits within a flat hierarchy create a considerable span of control. The IT director thus needs to be a proven functional manager. Second, IT and IS departments are specialist units. Thus the director needs the competence to manage specialist groups; in this case it is principally technological confidence that is required.

Four 'leadership' qualities now emerge for the directors of IT activities, namely:

1. Business leadership – connecting use of IT with business needs and strategy.
2. Technology leadership – shaping appropriate technology policies for the organization.
3. Organizational leadership – steering IT arrangements and making them work.
4. Functional leadership – managing the function and its specialist groups.

The balance of these qualities will vary with whether the role is that of 'IT director' or 'IS director', and with the heritage and organizational dynamics of IT at a point in time (see Chapter 9). It can also vary by sector. The IT director of a company in a delivery sector, where infrastructure matters so much, must be strong on technology leadership. In a dependent sector company, business leadership is mandatory. In drive sectors, organizational skills must complement technology and business confidence.

A recent survey by Price Waterhouse[6] found that, whereas in 1981, 66 per cent of IT executives reported to a board member, by 1986, 80 per cent did so. Furthermore, nearly 42 per cent expected to be on the board in five years' time. Reporting to, or being a member of, the board probably qualifies these IT executives to be classified as 'IT directors' (or vice-presidents). In an interview survey of such IT directors of leading UK companies, Earl *et al.* found two recurring characteristics:

1. Fifty per cent of the IT directors felt they spent most of their time outside the IT department focusing on strategic and organizational aspects of IT. Forty per cent spent most of their time inside the department managing the function on a day-to-day basis. Ten per cent felt that 'inside' and 'outside' were in balance. In three years' time, there was a feeling that managing inside the Department would become more significant again as the function was expected to deliver a new level of information services to the business.
2. Thirty per cent of the IT directors had general management backgrounds and were appointed to 'turn around' IT activities into a strategic capability. Seventy per cent

had DP/IT career histories, the majority having worked in more than one company.

A picture of the IT director, then, is beginning to emerge. As the functional head, he differs from the DP manager of the DP era in several ways. Table 7.5 summarizes the differences.

Table 7.5 Directing the DP and IT eras

From the DP manager	*To the IT Director*
A technical manager	A functional executive
Technical and management skills	Plus business and organizational sense
Planning and control focus	Strategic and political posture
Structured and accountable tasks	Conceptual and visionary charter
Clear role and relationships	Mixed roles and multiple relationships
A senior position	A board or near board position
A DP career	An IT or general career
Reactive external posture	Proactive external posture
Hands-on internal style	Hands-off internal style

Description and specification

Rockart *et al.*, in 1982, highlighted the changing role of the 'information systems executive'. Using his critical success factors framework, he suggested four priorities for what we may now call the IT Director:

1. Service – organizations expect IT departments to provide effective and efficient operations and high quality service. Measurement tools and accountability procedures are needed to help achieve these goals.
2. Communication – users need to know the potential of IT and be able to explicate their needs and priorities. Accordingly, strategic planning, top management responsibility, steering committees, inside and outside the IT department managers, and user-aligned development teams are required.
3. Human resources – technical and managerial competence are required in the IT function and both development and maintenance have to be adequately resourced. Thus, career and management development, personnel recruitment and retention, and image building for the IT community are critical success factors.
4. Repositioning – IT departments have to focus on user needs, provide IT support, treat information as a key resource and become a staff rather than line function. Thus, data management, organizational devolution of IT, building decision support systems as well as transaction processing systems, and technology transfer are new imperatives.

Rockart then specified the attributes the IS executive should possess to achieve these goals. They are perhaps the job specification implicit in the IT director charicature of Table 7.5. Successful IT directors ideally:

(a) see themselves, and are seen, as corporate officers;
(b) are general business managers, not IT specialists;

(c)   are candidates for top line management jobs;
(d)   see the IT function as critical to company success;
(e)   have a high profile image in their organizations;
(f)   have political as well as rational perspectives;
(g)   have a clear view of their own critical success factors.

A situational approach

The above specification may explain why finding the successful IT director is often thought to be impossible and why IT executive searches are continuous. It may be sensible not to create or appoint an IT director, if the appropriate person cannot be found. Often, organizational expectations tend to be too high, performance measurement full of intangibles and problems, and the full mix of talents rare. It therefore is important to ask what is the priority task and what are the dominant critical success factors.

Positioning the company on the McFarlan and McKenney strategic grid can help as demonstrated in Figure 7.3. Factory situations require strong, hands-on, performance-oriented executives. Strategic firms require business-oriented IT directors present in board-room discussions. Turnaround situations require visionary, strong champions as their IT directors with business credibility. Support firms can tolerate a service-oriented technical manager.

In the factory and turnaround situations, the IT executive or director can be recruited from line functions, in the first case having strong operations credentials and in the second being experienced in business development and leadership. By the time a firm places itself in the strategic quadrant, the four types of leadership identified earlier are all required – technological, managerial, business and organizational. This can be achieved by experience, especially if the IT director has survived the turnaround stage. The message of this analysis is therefore that IT directors can be recruited internally as well as externally and can be developed by experience. If a line manager finds himself in the position of IT director, he may have to recognize that perhaps 30 per cent of his time is initially spent on learning – by experience, by a variety of formal educational events, and by enlisting the support of one or two gurus. This was a pattern discovered in the Earl *et al*. study.

Finally, should the IT director be on the board? Again, using the strategic grid, the IT director of a business in the strategic quadrant normally will be a board member. Here IT is integral to the business and cannot be delegated to the 'next floor'. In turnaround contexts, the IT director will probably need the ear and support of the chief executive or a strong board member, in order to enlist ongoing support and check out initiatives. In the IT era, it is certain that, whatever his precise position, the IT director must cultivate and maintain close board relationships keeping members informed about IT matters and becoming informed about business matters.

In the case of the IS director in business units, there is no equivocation. The Feeny *et al*. study indicated that he must be a member of the executive management team or board – not least because the business units have been given responsibility and authority for IS direction.

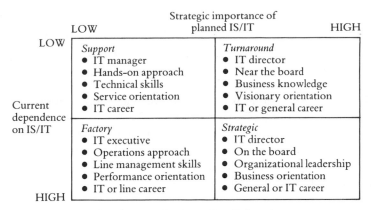

Figure 7.3 IT directors for all situations.

IT STEERING COMMITTEES

One of the mechanisms for making any of the ideal forms of IT organizational arrangements work, is the creation of one or more steering committees. These committees are formed to plan and control IT resources at the enterprise or corporate level. They have become an IT phenomenon in most organizations. Steering committees are often created by knee-jerk reaction as firms enter the third control stage of technology assimilation or the turnaround quadrant of the strategic grid. They are often recreated as firms enter the fourth maturity stage or strategic quadrant. They will be frequently 'tinkered with' in between. In short, steering committees appear to be an obvious necessity in managing IT, yet successful steering committees are difficult to find.

Important questions therefore include the following:

1. Why are steering committees necessary?
2. Are there different forms of steering committee?
3. What are the difficulties that may be encountered?
4. How can steering committees be managed?

These are discussed in the following sections.

Rationale

It has often been said that other functions like marketing or finance 'are not run by committees, so what is different about IT?'. The immediate answer is that information systems span all departments and functions and a coordinating mechanism is required both to decide how to allocate scarce IT resources and to plan system developments. The archetypal format is a membership comprising senior representatives of main divisions or functions, chaired by a top executive, meeting periodically to agree IT direction, approve and rank projects, review performance, formulate or approve technology policies, determine resource levels and perhaps recommend major initiatives.

In practice, at least 11 reasons can be found for the existence of steering committees.

1. When IS development needs strategic direction – common in turnaround and strategic contexts, the committee is charged with steering IT activities in line with the strategic direction of the organization.
2. When IT users express concern – common in stages three and four of technology assimilation. A committee is formed to provide organizational leadership for exploiting and managing IT.
3. When resource allocation is an issue – in most organizations, IT resources are scarce. Even if funding is not constrained, the ability to develop systems on a broad front and to recruit enough personnel is limited so that resource allocation becomes important and contentious. The committee is asked to make the difficult choices.
4. When top management seeks control – again a phenomenon of stage three of the technology assimilation curve, whereby a senior management group is appointed to wrest control from the IT specialists.
5. When top management support is needed – often engineered by the IT function, a senior management committee is instituted to enlist top management support for IT activities.
6. When visibility or revamping of IT is required – again prompted by the IT function, creation of a steering committee (or a new one) is a signal that the old ways are redundant. 'DP is dead; long live IT' might be the slogan!
7. When the IT function is centralizing or decentralizing – if centralization is under way, a steering committee provides a mechanism for coordinating requirements and practices. Conversely, if decentralization is in process, a steering committee may provide a mechanism for keeping and sustaining necessary reserved powers centrally.
8. When information technologies are dispersing or converging – if dispersion is in progress, and organizational mechanism is often required to address and implement architectural issues so that wholesale anarchy does not prevail. If convergence is strong, a steering committee can help ensure convergent trends fit business needs.
9. When the IT function is being run as 'a business within a business' – here the business unit or business venture arrangement has vital policy responsibilities, and perhaps monitoring duties, vested in an organization-wide committee.
10. When the host organization is restructuring – new organizational designs and changes often prompt the need for guidance on how the IT function should respond and the transition managed. A steering committee is given this task.
11. When the organizational culture permits or insists – some organizations have a committee or consensus style. If IT activities were not overseen by a committee, managers and businesses would feel uninvolved and alienated and IT would not be perceived as a serious function. Equally, expecting IT to be directed by committee in organizations where committees and bureaucratic procedures are taboo is foolish.

This set of rationales may not be exhaustive. Perhaps the principal reason why organizations create IT steering committees is that the key information management policy issues identified in Chapter six cannot be delegated to the IT function, and, because IT is cross-functional and impacts on the whole organization, only a senior corporate or enterprise level body can be given both the policy responsibility and authority for these decisions. In many ways, a steering committee is the board for IT. However, the existence of 11 or more rationales helps explain why steering committees are so difficult to run. In short, different forms of steering committee are required for different purposes. Yet, experience suggests that few organizations ask what are the principal objectives or expectations of their steering committees and design and manage them accordingly.

Four types

Clarifying the purpose of the steering committee helps define agendas, membership frequency, chairmanship and organizational level. For example, if resource allocation is the major rationale, it is clear that the process will be political and that representatives with authority must be appointed, chaired by a top executive with a 'corporate' view. Conversely, if the committee was created to guide IT under dispersion or convergence, it is unlikely to succeed if technological expertise is absent from meetings. If strategic direction is key, it is vital that some members have a vision of tomorrow's business and not just today's. It is also important that the committee meets as frequently or infrequently as strategic changes and signals need examining. Indeed, my work on strategy formulation has led me into observing, joining and understanding steering committees. What unfolds is the existence of, and possible need for, four ideal types of committee – each different in purpose and functioning. These are tabulated in Table 7.6.

The *steering group* label is given to a body responsible primarily for guiding and approving the IS strategy. It is concerned with the 'what' rather than the 'how'. In decentralized organizations, each division and/or business unit might be expected to have one if IT is important to its business. There may also be a corporate steering group tackling corporate IS strategy and perhaps overseeing the business IS strategies where reserved powers for direction and resource allocation exist.

The steering group, then, is expected to give business direction to IT and to set priorities. Its outputs therefore are strategic and long-range plans, or the approval of the applications development portfolio. However, it will also pronounce on questions like balancing the resources allocated to development versus maintenance or funding infrastructure and research and development. The critical success factor for the steering group is that it must give business clarification to IT activities. Thus, its membership is likely to comprise senior businessmen with functional and enterprise experience plus the IS or IT director and probably the executives in charge of strategy and development in the IT department. In some businesses – small ones or where IT is particularly important – the group may be an enhanced or reduced version of the board. It certainly should report to the board. Rationales 1, 2, 3, 5 and 6 particularly spawn this type of committee. It may be complemented by a corporate 'policy committee' (see below) to oversee technology matters, and temporary project steering groups to plan and control individual IT projects.

The *policy committee* label is given to a body responsible primarily for guiding and approving the IT strategy. It is concerned with the 'how' rather than the 'what'. Policy committees are often corporate committees overseeing technology policy across the business. They will focus on architectural, delivery and functional management questions. Examples might include vendor policies, hardware standards, resource acquisition, development and stewardship, and information management planning and control procedures.

Table 7.6 Steering committees: four ideal types

Type/attribute	Steering group	Policy committee	IT board	IT forum
Task	IS strategy	IT strategy	Departmental strategy	IS/IT coordination
Thrust	Direction and priorities	Capability and delivery	Planning and controlling	Sharing and cooperation
Outputs	Plans	Policies	Actions	Learning
Critical success factor	Business clarification	Technological vision	Clear mission	Process skills

The policy committee, then, is expected to give technological direction to the business and focus on IT capability and delivery. Its outputs therefore are policies and procedures. The critical success factor is adequate understanding by the committee of IT but enhanced by visions of what can be achieved for the particular organization. The policy committee thus must be 'informed' by the plans of the steering groups. It requires members who are knowledgeable on the technologies important to the business, executives who have experience of using IT, and executives who have the conceptual ability to see where IT can take the businesses and vice versa. Thus, the criterion for membership is primarily ability to contribute to technology policy. However, some of these members must also, by their position, status or involvement, be able to ensure the resultant policies and procedures are understood and carried out. Too many policy committees fail on these two success factors. Rationales 2, 4, 5, 6, 7 and 8 can spawn this type of committee.

The *IT board* label is given to a body primarily responsible for directing IT departments structured as business units or business ventures. The archetype is the board of the IT business within a business. It often, therefore, is the mechanism for ensuring IT is run as a business and will insist on a business strategy for the department, approve and monitor revenue and capital budgets, and discuss and suggest resource policies and operational *modus operandi*. Besides the senior executives of the IT business unit, it is likely to have one or two directors appointed from customer departments or divisions, perhaps one or two outside non-executive appointments to inject experience and missing knowledge, and perhaps a chairman from the host organization's top management.

The 'IT board', then, is expected to formulate and monitor the business strategy for the IT department. Its concern is the management, planning and control of the unit and its outputs therefore are agenda actions for the department. The critical success factor is establishing a clear mission, determined as much as anything, by the IT and IS strategies of the host organization – plus the needs of the external market if it is a business venture. Rationales 4, 6, 7 and 8 can spawn this type of committee.

The *IT forum* label is given to a body whose purpose is much 'softer' than the other three types. It commonly arises in multidivisional, multinational organizations where the dispersed IT community wishes to exchange ideas, concerns and experiences. The intention often is to influence or initiate policies not in place and perhaps made by other bodies, and to facilitate technology transfer. Thus the IT forum is generally a corporate body at country, regional or world level. It commonly exists alongside the other three types of committee. It may be called a conference, seminar, or meeting, but 'forum' is the keyword implying unbounded agendas and the importance of process.

The IT forum, then, is expected to help the IT community and is a soft mechanism for coordination. It is concerned with sharing knowledge and experience and identifying areas for cooperation formally or informally. A measure of success is how much the participants learn and so the critical success factor is the process skills applied. These include knowing when to meet, sensitive structuring of agendas, being eclectic on membership, judging when to make unofficial matters official and informal behaviours formal, and balancing learning with some more concrete achievements. The chairman may have to be the overall head of IT but he may need process help to do the job. Rationales 1, 6, 7, 8, 10 and 11 can spawn this type of committee.

These four types are not mutually exclusive and not all organizations need each of them. Often there is an evolutionary discovery that each is required over time. The following case illustrates this pattern.

A multidivisional manufacturing company had run down its IT activities over several years as it decentralized very aggressively and fought for survival. In 1984, a corporate realization emerged that IT was becoming a strategic matter of exposure for some of its businesses. A central push was given to IT and some businesses were exhorted to appoint IT managers and formulate IS strategies. An IT forum was created to bring these managers together and establish a common understanding of where and how IT was becoming strategic in the different businesses. A new IT function was arising and cooperation between divisions began to flow. At the same time, divisions started to set up steering committees to guide their IT managers on business needs. Often these were chaired by finance directors who had always been responsible for DP. Some of them attended the IT forum. As the importance of IT in some businesses was realized, chief executives began to take over as chairmen and their IT managers then attended the IT forum with more authority and a desire to achieve as much as to learn.

By 1987, it was clear that the IT forum was running out of steam as a learning vehicle and that the group was in need of some cross-divisional IT policies. In late 1987, the forum was replaced by an IT policy group, chaired by the main board member with overall responsibility for IT, and charged with initiating and formulating any necessary IT policies and procedures. Members were to be invited by the chairman for their ability to contribute; no longer was the committee representational and 'soft'. At the same time, the central IT department inherited from earlier days was given a board to direct it. Its task was to judge what the internal divisional market required and direct the IT department accordingly. If needs were insufficient or inadequately met, the board would disband or restructure the IT department. To ensure a satisfactory principal-agent relationship through the board, directors would be appointed from each major division.

By late 1987, the IT community asked if a revised version of the IT forum could meet infrequently in order to ensure interchange and cooperation still continued across the business. In three-and-a-half years, the corporation had discovered the need for all of the four types of committee.

The above case study is not an exemplar for all to follow. Some steering committees are hybrids of the four ideal types and do work effectively. Even then, however, it is important to ask which purposes are to be tackled by the hybrid and then structure and manage the committee accordingly. As argued below, in time the hybrid may well have to be recast into one or more of the ideal types.

Typical tensions

Steering committees are born, splutter, die, are rejuvenated or resurrected and generally enjoy a hazardous life. A number of tensions arise in this series of life-cycles and most are the consequence of not specifying the committee's purpose, reviewing it occasionally, or running the committee to fit the purpose. The case quoted above demonstrates how there may be a diversity of these committees, but that one type can be an outgrowth of, or a replacement for, another. Thus, it is important to anticipate such changes of requirement.

The following tensions are typical of steering committees and provide the signals to monitor.

Knowledge base
The skills and education of the membership do not, or no longer, fit the purpose. Lack of business understanding can bedevil steering groups, poor technology appreciation can hinder policy groups, inadequate business management sense can imperil boards, and sleepers can mar a Forum.

Hierarchy
The locus of the committee in the organization and the status of the members can be a crucial factor. Put simply, do not raise the level above its need, otherwise IT is oversold and members do not attend. Conversely, raise the level as issues and applications of IT become more central to the business.

Constitution
The classic tension is of representation versus contribution. Most steering groups and policy committees need to be alert to different constituencies and be accepted by them with authority; yet, the knowledge base must not be impaired. Put simply, if in doubt seek a balance.

Linkages
Steering committees have a habit of not communicating upwards and downwards in the organization (often ignoring the IT departments themselves) and not connecting into other boards and committees. Lack of communication generally means the committee becomes an invisible, distrusted body. Lack of connection (for example through minutes or policy papers) generally means the committee has no support or mandate and is isolated.

Calendar
Many steering groups and policy committees meet too frequently. As a result, the

focus becomes tactical and project oriented and members lose commitment. An IT board, conversely, may need to meet monthly since it is a business executive body. Second, the timing of meetings can be haphazard. It clearly helps if key steering group meetings fit in with budgetary and long-range planning cycles and IT board meetings with budgetary control cycles. Forum meetings should be infrequent or *ad hoc* rather than frequent or routine, to present role invention or stagnation.

Evolution

As business, organizational or technological issues change and, as information management matures, the purposes of the committee can multiply, fuse or diminish. The charter and membership – or the purpose and style – may have to evolve gradually until such time that radical restructuring within the four types is required.

Process

Because steering committees are tackling complex and often political matters, the process is as important as the structure. Thus, how it works should be reviewed as well as what it does. This is developed in the next section.

Managing steering committees

The notion that steering committees evolve and that changes of purpose should be anticipated implies that they should be managed over time. Drury, in a study of steering committees, noted that managements tended to have several expectations of them. From his research, he found some clear advantages, some expectations that were not met, and some areas where evidence was unclear. Benefits included gaining top management attention, improving user awareness and involvement, and improving IT awareness of, and involvement in, user matters. Whether resource allocation, user service or evaluation of alternative ideas improved was unclear. There seemed to be no impact on IT operations performance, equipment purchase or performance measurement. However, Drury did not report or discover that different types of committee were needed; it would appear that the objects of his studies were committees concerned with both IS and IT strategies.

What Drury did discover was that some of the *process* aspects of managing steering committees were crucial. In particular, effective committees adopted a decision-making style that was participative and open. Decision by agreement was practised rather than decision by imposition. Likewise, agenda-management was communal and open and not manipulated and closed. Agenda items were raised from the breath of membership and not placed just by the IT department and the chairman.

To these two process variables, may be added two more which are derived from the tensions listed earlier. The committee must be visible in the organization, connecting with other bodies and communicating to general management, users and specialists alike. Second, the importance of the knowledge base and the contribution of all members means that the committee may need educational support. This includes both formal events, for example occasional briefings on IT supply, use and management trends, and learning by doing, particularly through the judicious use of items that get on the agenda.

Table 7.7 Steering committees: the manageables

The set	The manageables	Time dimension
Structural	Task – purpose and type	Variable
	Level – locus and status	Variable
	Calendar – frequency and cycles	Variable
	Membership – skills and balance	Variable
Process	Decision-making – agreement not imposition	Constant
	Agenda items – open not closed	Constant
	Visibility – integrated not isolated	Constant
	Education – to be active not passive	Constant

An early article on steering committees by Nolan emphasized the structural variables. He pointed out that the task, the level, the calendar and the membership are all structural factors that can be varied over time. Some of these were listed as potential tensions in the previous section and they all tend to be a function of the committee's purpose. When added to the process variables just discussed, two sets of manageables emerge. These are summarized in Table 7.7 and provide the framework for managing steering committees over time.

SUMMARY AND CONCLUSIONS

Four levels of organizing IT activity have been analysed: the IT function; the IT department; the IT director; and the IT steering committees. Each level is characterized by frequent change. It is important to understand what drives their dynamics and then organize IT activities accordingly.

Currently, the structure of the IT function is becoming more decentralized and is getting closer to the user. This results in a mix of arrangements in many companies, often representing a federal structure. However, the particular mix in each organization should be contingent upon the organizational, technological, strategic and historiographical characteristics over time.

The structure of the large IT department is becoming flatter, as more tasks have to be embraced and the orientation is towards customer service. This is creating qualitative and quantitative gaps in IT human resources.

The head of the IT function is getting closer to the main board and generally is a director in action, if not in title. He has to exercise four leadership skills: business direction; technology policy; organizational politics; and functional management. This requires spending much of his time outside the IT department itself.

Steering committees are a common phenomenon in the organization of IT. They are created for many reasons and face many potential hazards. It is important to determine the purpose of a steering committee and establish which of four generic types are required. These have been called steering group, policy committee, IT board and IT forum and are variously required at different times and in different situations. For each type, however, it is important to pay attention to managing the process, if steering committees are to succeed.

Some thoughts on how these four levels of analysis can be welded into an effective whole which takes the organization finally from the DP era into the IT era are discussed in Chapter 9.

NOTES AND REFERENCES

1. For source material, see Hubinette K. H., 'Organisation and control of development in information technology: Volvo Data AB', in Earl M. J. (ed.), *Information Management: The Strategic Dimension*, Oxford University Press, 1988.
2. *Source:* La Belle A. and Nyce H. E., 'Whither the IT organisation?', *Sloan Management Review*, Summer 1987.
3. See, for example, Lawrence P. R. and Lorsch J. W., *Organisation and Environment*, Division of Research, Harvard Business School, 1967, and Galbraith J., *Designing Complex Organisations*, Addison-Wesley, 1973.
4. See, for example, Feeny D. F., Edwards B. R. and Earl M. J., 'Complex organisations and the information systems function. A research study', Oxford Institute of Information Management research and discussion paper (RDP 87/7), Templeton College, Oxford, 1987, and Lockett M., 'Strategies for end-user computing', in Earl M. J. (ed.), *Information Management: The Strategic Dimension*, Oxford University Press, 1988.
5. See Alloway R. M. and Quillard J. A., 'User managers' systems needs', *MIS Quarterly*, June 1983.
6. Price Waterhouse/computing opinion survey, *Organisation of IT*, September 1986.

FURTHER READING

Buchanan J. R. and Linowes R. G., 'Making distributed data processing work', *Harvard Business Review*, September–October 1980.

Drury D. H., 'An evaluation of data processing steering committees', *MIS Quarterly*, December 1984.

Earl M. J., 'Emerging trends in managing new information technologies', in Piercy N. (ed.), *The Management Implications of New Information Technology*, Croom Helm, 1984.

Earl M. J., Feeny D. F., Hirschheim R. A., and Lockett M., 'Information technology executives' key education and development needs: a field study', Oxford Institute of Information management research and discussion paper (RDP 86/10), Templeton College, Oxford, 1986.

Edwards B., 'IS policy, strategy and organisation', unpublished IBM discussion paper, 1984.

Gibson C. F., and Nolan R. L., 'Managing the four stages of EDP growth', *Harvard Business Review*, January–February 1974.

Hedberg B., and Mumford E., 'The design of computer systems: man's vision of man as an integral part of the system design process', in Mumford E. and Sackman H. (eds), *Human Choice and Computers*, North Holland, 1975.

McFarlan F. W., and McKenny J. L., *Corporate Information Systems Management: The Issues Facing Senior Executives*, Dow Jones Irwin, 1983.

Nolan R. L., 'Managing information systems by committee', *Harvard Business Review*, July–August 1982.

Rockart J. F., Bullen C. V. and Bull L., 'Future role of the information systems executive', *MIS Quarterly*, December 1982.

Tricker R. I., *Effective Information Management*, Beaumont Executive Press, 1982.

Chapter 8
CONTROLLING
IT ACTIVITIES

INTRODUCTION

In Chapter 2, information management at the corporate level was seen essentially to comprise planning, organizing and controlling IT activities. This chapter examines management control of IT. In principle, control systems and procedures for IT should fit the firm's planning approach and organizational arrangements, so that all three information management practices pull in the same direction. Unfortunately, corporate pressures for control often generate behaviours which subvert both planning and organization philosophies and lead to suboptimization. Equally common, the technologists' views of control tend to be in conflict with the philosophy of the management control system at large in the organization, so that tension and questioning are typical in this area. Finally, as IT becomes perceived as a strategic resource, traditional control questions have a sharper edge. Indeed, they often indicate an erosion of corporate support for IT, despite the external and internal rhetorics about IT being a source of competitive advantage. Such questions include the following:

1. How much should we be spending on IT?
2. How do you assess the benefits of an IT project?
3. Should we charge for information services and, if so, how?
4. How do we know if we are getting value for money from all our activities?

The first question is often referred to as 'the funding issue' and is asked frequently as companies' year on year spending on IT continues to grow at high compound rates. The second question reflects the recognition that perhaps 50 per cent of all capital expenditure today is on IT,[1] together with an anxiety that returns often seem more intangible than for many capital projects. This appraisal question is tackled in the section beginning on p.164. The concern about chargeout is traditional, but today it reflects the desire to improve accountability for IT without creating arcane accounting procedures and bureaucratic attitudes. Thus, responsibility accounting in IT is examined in the section beginning on p.174. The final question is frequently asked by chief executives who know from experience that there is no easy answer to it, but demand in the contemporary climate of 'leaner, meaner, fitter' business that all functions must justify their existence. Therefore, performance measurement is the subject of the final section beginning on p.184.

FUNDING IT

A host of questions are raised by 'the funding issue', some at the very heart of understanding and managing information systems resources in the IT era. How much should we spend on IT is the dominant concern; other questions include:

1. Do we know how much we are spending on IT?
2. Will IT budgets continue to rise as unit hardware costs fall?
3. Why is corporate support for IT running out?
4. Why do technologists generally wish to expand IT activities and top management contract or stabilize them?
5. How should we finance IT?

Rationally, as we shall see, many of these are 'non-questions' and thus are inherently spurious or dangerous. Yet, managerially they have to be answered, for they reflect both the recognition that IT – at least in *spending* terms – has become important and the limited organizational understanding of the nature and purpose of IT *investment*. The spending frame of reference is examined first.

Ratio analysis

As managements observe the growth of IT spending (seen in Chapter 1 to be growing perhaps by a factor of seven times in the 1980s decade and at growth rates from 20 to 100 per cent p.a.) and realize that IT/IS are discretionary expenditures in accounting terms, they like to know what others are spending. Thus, computer manufacturers and management consultants seek to analyse and publish IT spending ratios to guide or give comfort or discomfort. Like all financial ratios, they should be issued with care!

Price Waterhouse[2] suggest that in the UK the average corporate spend on IT is 0.97 per cent of sales revenue. A competitor consultancy suggests it is 1.43 per cent and many observers insist that the average value of this ratio varies between 1 and 5 per cent according to sector, posture, history and so on. All that can be deduced thus far, then, is that IT spend in absolute terms is material and that differences in ratios could be interesting to analyse.

One source of difference, as might be expected in any analysis of IT's strategic contribution, seems to be industrial sector. Price Waterhouse reported sector forecasts (from budgets) for 1987 and these are reproduced in Table 8.1. The immediate reaction might be that, although some significant percentage differences appear, they are not dramatic. However, they are *average* figures; within sectors there can be much wider ranges. For example, the following IT expenditure levels have been recorded in organizations well known to the author:

A major chemical company, 1.45 per cent compared with the process industry ratio of 0.64 per cent in Table 8.1.

Table 8.1 IT spending by industry

Sector	Ratio of IT expenditure to sales (%)
Engineering	0.68
Process	0.64
Retail	1.10
Other industrial	0.86
Public utilities	1.04
Finance	1.08
Education and research	4.12
Service bureaux	11.90
Average	0.97

Source: Price Waterhouse

A leading retail company, catching up on IT investment it would claim, 1.7 per cent compared with 1.10 per cent for the sector in Table 8.1.

An airline, 3 per cent compared with ratios of below or just over 1 per cent for most industry sectors in Table 8.1.

A financial services group, 20 per cent compared with 1.08 per cent for the finance sector in Table 8.1.

A retail distribution company that created substantive competitive advantage with IT and disturbed the whole sector, less than 1 per cent.

In other words, IT expenditure to sales ratios are meaningless as isolated numbers. Comparison with an industry average may be helpful in forcing a firm to ask why its own ratio is much less or much more, but a variance does not automatically indicate good or bad performance.

Ratio *ranges* can be more helpful for checking out and analysing relative positions. For example, the chemical company with 1.45 per cent reckoned that the range in its industry was 1 to 2.5 per cent of sales and asked itself questions about comparative value-added structures, investment strategies and IT histories.

Since these ratios have become a metric of the industry, it is worth noting some of the technical and other problems they pose. Accounting problems are rife. Different industries account for sales turnover differently and have different turnover structures. For example, in banking, it is quite difficult to determine a turnover definition equivalent to measures used in manufacturing. In banks, it often makes more sense to relate IT spend to operating costs, frequently yielding levels of roughly 15 per cent or more. Then accounting for IT itself is also problematic: Is all IT included? How is IT defined? Is some IT capitalized? etc. Price Waterhouse, for example, opined that perhaps one third of IT expenditure did not appear on IT budgets and so suggested that the industry average ratio could be 1.5 per cent rather than 0.97 per cent. This seems realistic, not least just to adjust for invisible end-user computing.

Then, while accountants might debate which technologies should be included in IT, noting that perhaps only 50 per cent, on average, of IT budgets anyway are explained by hardware, they would find even more confusion and contention (as would managers and technologists) about the place of training costs, user support costs and the like. They would then notice that, even in their own profession, some accounting firms were spending probably twice as much in ratio terms as others and would wonder whether this should be highlighted in the audit report. However, intuitively they would probably feel that, whilst low spending buys very little, high spending in itself is not sufficient for success. Yet, some surveys have opined[3] that leading companies in profitability terms spend much more on IT than the profitability laggards in any industry.

So what do ratios tell us about the funding issue? When compared with ranges for industry sectors, they can suggest some global questions to be asked. A low or high number perhaps psychologically prompts more questions than an average score. Yet an average score does not necessarily tell us that our firm is satisfactorily efficient and effective in IT usage, that we are doing what most are doing, that we will not be exposed by competition, or that we have a safe risk-averse posture. To be helpful, the ratio needs to be supported by expenditure numbers by division, technology, application area, user type, year etc., and informed by knowledge of the IT spending patterns in our competitors, suppliers and customers.

> A manufacturing and wholesaling company convened its board to consider its response to a competitor who was making major year on year gains in market share through aggressive use of IT. The competitor had used on-line order entry links with customers and integrated inventory control and distribution systems to revolutionize the industry. In view of the special nature of this one-day board meeting, the DP manager was invited. He thought it somewhat ironic that he had just been given a bonus for achieving a 10 per cent reduction in the DP budget in line with across-the-board cuts, partly forced by the company's current embarrassment in the market place.

In other words, expenditure on IT should be determined by demand and the 'right' level of spend is a function of the threats, opportunities and capabilities for each organization. In short, IS strategy formulation drives the answers to these two questions, just as it determines how much we spend on development versus maintenance versus R & D etc. Ratios can only provide a few crude clues. They help in forcing us to measure and know what we are doing in aggregate and disaggregate. But they can imply and impute a false logic. What we should spend is not an accounting problem, and on the whole, funding is not a proper issue. Once we adopt an investment, rather than expense, frame of reference, these two assertions become clear.

Capital investment

Whatever ratios do and do not tell us, it is clear that information technology can be a sizeable fixed asset, that IT expenses are material, that continued expenditure on IT is contributing significantly to industrial capital formation and that today many firms see IT as a strategic resource. In other words, IT in most organizations needs to be seen as capital investment not period expense. Indeed, in one major financial services group known to the author, 50 per cent of planned capital expenditure in the three-year period 1987–90 will be on IT.

Acknowledging that IT expenditure is more a form of capital investment than a line in operating expenses is more than an accounting revelation. It changes the entire picture of management control of IT; the 'funding issue', project appraisal, responsibility accounting and performance measurement all change. In particular, if IT expenditure is seen as capital investment, then the following factors apply:

1. Resource allocation is crucial – correctly appraising individual projects and optimizing the risk and return profile of the project portfolio.
2. Financial planning is necessary – ensuring that funds are available to finance IT projects as they need cash.
3. Strategic factors have to be considered – since capital investment is a major means of implementing strategies (and, as Brealey and Myers, from their corporate finance perspective, put it: strategic planning is really capital budgeting on a grand scale).
4. Managing the returns from IT becomes important – making good investment decisions is one thing, ensuring good implementation and adequate pay-off is another.
5. Accounting for IT changes character – in external and internal accounting, transaction-based, accrual, historic, expense accounting will have its limitations.

These and related consequences are summarized in Figure 8.1 and some are developed later in the chapter. Conversion from expense to investment thinking, however, is not yet commonplace. Nolan, Norton and Company reported survey evidence in 1985[4] that, whereas all companies constructed annual budgets for IS, only 10 per cent did five year capital appropriation planning for IT. Likewise, 70 per cent formed long-range IS plans, but only 30 per cent translated these into long-range financial plans. In similar vein, 90 per cent of companies did cost benefit analyses of new IS projects but only 40 per cent did post-implementation reviews.

Such empirical evidence is interesting. Adopting investment concepts, however, allows much more compelling normative analysis. If we adopt capital investment frameworks from corporate finance theory, we see that 'the funding issue' is relatively unimportant, if not illusory. In short, the concern over spending on IT should not be justified on grounds of limited funds. Most firms do not face funding constraints – capital rationing is the technical term. They can raise capital in large amounts at a fair price as long as capital markets are perfect (or reasonably so) and the firms have good projects and present adequate information. Capital markets are in the business of financing profitable ventures and few businessmen (in established businesses) really complain that financing is difficult[5].

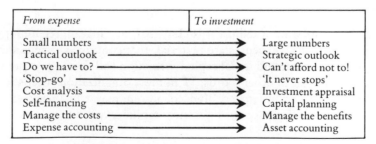

From expense	To investment
Small numbers ⟶	Large numbers
Tactical outlook ⟶	Strategic outlook
Do we have to? ⟶	Can't afford not to!
'Stop-go' ⟶	'It never stops'
Cost analysis ⟶	Investment appraisal
Self-financing ⟶	Capital planning
Manage the costs ⟶	Manage the benefits
Expense accounting ⟶	Asset accounting

Figure 8.1 Managing IT as an investment.

'Soft rationing' of capital can exist, but, as Brealey and Myers argue, this is often due to internal, rather than external, factors. These include head office imposed capital limits on divisions to limit over-optimistic investment, or to impose investment priorities across business units, and limitations on non-capital resources, such as skills or management time. Indeed, in IT projects, it is often skills, hardware or software availability, management capability, organizational resistance, or system dependencies which constrain IT plans and budgets. These are not funding factors.

'Hard rationing' may exist if capital markets are imperfect, if firms are in financial distress, or if firms manage their relationships with investors badly. In this case, IT projects may be held back by lack of funds; but so will, or should, all other capital projects. Thus, if IT is seen as investment and not expense, its funding should be treated no differently from other capital projects. Indeed, if there is capital rationing, the firm should invest in those capital projects – whether IT or not – with the highest net present value, until the money runs out.

The 'funding' or 'spending' argument, then, should not be about capital availability. The decision rule is clear: invest in IT projects with a zero or positive net present value, for then firms will be investing in projects whose benefit equals or exceeds their cost (or whose marginal revenue equals or exceeds their marginal cost). Any increase or decrease in spending on, or funding of, IT therefore becomes a matter of meeting business goals with profitable projects. If this decision rule is accepted, then the profitable projects should be naturally championed by senior executives from the business area most involved. Indeed, they may be able to sponsor and fund them themselves, depending on the capital expenditure limits imposed at different levels of the organization. This corollary of the analysis is very important. IT directors frequently complain of inadequate corporate support. This is not the same as traditional 'top management support', but refers to the felt need to continually justify IT expenditure levels or the feeling that recent financial support is about to disappear. The reported cause is 'boards who don't understand' or 'top management movers, shakers, visionaries' who have moved on and not been replaced. Yet, it is senior user executives and line managers who often believe in, depend on or drive IT applications. Under the profitable project decision rule, they should be the *business supporters* of IT and the corporate support problem should wither away.

This normative analysis, of course, has to be modified by some managerial pragmatism. First, some applications are self-financing – for example, cost displacement projects – and the only funding question is smoothing out the cash flows in a relatively short time-frame. Second, the devolutionary spirit of the last chapter (and the analysis of the preceding paragraph) implied placing many IT investment decisions on users and local business units. This may lead to 'soft rationing' in the interplay between the centre and divisions and between specialists and users. Solutions here lie in some of the IS strategy principles of Chapter 4 – ranking mechanisms, 'wild hare funds' and experimentation. Also, funding control of new or local technologies may be relaxed, at certain times, points discussed in the section on responsibility accounting and the summary of this chapter. Third, however attractive IT projects may be, top management is often nervous about sanctioning too many of them for fear of creating an unstoppable, intertia-driven IT function which in time becomes a non-productive overhead. This may be a danger, but it perhaps points to delivering IT projects, where possible, by discrete and finite means, such as sub-contracting, use of packages, and hiring of temporary resources. Finally, all capital investment decisions take place in an arena of 'strategic control' – the mission, mandates, and climate of organizations over time. Here, Parsons' mandates described in Chapter 6 are relevant. Under a centrally planned mandate, strategic and political factors may outweigh the rationality of net present value. In free market regimes, short-term views may dominate, and in scarce resource contexts, operating budgets may still drive funding and investment of IT.

Parsons' leading edge regime, perhaps, most confronts the normative analysis. Investing in leading edge IT to create opportunities is not easily accommodated by net present value calculus, unless dominated by risk and sensitivity analyses. Likewise, funding a leading edge mandate requires a considerable psychological leap. Moreover, any investment in IT which crosses different applications and organizational boundaries is difficult to justify and fund on a project-led basis. Data centre enhancements and corporate communications networks are examples. Here, the 'funding issue' is substantial – whether it means affordability, desirability, fundability or viability. If operating under a leading edge mandate, or seeking a quantum jump in exploiting IT for strategic advantage, there are occasions when 'projects must speak for themselves but be championed by users' is an ineffective maxim. Here, loosened controls, business-case risks, strategic vision and directional planning must take over for a time. In this case, the organization explicitly relegates 'funding' and its associated questions as a factor in the management control of IT.

Funding questions

The conclusion to be drawn from this section is that in principle there is not a funding issue or question in IT. Nevertheless, there are some useful questions at the policy level that executive teams should ask.

1. What are we spending and where on IT – and, occasionally, can we explain this against spending patterns in our sector?
2. Is business strategy driving our expenditure on IT – in both amount and allocation?
3. Is financial planning of IT being done as for other capital expenditure?
4. Are any positive net present value IT projects being rejected?
5. Is our funding of, and are our investment decisions in, IT consistent with the mandate we have given to IT?

Throughout this section on funding, the connection between appraising IT projects and funding them has been clear. 'Discover profitable projects and the funds should be made available' has been the maxim. However, the methods for assessing desirable projects often come under criticism and it may be that one of the apparent funding difficulties in IT actually arises from the use of inappropriate investment appraisal techniques. This is the subject of the following section.

APPRAISING IT

Besides reducing organizational aggravation over funding of IT, several other arguments can be made for formal appraisal of IT projects. These include the following points:

1. IT projects can be very expensive, so rigorous evaluation is necessary.

2. Often IT projects require significant investment now in return for profit flows in the future, so time value analysis is necessary.
3. IT resources are usually scarce. It is not necessarily hardware or capital that is the problem, but software, human skills and managerial capability. So screening and ranking appraisals are required.
4. IT projects compete with other projects for these different resources, so they should be appraised on a like basis.
5. Organizations need to be confident of the viability of IT projects and a visible appraisal procedure is necessary.
6. IT projects may have considerable strategic impact on the firm and should be rigorously evaluated.
7. *Ex ante* appraisal provides standards for later performance measurement.

All these arguments can be applied to any capital investment project – IT is, in fact, no different. However three more reasons arise in the case of IT projects:

8. IT project appraisal provides a mechanism for enlisting top level support and involvement.
9. Formal appraisal methods may force both managers and specialists to check application objectives and consider alternative methods or designs.
10. Time, cost and benefit evaluations inherent in appraisal methods provide benchmarks for project planning and control.

In short, if we regard IT as an investment rather than an expense, then capital investment appraisal techniques would seem to be relevant. However, the problem is which techniques are appropriate? Increasingly, conventional methods have come under attack, not only from managers, but also from theorists and policy bodies.[6] The issues raised in this debate include the following:

1. Conventional methods such as internal rate of return or payback calculations may suit cost displacement or savings projects, but do not cope with competitive edge projects or strategic thrusts to change sector dynamics, where the cases are multivariate, soft and uncertain.
2. Innovation and new ideas may be determined or ridiculed by 'hard-nosed' quantification.
3. Benefits of some IT projects are so immense in productivity, leverage or business development terms that net present value, accounting rate of return or payback calculations become outrageous and incongruous.
4. Formal appraisal is not standard practice and may reflect intractable difficulties in data collection, decision analysis, risk assessment and communication.

There is some validity in all these doubts. Yet most executives or theorists would find it difficult to dismiss the ten reasons for appraisal cited earlier, just because current techniques are outdated or appropriate methods are difficult. Alternatively informal methods might be accepted in some cases, but arbitrary methods might be worse than none at all.

Kaplan quotes the following example in his discussion of justification approaches for computer-integrated manufacturing.

The Yamazaki Machinery Company in Japan installed an \$18 million flexible manufacturing system. Productivity benefits included reductions in machines from 68 to 18, in employees, from 215 to 12, in floor space from 103,000 to 30,000 square feet and in average processing time from 35 to 1.5 days. After two years, savings, however, only totalled 6.9 million, much of this figure coming from one-off inventory reduction. Even if labour savings continued at \$1.5 million for twenty years, the project's return would be less than 10 per cent p.a. Since many UK and US firms use hurdle rates of 15 per cent or more and payback periods of five years or less, this project would have been appraised as unprofitable. Yet, the productivity and performance benefits were outstanding – and flexibility was acquired as well.

Another case, known to the author, hit similar problems:

The board of a UK textile manufacturer examined a proposal for a computer-based production planning and control system. The rationale for the system was that to quicken response to consumers' buying habits as recorded by retailers' electronic point of sale systems, an integrated and dynamic approach to production planning and control was essential. Unfortunately, because of the slow and uncertain stream of increased business that might result, the IT project produced a poor net present value and a payback well in excess of the corporate requirement. The board concluded that it did not matter whether the appraisal method was wrong or the data inaccurate, the business case was strong. It approved the project on the grounds that 'we cannot afford not to, because our competitors will do so and our retail customers expect it'. Fortunately, the level of investment required could be approved by the firm's board without its being referred to the corporate headquarters.

These two examples illustrate why managers and specialists increasingly campaign for rejection of conventional methods, more 'practical' and less 'theoretical' techniques, or completely different approaches altogether. Before we examine whether new frameworks are possible, however, it is important to consider the relevance of the theoretically correct technique for capital investment appraisal. For the net present value method arose from an earlier technological discontinuity in the early 20th century and has some powerful logic.

Net present value and IT

Net present value (NPV) or discounted cash flow (DCF) techniques are generally regarded as the theoretically correct and practically feasible approach to capital investment appraisal. This is not the place to rehearse the mechanisms,[7] but it is perhaps useful to note that the NPV method:

(a) estimates and evaluates cash flows not accounting numbers;
(b) recognizes and discounts for the time value of money;
(c) establishes whether the marginal or incremental revenues of a project exceed the marginal or incremental costs; and
(d) gives a figure which indicates both absolute and relative project viability.

In short, it copes with the nature of capital investment projects. For IT projects, it has two particularly attractive attributes. The NPV method allows delayed or slow build-up benefits to be evaluated. Second, it provides a structure and detail which can help overcome the political and emotive claims often attached to IT projects. Typical arguments of this sort include 'we won't survive without it', 'the competition are doing it already' etc.

There are, however, four principal difficulties with NPV for IT projects, some more serious than others. The first is the identification and evaluation of alternatives. In principle, different alternatives can be tested by NPV, but the structure and process of it tend to encourage thinking that this project is the only way. Three sorts of alternatives matter:

1. Base case alternatives – IT projects often are aimed at improving or replacing current practices. Thus the IT project's cashflows are compared with the current picture. However, if IT is being proposed because of threats to the *status quo*, the realistic base case alternative is not current practice as if nothing changes but current practice evaluated under the likely threats. McCosh *et al.* call this scenario a null strategy.
2. Replacement alternatives – increasingly IT projects are proposed which replace existing IT projects – the system renewal problem. If these are subjected to investment appraisal, other alternatives may be obscured. For example, a non–IT project may now be more appropriate because the main benefits have been already realized from the old project, or because alternative means may exist which were not available earlier.
3. Design alternatives – by the time the NPV analysis is done, a system design is frozen. Although sensitivity analysis of the NPV may stimulate discussion of design alternatives, this cannot be relied upon. It is important that executives look out for design (and objectives) alternatives at the appraisal stage.

The second difficulty with NPV methods is selection of the hurdle or discount rate. Finance theory tells us that this should be the opportunity cost of capital (or possibly the weighted average cost of capital) adjusted for project risk. There are two problems here:

1. It is difficult to sensibly adjust discount rates for project risk in any capital investment appraisal. IT projects in principle carry so many different risks (and for innovative or strategic IT projects they may not be apparent until late in the project's life) that risk adjustment of the discount rate may be unhelpful. Risk analysis might be done by other means (see later).
2. Where IT projects are truly strategic – pursuing competitive advantage or creating new businesses – discount rates may need to be modified downwards to encourage bold initiatives. This may be dangerous practice before the NPV computation is done. Instead, it may be safer to accept a lower NPV at the normal discount rate if the strategic case looks strong or 'worth a bet'. However, if corporate management is looking to encourage IT projects from youthful, venturing divisions and discourage any but the most profitable from mature and declining business units, then different hurdle rates might be applied – lower to the former class and higher to the latter. McCosh *et al.* have advocated this tactic.

The third difficulty with NPV methods is coping with 'intangible' benefits. These can arise in IT projects pursuing improved performance, competitive advantage or new businesses. Kaplan notes that many benefits of advanced manufacturing technology (AMT) – flexibility, quality, responsiveness – are of the intangible class. However, intangibles are not necessarily unquantifiable; indeed, they should become tangible and often quantifiable after project implementation. Thus, ignoring them or giving them a zero value may be even more arbitrary than guessing their value. There are three possible approaches here:

1. Test alternative estimates of intangibles in the NPV model to examine the project's sensitivity (or uncertainty).
2. Treat intangibles as options.[8] This involves calculating expected values (probability times estimated value) for the intangible or possible opportunity in the project and adding it to the more certain cash flows. The analogy here is buying financial options.
3. Calculate the NPV for the certain cash flows. If it is acceptable, accept the project. If not, examine what value the intangibles should attain to make the NPV zero and then assess whether such values seem realistic. Kaplan has suggested this approach. It would seem sensible for many IT projects which have displacement savings benefits and productivity gains, together with performance improvements or competitive advantage potential.

The fourth difficulty in a way encapsulates the other three. It is the notion that NPV is too mechanistic, economistic and 'hard' for many IT projects which are complex, multivariate and 'soft'.

Meredith and Hill, in discussing justification of AMT, propose, in several guises, multi-stage approaches for such projects. Adapting their suggestions, perhaps three stages make sense for complex IT projects.

1. NPV methods for appraising the 'hard', tangible elements of the project.
2. Multi-factor qualitative analysis for the 'softer', intangible elements of the project, often the benefits of new ways of doing things or of competitive edge.
3. Risk and uncertainty analysis of the whole project, where there are elements of the unknown, particularly in exploiting IT to create new businesses. Classic techniques here include sensitivity analysis and deterministic or probability modelling.

Such a three stage process not only tackles the different attributes of IT projects, but each stage provides a check on the others. For example, an NPV calculation can provide a cool, dispassionate view of the qualitative arguments presented for a strategic project.

However, classical financial appraisals of investment and strategic decisions have been described as 'ammunition machines' by Earl and Hopwood. They tend to impute a financial or economic rationality to decisions which are not unidimensional. Earl and Hopwood therefore argue that decision aids should be more like 'dialogue machines', ensuring that different factors, dimensions and viewpoints are explicated. The multi-stage approach proposed about might facilitate this – and still provides the NPV calculus to render some comfort to the organization (a 'rationalization machine'). Alternatively, it could be argued that, if an IT project has very clear competitive advantage or strategic potential, financial appraisal is unnecessary. The important thing here is to press on and gather the economic rents promised. Indeed, too much financial appraisal of such opportunities could make the firm worry about the tangible costs and benefits so much that it takes its eye off the obvious comparative advantages it should be exploiting. As Brealey and Myers put it, good techniques do not guarantee good decisions (or, incidentally, good implementation).

The ultimate version of this argument would be to suggest different appraisal methods for different types of project. Meredith and Hill proposed this for AMT justification. Different types of project, of course, are not a function of the technology being applied, but of the use of the technology or purpose of the project. A classification of IT use presented in Chapter 1 provides a framework for this line of attack.

Four-way framework

The point about different applications or uses of IT is that they differ in purpose, nature, certainty and risk. These differences often are expressed in practice by statements such as:

(a) 'You can't prove competitive advantage through discounted cash flow';
(b) 'To get strategic IT applications approved, we have to circumvent appraisal procedures';
(c) 'We didn't know the real benefits until after we experimented with and installed the system'; and
(d) 'To get the project started, I had to tear up the formal appraisal'.

Furthermore, as these statements demonstrate, innovative and competitive advantage applications of IT often have escaped or avoided formal appraisal and have been proven by trial and error methods, such as prototyping. This has been a clear message from research done in the Oxford Institute of Information Management.[9] So, although political and entrepreneurial approaches will always be practised and often required, there seems to be a good case for formulating and adopting a variety of appraisal methods for different purposes.

The classification of IT application introduced in Chapter 1 forms the first column of Table 8.2. The second column suggests the sort of goals that these applications pursue. Column three summarizes the nature or character of each use and the final column accordingly suggests the appropriate approach and technique to be adopted in appraising the project. Of course, the classification of use or aim is not watertight and the aims are not mutually exclusive for all IT projects. Thus, the approaches and techniques suggested in the final column may have to be combined for some projects. However, it is worth exploring the differences in more detail.

If *productivity and performance* are being pursued, the goals are likely to be efficiency and effectiveness. They may be expressed in terms of productivity, quality, responsiveness, throughput etc., but there is nothing soft about the intent. Indeed, benefits often will be tangible *ex ante* and certainly should be so *ex post*. Even where the aim is improved performance wider than productivity gains, a clear argument will be available on how this can be achieved – by levering managerial time, introducing new skills, aiding important decision making and so on. Here, financial appraisal methods are appropriate. Productivity and performance gains ideally can be quantified in NPV calculations; alternatively, paybacks, financial statement impact, or rate of return targets can be specified.

Table 8.2 Four-way framework for appraising IT

Aim	Goals	Nature	Approach/technique
Productivity and performance	Efficiency Effectiveness	Tangible benefits Clear argument	Financial Net present value
New ways of managing	Change Flexibility	Radical concept Multi-dimensional	Multi-factor Metrics
Competitive advantage	Product-market positioning Competitive disequilibrium	Concrete vision Commercial judgement	Strategic analysis Tests
Developing new businesses	Diversification Growth	Business venture Risk and uncertainty	Business case Business plan

If IT is being deployed to facilitate or engineer new ways of managing, the probable goal can be summed up as *change*. Often it will be expressed in terms of flexibility or removing constraints. Behind these applications will be a somewhat radical concept – for example, a new way of designing the organization, revolutionary production processes and procedures, or restructuring of work. There will be many dimensions to the application: social, economic, organizational, ethical etc. Thus, the approach to appraisal can only be multi-factor, presenting non-financial and financial justifications. Some of the qualitative arguments may be made quantifiable by inventing non-financial metrics and by agreeing a rubric for weighing and scoring them.

Where IT is being exploited for *competitive advantage*, the focus is on product-market positioning. Goals relate to external as much as internal operations and the ultimate objective is to cause competitive disequilibrium. However, it is all too easy to have vague ideas and make wild claims. The nature of successful competitive advantage applications of IT is that they are based on a concrete vision of what is required.[10] Because they are innovative and involve consideration of non-IT factors as much as IT itself, they require commercial judgement for their proposal and support. What is clear from many unsuccessful competitive advantage ideas, and from companies who resist the idea that IT can yield competitive edge, is that competitive strategic analysis is not done to either test or prompt the idea. It is here that Porter's frameworks for analysis can be used, examining the impact of the IT idea on competitive forces and generic strategies. Thus, strategic analysis is the approach to adopt. However, research then shows that it may be best to test the idea by prototyping, rather than either subject it to tight and heavy financial appraisal or adopt and implement it wholesale.[11] Costs and benefits (foreseen and unforeseen) can then be evaluated in the competitive arena and possibly further ideas suggested.

Where IT is being exploited to generate *a new business*, the goal is likely to be either diversification into an information business or further growth in the information services sector. In other words, the IT application is actually a business venture and the investment characteristics can be summed up under the label, 'venture capital'. Inevitably, the project comprises risk and uncertainty. The approach to adopt therefore is formulation and presentation of a business case for the application. The method is as an entrepreneur uses with his/her banker – construct a business plan. This will focus on financial needs and returns, market research and planning, and operations logistics and management. It will comprise alternative scenarios derived by risk and uncertainty modelling.

This four-way framework is a managerial prescription for IT appraisal. It is based on three premisses or principles:

1. Different IT uses have different attributes.
2. In reality, many investment and strategic decisions are not made as finance theory prescribes.
3. IT appraisal should not differ fundamentally from investment appraisal in general.

Cost benefit analysis

Whichever approach from the four-way framework is adopted, data is needed on costs and benefits of the IT project. This is an area where in capital investment appraisal in general there are significant difficulties which often are understated. Also, in IT projects, it is important to widen the appraisal beyond the economic analysis which was the focus of the last section.

McCosh *et al.* proposed in 1981 a cost benefit framework which recognized not only economic viability, but also technical and operational viability. This seems to be even more valid for the IT era as it was for the DP era. Economic viability is evaluated in terms of costs and benefits to the business. The last section concentrated on how to measure benefits and was summarized in Table 8.2.

Benefits and costs should always be differential, i.e. only those which arise from adopting the project under consideration rather than the alternative base case. Collecting costs is much easier than assessing benefits; the only difficulty is recognizing what cost items may occur. Table 8.3 provides an *aide-memoire* which reminds us that many are located in, and the responsibility of, the user area. It also reminds us that there are start up costs and ongoing costs.

Table 8.3 Cost analysis

	Technical	*User*
Development	Hardware/software purchase Hardware/software use Systems analysis and programming Professional education and training Application selling and marketing Communications	Development effort Implementation and conversion Education and training Data development and collection Displacement and disruption
Operations	Hardware/software use Data preparation Supplies and services Maintenance Communications	Support staff Data management Data collection Maintenance

Technical viability has to be assessed largely by the specialists, but needs sharp management verification. Questions to be asked include the following:

1. Is the requisite technology available and proven?
2. Are the relevant technical skills available to exploit it?

3. Are there other system dependencies involved?
4. Does the project represent a new technological risk posture?
5. Have all the technologies and interfaces been thought of?
6. Are all the technologies and interfaces necessary?
7. Does the proposal fit the architecture framework?

Asking these questions not only helps assess the project's viability, but indicates the risks and difficulties that have to be carefully managed.

Table 8.4 Cost-benefit framework

Application: shop floor data collection	Viability	Risk	Opportunity
Economic	High: could lead to improvements in production performance with up to 50% savings in waste and 30 % reduction in downtime	Dependent upon management's use of information and follow-up actions and investment	Could be a step towards automation and to achieving low cost production
Technical	Medium: some new methods involved	New technical interfaces required in new type of application for us	Chance to learn about integrated production and management systems
Operational	High: because few direct consequences for shop floor	Could be workforce anxiety on implications: consultants required	Could be means of starting quality circles

Operational viability is much more a user assessment. It is necessary because it is the implementation and use of IT applications which are critical to yielding the benefits. Thus, management should ensure the following sorts of questions are asked:

1. Is the necessary data available and reliable?
2. Do operational procedures and disciplines exist?
3. Is there support and commitment for the project?
4. Have job and organizational impacts been considered?
5. Are there opportunities for social, organizational or logistics improvements?
6. Have implications for third parties been considered?

These three tests of application viability can then be aggregated into the cost-benefit framework in Table 8.4. This is not a calculus or answer matrix. Its purpose is to aid the breadth of 'dialogue' needed to finally approve a project, rather than just concentrate on the 'ammunition' of financial returns. The matrix shown here is completed for a proposal to introduce shop floor data collection into a process plant. The framework explicates not only the three tests of viability, but also highlights any risks or special opportunities. In this way, not only is a breadth of analysis encouraged, but management, specialists and users should be prompted to recognize and understand all the implications.

This three-dimensional framework allows a subjective view to be made of risk and return for each project. It is then a short conceptual step to construction of an efficient portfolio of projects which seeks an acceptable trade-off between risk and return in total. Reducing overall risk would imply selecting only a few risky projects. Diversification of risk – as in finance theory – would imply selection of projects with negative, co-variances (i.e. whose risks are not heavily interrelated). The portfolio matrix introduced in Figure 4.4 described the mix of a manageable risk–return portfolio. To achieve this, the viability and opportunity columns of Table 8.4 indicate the returns of each project and the risk columns subjectively assess the risk. This suggests one of the linkages required between IT appraisal and IS strategy formulation.

Interlocking plans and appraisal

If IT applications are subjected to investment appraisal, it is important that the procedures are connected into strategic planning, medium-term planning and budgetary planning. Why is this?

1. Capital projects are strategic actions – equally strategic plans are implemented through capital projects.
2. Benefits of capital projects should be targeted in, and consistent with, medium-term plans – not least because other business changes will be required to ensure project success.
3. Benefits and costs of capital projects should be made accountable through budgetary planning and control, and project performance measured.

As Brealey and Myers assert:

> A good capital budgeting system does more than just make accept-reject decisions on individual projects. It must tie into the firm's long range planning process – the process that decides what lines of business the firm concentrates in and sets out plans for financing, production, marketing, research and development etc. It must also tie into a procedure for measurement of performance. Otherwise the firm has no way of knowing how its decisions about capital expenditure finally turn out.[12]

Again, IT projects are no different from capital projects in general in this regard.

The *strategic planning linkage* is threefold. First, as Chapter 4 emphasizes, IS strategy formulation is most likely to suggest priorities, directions and potential applications. When more detail is known, projects can then be appraised to ensure economic viability using the appropriate method according to application class (Table 8.2) and to assess broader criteria using the matrix in Table 8.4. Second, if an IT project arises *ad hoc* and is subjected to formal appraisal, it should also be checked against the strategic directions which will have been clarified in the IS strategy formulation process. Finally, if an IT application is discovered accidentally and perhaps through prototyping (or just strategic analysis) has been demonstrated to yield substantial competitive advantage, then further appraisal should be forgone. Formal methods should not obstruct or delay projects which will earn demonstrably good economic rents. Equally, unanticipated projects with good returns should not be rejected because they cannot be accommodated in the strategic planning or capital budget cycles.

The *medium-term planning linkage* is more subtle. First, in some organizations who practise medium-term planning, all projects would be expected to be presented in outline in the plan. This is a way of 'normalizing' the management of IT. Second, the expected benefits should be targeted or goaled in the plan and the likely costs scheduled. At the same time, all consequential or complementary changes should be identified and planned. Finally, the medium-term plan can be the vehicle by which tangible benefits are aggressively scheduled and perhaps large IT projects made more manageable by breaking down the application into modular deliverables.

> Friends Provident, the UK insurance company, has planned all its IT projects (including its successful competitive advantage applications, 'Gladis' and 'Frentel') by factoring them into manageable modules. The company's aim was to deliver a 'plum' each year to gain and retain management credibility and confidence. No single module had to take more than two years to develop and implement or consume more than seven man years' effort.

The *budgetary planning linkage* is concerned with implementation and results. IT projects for reasons of cost control and tying down benefit responsibilities should be incorporated into budget plans. Development and operational costs should be included to raise cost consciousness and aid cost control. More important, release and achievement of benefits should be built into user departmental budgets, where possible. This is one way of emphasizing that benefits are tangible. However, as for capital projects at large, there is also a good case for use of post-implementation audits of costs and benefits. This topic is discussed from p.184. Experience, and research,[13] however, suggest that post-audits are not commonly practised, and where applied usually concentrate on technical evaluation. Indeed, this finding suggests the conclusion for this section.

There are many reasons for treating IT projects as capital investments and appraising them accordingly. However incorrect or inappropriate methods should be queried and rejected. Perhaps for IT projects above all, eclectic and pragmatic approaches are required, as long as they are based on sound principles. Equally, in some cases formal appraisal should be limited or forgone – as long as management understands why the project is being approved and what needs to be done to ensure its success.

RESPONSIBILITY ACCOUNTING FOR IT

Responsibility accounting is concerned not so much with the level of the IT project but with the relationships between the IT function and the rest of the organization. Responsibility accounting is concerned with issues such as those shown in the following examples:

1. Whether IT is to be run as a business within a business and whether it should be managed as a profit centre.
2. Whether IT should be seen as investment rather than expense, and whether it should be managed as an investment centre.
3. Whether IT services should be charged out at market or cost-based prices.
4. Whether chargeout procedures can facilitate user involvement and avoid specialist control.
5. How chargeout procedures and IT accounting should interface with the host management control system.

Each of these issues is interrelated. However, their complexity demands that they be tackled in two parts. The first two issues are about responsibility centres and the other three about transfer pricing.

Responsibility accounting

Responsibility accounting is concerned with defining the performance (usually financial) expected of an organizational unit, and the accounting numbers and procedures to be adopted to measure that performance. This section therefore is conditioned by conventional theory from management accounting and management control. It is also influenced by, but not identical with, earlier writing of McFarlan and McKenney. The principal question for IT activities is what sort of responsibility centre should the IT function become on a continuum from service centre through cost centre to investment centre. Since responsibility accounting is much determined by organizational structure, the analysis of Chapter 7 is relevant. Indeed, it was suggested that control procedures were part of the total mix of organizational arrangements for IT that unfolds in the tensions between centralization and decentralization and between users and specialists.

McFarlan and McKenney use the term, 'control architecture', to describe this structuring of management control of IT. We can posit four ideal positions on the architectural continuum: service centre; cost centre; profit centre; and hybrid centre. The service centre concept is summarized in Table 8.5. 'Service' implies perhaps three characteristics:

1. Users receive no charges or cost allocations for IT resources consumed.
2. Non-financial goals are more important than financial ones in the use of IT.
3. IT is not funded from revenues or cost recovery.

The first characteristic means that users can either ignore IT or make untutored and uneconomic requests and that the specialists become insulated from user (market) influenced control. The second characteristic suggests that the mechanism may be appropriate as firms experiment with or wish to diffuse a new technology, as firms wish to stimulate investment and actions required of the turnaround quadrant of the strategic grid, or where benefits of IT services clearly far outweigh costs.

Table 8.5 Service centres for IT

Service centre Advantages	Disadvantages
Stimulates usage and experimentation	Can create uneconomic requests
Suited to stages 1 and 2 of assimilation	Can protect IT unit from accountability
Avoids accounting (charge-out) complexities	Requires good funding decisions
Avoids organizational conflicts	May dilute organizational learning
Fits turnaround (and support) quadrants	Inappropriate for strategic or factory quadrants
Promotes network/service use	Can create excessive demand
Can fit centralized IT unit	Rarely fits management control system at large

The third characteristic means that either the IT function or the organization as a whole has to propose the level of IT investment (spending) and fund it corporately.

This approach is equivalent to the McFarlan and McKenney concept of an unallocated cost centre where IT activities are a 'free resource'. There are clearly situations where this philosophy is appropriate – as Table 8.5 shows and as we shall conclude later.

> An accounting firm was very much in a turnaround situation. It was moving from little IT support in the business, other than in auditing, to aggressive use of IT for automation and competitive advantage. To facilitate interest, exploitation and usage, it did not introduce chargeout, especially as the step changes in cost were significant. However, the decision to make the overall change in IT investment level was carefully made with all partners consulted 'not least because funding came from 'partners' pockets'. When the firm began to look for structural cost improvements in its business, the IT group, like other major activities, was subject to zero base review of its budget.

The cost centre approach is summarized in Table 8.6. It implies three characteristics:

1. Costs of IT services are allocated to users through chargeout.
2. Cost consciousness and financial accountability are perceived as responsibilities of users as much as of specialists.
3. IT investments are intended to be influenced by cost and benefit analysis but not necessarily funded by cost recovery.

The first characteristic means that costs are either fully recovered by *ex post* allocation or roughly covered by apportionment rates, perhaps with efficiency and volume variance accounting, agreed through the accounting year. The second characteristic is founded on the premise that, if users incur costs for use of IT, they will:

(a) be concerned to use and conserve information services;
(b) compare benefits with costs in important IT decisions; and
(c) begin to influence the behaviour of the IT specialists and accept their responsibility in both decision-making and operation of IT activities.

The third characteristic means that funding of IT investment which is required 'up front and in chunks' has to be done from capital, not revenue, sources. Overall, the philosophy behind the cost centre approach is to introduce cost consciousness in all parties. It obviously makes sense for organizations with a cost centre architecture for management control. However, IT departments often work out how to survive this control structure, by charging for everything, balancing their payments come what may, and introducing chargeout algorithms which confuse and divide the 'opposition'. So, although it is applicable to many situations, it can lead to dysfunctional behaviour unless carefully implemented. The case below demonstrates what can go wrong.

> A chemical company ran a central IT bureau which was created to develop and operate common computer systems worldwide. This was justified by the board as necessary for implementation of a global marketing and distribution strategy. All the businesses worldwide were profit centres with considerable autonomy, their chief executives being remunerated on a profit-related scheme. The board also expected the IT bureau to be cost-conscious and from time to time, surprised by rising cost levels, imposed cut-backs. It also instructed the IT bureau to recover all its costs by chargeout, the apportioned costs being items above the profit line in businesses' management accounts. Consequently, the businesses worldwide resisted the common systems; some set up their own IT operations; and all complained and argued about the costs and benefits. As support and use of the bureau faltered, the board applied more budget constraints on it. By the time the necessary

Table 8.6 Cost centres for IT

Cost centre Advantages	Disadvantages
Encourages reasoned use requests	Can be a deterrent to IT use
Creates controls on IT	Can focus on costs not benefits
Suits stage 3 and 4 of assimilation	Can cause arguments
Satisfies desire for chargeout	Many accounting choices
Relatively simple accounting	Disliked in profit centre organizations
Fits cost centre organizations	Often unsatisfactory in practice
Suits all quadrants of strategic grid	

finesses were made to the responsibility accounting, the business strategy was being questioned and the whole organization restructured.

The profit centre approach is summarized in Table 8.7. It suggests three or four characteristics:

1. IT services are charged out at cost plus – often market – prices.
2. 'Market forces' and 'customer orientation' are brought to bear on the IT function and its relationship with users.
3. The IT department is set up more as a business unit or business venture (see Chapter 7) on the principle of 'a business within a business'.
4. The IT business venture may be funded by a capital injection and capital issues, and/or through long-term business planning and be expected to earn a targeted return on investment centre. In other words, it is an investment centre.

The first characteristic means that *prices* for IT services are preferably guided by those prevailing in the market place or based on a cost–plus profit margin principle. The second characteristic means that users often have a choice whether to buy their services from the internal IT group or from outside. Equally, the IT group may have the freedom to sell services externally as well as internally. The third characteristic is commercially appealing, but has many pitfalls; however, it clearly suits bureaux and information services agencies. Indeed, these organizations may possess the fourth characteristic and become another business stream in the host organization's portfolio. Almost certainly, an investment centre will feel it should influence both the level and use of capital investment and thus will pursue external as well as internal business opportunities.

Table 8.7 Profit centres for IT

Profit centre Advantages	Disadvantages
IT function has to control costs	IT function can cut costs and service
IT function has to market itself	IT function may go external
IT user partnership can be forged	Users may act as short-term traders
IT activities may become innovative	IT function may become too entrepreneurial
Suits stages 3 and 4 assimilation	Can discourage experimentation and risks
Suits support and possibly strategic quadrants	Can conflict with business strategic need
Fits profit centre organization	Can be seen as a game
Suits bureau or business ventures	Can create under–utilized IT resources
May focus attention on assets	Can lead to ROI management

Table 8.7 summarizes many arguments for and against profit centres. What stands out is:

(a) the ability (or desire) to change the behaviour of IT departments; and
(b) the risk that this will change too much.

Also, specifying and agreeing the transfer price is not at all easy – see later – and treating IT departments as profit centres can often lead to dilemmas of direction, funding and performance measurement which would be simpler or non-existent if profit accountability were not so strong.

> An engineering services division of a conglomerate was set up as a profit centre in line with all its customer divisions. It was told it must stand on its own feet. Accordingly, it chose to sell its services outside as well as internally. It developed its capabilities in advanced CAD. Ninety per cent of this business was external, some being with the host firm's competitors. The host firm became quite backward in engineering applications of IT in general and CAD in particular.

> A manufacturing company set up a central unit separate from the central data processing department to drive, develop and facilitate end-user computing in the group. Known as the microsystems unit (MSU), it was set up as a profit centre business venture. It was expected to meet a profit plan and finance itself. Thus it chose to supply microcomputers, buying at a group discount and selling internally at a margin. It also offered microcomputing support and microsystems development. In theory, the computer sales would generate the early profits and create funding to subsidize and pump-prime development activities. After three years, computer sales fell away as demand reduced and local external agents offered similar or better deals. Meanwhile, the MSU had become very good at selling computers because this generated cash, it was easier than development and local businesses did not have faith in the ability of a central unit to develop relevant applications. It became clear that the MSU could not survive as a profit centre business venture and it was wound up. What had been achieved was reasonable standardization of personal computer acquisition. However, the profit centre policy mitigated against achieving the other non-financial objectives of the MSU.

Given that in Chapter 7 it was suggested that organization and control arrangements for IT tend to be a mix of solutions in complex organizations, neat, black and white responsibility centre charters may sometimes be inappropriate. Not only may service centres, cost centres and profit or investment centres for IT exist in the same organization, but an IT department may be given mixed financial responsibilities. Such 'hybrid centres' can be thought of as a mixed economy. This approach is summarized in Table 8.8.

Table 8.8 Hybrid centres for IT

Hybrid centre *Advantages*	*Disadvantages*
Can manage IT loosely and tightly	Can be confusing
Suits stage 4 assimilation	May be misfit with host management controls
Suits different assimilation stages for different technologies	Can cause internal (functional) conflicts
Fits turnaround and strategic quadrants	Can encourage cross-subsidies
Facilitates central push in decentralized context	Needs strong direction
Can separate development from operations	Can be complex accounting

The hybrid concept has three characteristics:

1. Some IT activities are charged out to users and some are subsidized centrally.
2. Innovative, imposed and turnaround activities are managed loosely and routine, requested and core activities are managed tightly.
3. The IT function is given clear financial and non-financial goals.

Collectively, these characteristics recognize the advantages and disadvantages of each of the other three responsibility centres. The hybrid approach states that some activities should be cost centre managed, some service centre and some profit centre – and these may change over time. The more mixed are the positions on the technology assimilation curves and the more the management implications of the firm's positioning on the strategic grid clash with the host organization's management control system, the clearer is the case for running IT as a mixed economy. It may well be that unofficially some cost centre, profit centre or service centre IT departments are *de facto* run as hybrid centres. For example, budget variances may be sanctioned; under- or over-recovery charging rates may deliberately create central suspense accounts which reflect a level of discretionary funding; some initiatives may be sanctioned and not accounted for in order to make a start.

> A corporate IS department was directed to provide corporate infrastructure, such as the communications network, manage facilities for divisions on request, provide software development and advisory services on a negotiated contract basis, and pursue innovative projects approved and funded by a corporate policy committee. Infrastructure was to be fully cost recovered over the project life-cycle. Facilities management was to be agreed and contracted for at negotiated market rates. Services were to be supplied at market prices on a competitive basis. Innovative projects were not to be charged at all. The host organization was structured into profit centres. The rationale of the hybrid solution adopted was to follow the profit centre philosophy except for synergistic infrastructure and centrally pushed innovation.

Frameworks for selecting appropriate responsibility centres and transfer pricing are offered later. However, the empirical evidence is interesting. Earl, in 1983, found that most European businesses still adopted cost centre philosophies in their management control of IT. Four years later, Feeny *et al.* found the same trend in their organizational study. Indeed, organizations placing themselves in turnaround or strategic positions on the strategic grid found that complex chargeout systems and profit centre accountability often got in the way of integrating the IT function with the rest of the business and impeded investment for innovation and strategic change. Of course, chargeout and responsibility accounting are intertwined. Thus, the next section addresses the difficulties of the chargeout question.

Transfer pricing

Transfer pricing for IT, or chargeout, is frequently an emotional matter. In principle, selection of any transfer pricing method should be a function of the management control system in operation. However, chargeout of IT is:

(a) sometimes designed and applied without thought to management control principles or to the behaviour it will stimulate; and

(b) in all situations an inherently complex issue.

There are four principal chargeout mechanisms available: cost-based; market price; dual method; and no price.

Cost-based approaches seem commonest. Table 8.9 summarizes the arguments. The advantages and disadvantages are similar to those for all cost-based transfer prices. However, defining and measuring cost can be very difficult, given the variety of resources involved, the fixed, variable and stepped behaviours of IT costs, and the frequent desire to recover all or most of them. Furthermore, full costs get compared with unlike external rates based on marginal, joint or discounted costs. Finally, the multi-factor chargeout algorithms which result, often producing varying costs over time, can cause endless confusion and conflict. Recent experience and trends suggest that three finesses of cost-based methods help:

1. Base the cost rates on units that users see they consume or feel they influence, e.g., cost per transaction, page, or screen and standard cost per development hour.
2. Ensure standard costing is applied where feasible so that efficiency variances are charged to IT departments and planned utilization variances applied to a central charging account; the latter implies setting activity levels in budget planning.
3. If user departments are profit centres, consider carefully whether it is motivationally better to account for chargeout items above or below their accountable profit line.

Table 8.9 Cost-based chargeout

Cost-based chargeout Advantages	Disadvantages
Fits cost centre control	Can pass IT inefficiencies to users
Can fit profit centre control by cost plus	Costs users more and provides no market comparison
Creates cost consciousness	
Simple in concept	Can be compared with irrelevant prices
	Complex in practice to define and apply

Market-based methods would seem to fit profit centre regimes, suit IT departments that are business ventures, and introduce market forces thinking to IT decision-making. The approach is summarized in Table 8.10. As in transfer pricing in general, market-based prices seem fair to users, might be regarded as efficient prices to guide decision-making and provide incentives to the supplier department. In IT, however, markets are rarely efficient and comparable services often cannot be found. There is too much marginal cost pricing, product discounting and user-provider asymmetry of information and knowledge. Furthermore, needs are often unique, unclear or not really price-sensitive. Moreover, the market philosophy can encourage users to buy outside and suppliers to sell outside – when this may not be in the firm's strategic interest or may cause underutilization problems and erode critical mass. Pragmatic guidelines for successful market-based pricing therefore are:

1. Restrict it to routine, mature and structured services and then use market prices as a guideline.

2. Consider carefully whether external supply or purchase of services should be prohibited.
3. Adopt it only for those IT resources or activities it really fits and adopt other methods elsewhere – the hybrid centre concept.

Table 8.10 Market-based chargeout

Market-based chargeout Advantages	Disadvantages
Provide external standards	
Suits profit centres and business ventures	Comparable or efficient markets may not exist
Can negotiate prices	May lead to users and IT entering the market
Avoids cost definition	May cause conflicts needing resolution
	Difficult for shared or common resources

Dual approaches involve sophisticating the chargeout system so that users are charged at standard cost but the IT department is credited with standard cost plus or minus the variances plus a standard profit margin. For bookkeeping purposes, the uncharged profit margin is charged to a central charging account. This implies that the IT supplier is a quasi-profit centre.[14] The approach is summarized in Table 8.11. It probably suffers the same general disadvantages noted by Dittman and Ferris. It is seen to be artificial accounting, it can be complex and costly to apply, and the IT department knows that it is not really a profit centre. It is more sensible to use market prices and cost-based prices appropriately in tandem, treating the IT department as a hybrid centre.

Table 8.11 Dual chargeout

Dual chargeout Advantages	Disadvantages
Motivates IT supplies and users	Often seen as artificial
Can fit profit centre organization	Expensive to administer
Can help supplier-user partnership	Still needs sound cost definition

'No chargeout' is not unknown. It is consistent with service centre responsibility accounting and with encouraging and funding innovation and early adoption of a technology. Table 8.12 summarizes the arguments. There are activities and times when no chargeout is appropriate. In practice, this approach may co-exist with any of the other three methods.

Table 8.12 No chargeout

No chargeout Advantages	Disadvantages
Suits service centres	Ignores cost consciousness
Encourages innovation	Encourages irresponsible use and demands
Avoids conflict	Often misfit with management control system

Whichever method is adopted, it is important to realize that chargeout is a form of transfer pricing and thus should meet the following criteria:

1. It must be understandable and predictable for users.
2. It must be fair to performance measurement of both parties.
3. It must be realistic in reflecting consumption of resources.
4. It must be capable of accounting and administration.
5. It must fit the responsibility accounting system.
6. It must facilitate goal congruence such that decisions are made in the interests of the organization as a whole.

A contingency approach

It is clear that the link between chargeout and transfer pricing is inextricable. Allen argues that profit centre responsibility accounting and chargeout can fit all circumstances and ensure IT services contribute to the corporate good rather than act as a drain on resources. With profit centre performance measurement, flexible budgeting, price rather than cost-based chargeout, authority of supplier and buyer to incur cost, and user responsibility for acquisition decisions, he argues that service levels improve, better investment decisions are made, users become more informed, the budget-setting and funding problems disappear and the adoption of new technology is facilitated. Allen's arguments are persuasive. The trouble is that empirical evidence suggests this normative solution is problematical. Important complications in practice seem to be maturing of management understanding, strategic importance of IT and the organizational control context.

These factors are depicted in Figure 8.2 which proposes a contingency framework for tackling the responsibility accounting and chargeout problem. In short, certain solutions seem appropriate to different situations, depending on the management behaviour desired. The earlier analysis and examples suggest this contingency framework. In complex organizations, however, a mix of conditions may prevail. That is why a mix of solutions may be adopted – but Figure 8.2 still helps in the selection of the mix.

Figure 8.2 makes the following suggestions:

1. Profit centre with cost plus or market based chargeout suits:
    (a) stage 3 of technology assimilation curves where control, profitability and market pressures are brought to bear on the IT function;
    (b) support positions in the strategic grid where IT applications can safely be made on make or buy and affordability criteria; and
    (c) decentralized contexts where most business units are profit responsible and managements have autonomous authority over input and output decisions.
2. Hybrid centre with mixed or dual chargeout suits:
    (a) stage 4 of technology assimilation curves where specialist and user managements are mature and working in partnership;
    (b) strategic positions on the strategic grid where development and operations comprise a mix of infrastructural, routine and strategic applications involving shared, competitively determined and up front costs; and

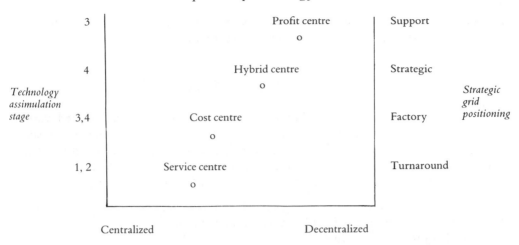

Figure 8.2 A contingent framework for responsibility accounting of IT.

(c) largely decentralized contexts where some central intervention and strategic control is practised, or matrix structures where functions have to strike a balance with line businesses.

3. Cost centre with fully recoverable or budgeted cost chargeout suits:
   (a) stage 3 or 4 of technology assimilation curves where users are expected to be accountable for IT costs and benefits;
   (b) factory positions on the strategic grid where tightly controlled but reliable performance is asked of the IT department; and
   (c) cost centre management control contexts where central directives set performance expectations for business lines and functions.

4. Service centre with no or budgeted cost chargeout suits:
   (a) stage 1 or 2 of technology assimilation curves where experimentation, innovation or diffusion are to be encouraged;
   (b) turnaround positions on the strategic grid where directional planning and earmarked funding override normal planning and control of IT; and
   (c) centralized organizations where bureaucratic control procedures decide who should do what with IT.

The positions on Figure 8.2 are ideal matches of the three contingent factors. Where compromises have to be made, the tendencies of each axis should not be ignored too much. This framework suggests a decision logic for designing responsibility accounting for IT. It comprises six steps:

1. Assess the stage of assimilation for each technology.
2. Position the overall business on the strategic grid.
3. Check the character of the organization's management control system.

Having assessed these primary determinants, take the final three steps:

4. Check that the accounting requirements can be met.

5. Assess, or simulate, whether the approach will generate the intended behaviours.
6. Ensure all parties understand and agree the approach.

EVALUATING IT

Funding, appraising and responsibility accounting for IT have all implied various degrees of evaluation. In this section, the concern is with *performance evaluation*. Although evaluation is riddled with theoretical, methodological and practical issues, most organizations ask themselves questions about IT activities which require different aspects of evaluation to be tackled. These questions include the following:

1. How do we know if we are getting value for money from IT?
2. How do we compare in IT with similar organizations?
3. Was that project successful?
4. Is that IT investment yielding the promised returns?
5. Is our IT department doing well or badly?
6. What are the information systems like in this potential acquisition?

Three levels of performance measurement are suggested by these questions: organizational; departmental; and system or project. In addition, there is a set of accounting questions in the background.

Performance measurement

At the *organizational* level, three approaches are found. First, organizations measure IT spending ratios – as discussed in the funding section of this chapter (p. 159) – and compare these with like organizations or sector averages. Common ratios are annual spending on IT divided by sales turnover or operating costs, annual spending on IT per employee or class of employee, and annual spending on IT by business function or IT activity. Large negative or positive variances from the average may prompt some sharp questions about efficiency, effectiveness or commitment – but it is important to be able to explain the relative positioning whatever the variance. Annual growth rates, as well as absolute levels of expenditure can be useful indicators of performance or intentions – of the competition as well as the host organization.

Another approach, where the organization has one identifiable IT unit, is to compare actual performance against the goals implied by the responsibility accounting system. This only gives an internal perspective. So largely does the third approach which is to compare annually in a subjective, multi-factor fashion, overall performance against the mission, mandate and objectives set by the information management strategy. This review will be done normally by an IT steering or policy committee.

At the *departmental* level, four approaches are available. Spending ratios again can be informative, for example, comparing development to maintenance cost ratios over time, or hardware to software cost ratios. Again, these measures only raise questions; they do not imply any right answers.

More objectively, synthetics or standards of performance can be employed. Comparisons of actual cost or resource units per program, system or computer run can be made with manufacturer-supplied synthetics or historical performance over time. One method which seeks to assess the relationship of input to output in performance measures is to divide development cost, maintenance cost, operations cost, or MIPS capacity by function points delivered.[15] Function points are valuable traceable system functionalities delivered to users. Such measures not only help assess departmental performance, but also indicate the power of alternative tools, techniques and methods.

Multi-factor approaches can comprise assessing ability over time to meet promised dates, comparing actual performance against responsibility accounting targets such as cost, profit or return on investment budgets, assessing responsiveness to business demands and user requests, asking if behaviour is consistent with positioning on the strategic grid, tracing movements in the level of systems backlog and commissioning user satisfaction surveys. Such multi-dimensional assessment is best done by the IT policy committee or the IT board.

Continuous evaluation routines within the department and between the department and users have the merit of linking management controls to operational actions. Examples include measurement of operations performance by downtime and recoverability reporting, measure of development performance by reporting on project costs, timescales and goal achievement, and checking overall performance by examining the level of customer complaints. Increasingly, such factors are being built into service agreements made between supplier departments and users. Since these are equivalent to supply, quality and maintenance contracts, the measures should be user-oriented not technology-focused.

At the *project or system level*, post-audits can be employed. Two types of post-implementation review exist: product review and process review. The first evaluates whether a system is achieving its intended benefits. The second assesses the performance of the project to ask what can be learnt next time.

The *product review* asks whether the objectives of the IT application have been met. These clearly include those identified in the economic, technical and operational technical assessment done in the *ex ante* cost-benefit analysis but now both benefits and costs should have become tangible. Thus, the review needs to be done at least one year after system implementation to give time for the costs and benefits to materialize. Equally, since benefits depend largely on users and costs on both users and providers, both parties must be involved – preferably aided by a third party who can provide process and method skills. Internal auditors sometimes fill this role; they should be skilled at verifying by factual, experiential and cross-referencing means, the benefits claimed.

There are four reasons for doing product reviews:

1. To check if cost and benefit goals have been met.
2. To discover any problems or further facilities that need addressing.
3. To discover what unanticipated benefits have occurred and whether these can be exploited further.
4. To learn about new applications and about future cost-benefit analysis.

All post-audit reviews, however, suffer from inherent difficulties. It is difficult to identify cause and effect between investment and subsequent performance, especially to separate out the effects of IT. Organizational members involved tend to feel they are being assessed and thus act defensively. Furthermore, most actors are adept at recreating history or have deficient or biased memories. Finally, it is often felt that the resource and skill required may be more effectively deployed on other matters. Perhaps this is why post audits seem to be rarely practised. There are perhaps three ways of helping to make them work:

1. Be content with measuring overall impact when assessing actual costs and benefits; looking for cause and effect and isolating the IT contribution may be impractical.
2. Estimate costs and benefits in broad numbers, remembering both costs and benefits are often twice the levels suggested.
3. Focus on what needs to be done now and what is new to be learnt, rather than on past performance and blame apportionment.

The *process review* asks what can be learnt from the project just completed about future project management and systems development. It should be done soon after system implementation while memories are fresh and relevant personnel available. However, it is as rarely practised as product review. Yet, since projects are temporary organizations, and organizations seem to learn about systems development only slowly or from catastrophes, process reviews make sense. There are some useful questions to be asked:

1. Was project performance – cost, timescales etc. – to plan?
2. What went wrong and why?
3. Were any new problems or challenges experienced?
4. What lessons can be learnt for the future?
5. Are there any early indicators about product review?

Since IT applications projects involve many parties, all should contribute to the review. The sensitivities involved suggest that the assistance of an organizational development specialist can help in detecting issues, resolving conflicts, explicating important issues and ensuring all relevant factors (technical, economic, personal, organizational and managerial) are considered. For routine projects, the process review report would form part of normal documentation and be received by a project management committee. For large or unusual projects, the report might be received by the IT steering committee, policy committee, board or forum, and perhaps be published for widespread reference.

Accounting for IT

One form of evaluation of IT is its treatment by financial statements. Whether IT is treated as an expense or as investment is not only a conceptual matter, it is an accounting problem. If we believe that financial reporting practice influences external and internal attitudes and decision-making it is worth examining how to account for IT. At the minimum, IT activities will be treated as period expenses on the income statement, probably subsumed within the cost of sales and administration items. Why might IT deserve more 'serious' treatment than this?

1. IT and its applications have the size, longevity and purpose of assets and investment, so should they not be capitalized on the balance sheet and depreciated

through the income statement?

2. The four classes of IT use identified in Chapter 1 all imply pursuit of substantial commercial returns, so should not valuation be based on concepts of economic value rather than historic cost of acquisition? ('Economic value' implies valuation of expected cash flows from the investment on a net present value basis. 'Economic depreciation' records the negative periodic change in this.)

3. Many IT applications have slow but progressively increasing returns, so might it not make sense to capitalize them and amortize their value by the annuity method or even on a basis of economic depreciation?

4. IT and its application represents a cumulative investment in, and an asset of, the business, so should they not be shown on the balance sheet?

These are technical arguments. Managerial issues include the following:

1. If IT is to be regarded as an investment rather than an expense, it should be valued and costed as such in the accounts to raise this consciousness.

2. If IT hardware and/or software are treated as items of expense, this may act as a deterrent to investment – not only because of the immediate but unexplained impact on reported profits, but because management accounts may adopt the same policy and have similar short-term impact on internal performance measurement.

3. If maintenance, enhancement and renewal of IT applications are to be tackled more aggressively, accounting for them as capital assets may encourage planned maintenance and renewal, adequate funding through explicit depreciation policies, and easier approval by being able to capitalize rather than cost some of the expenditure.

4. If IT spending (wholly defined) is a major part of a firm's capital expenditure, it should be shown on the balance sheet as part of the asset structure of the business.

A UK firm was acquiring a subsidiary of a US conglomerate. At the last stage of legal proceedings, the acquirer's IT director was asked to look at the clause 'which says something about systems'. It turned out that the firm was to be sold without its systems (because they ran on the holding company's computer). The negotiators had not hitherto realized that:

(a) the firm without its systems was not a going concern;
(b) lack of systems might represent a decrease in company valuation and certainly extra cost of the acquirer, and
(c) the balance sheet and income statement had provided no meaningful information on an important aspect of the business capability and advantage.

The technical and managerial arguments above neither represent a revolutionary concept nor specify major practical steps to be taken. However, in the author's experience, the accounting treatment of IT is varied, *ad hoc*, often arbitrary and sometimes absent. For example, hardware lives for depreciation purposes vary significantly. Software is rarely capitalized. IT expenses are not identifiable in income statements. Maintenance and enhancement is rarely capitalized. Merger and acquisition assessments are rarely informed from financial statements about IT. Yet the accounting standards of England and Wales and the International Accounting Standards body give useful scope for more serious accounting treatment, viz:

Fixed assets are those which are intended for use on a continuing basis in the enterprise's activities.[16]

Depreciation is a measure of the wearing out, consumption or other permanent loss of value of a fixed asset, whether arising from use, effluxion of time or obsolescence through technical or market changes. Depreciation should be allocated so as to charge a fair proportion of cost or valuation to each accounting period expected to benefit from the use of the asset.[17]

The assessment of depreciation, and its allocation to accounting periods, involves consideration of three factors . . . the carrying amount of the asset . . . the length of its expected useful economic life to the business of the enterprise, having due regard to the incidence of the obsolescence . . . the estimated residual value of the asset. . . .[18]

The useful economic lives of assets should be reviewed regularly, and where necessary revised.[19]

There is a range of acceptable depreciation methods; management should select the method regarded as most appropriate to the type of asset and its use in the business, so as to allocate depreciation as fairly as possible to the periods expected to benefit from the use of the asset. . . .[20]

The term, 'research and development', is currently used to cover a wide range of activities . . . it is generally possible to recognise three broad categories of activity, namely, pure research (work directed primarily towards the advancement of knowledge), applied research (work directed primarily towards exploiting pure research other than work defined as development expenditure), and development (work directed towards the introduction or improvement of specific products or processes). . . . The definitions . . . have been based on those used by the Organisation for Economic Cooperation and Development. . . .[21]

Expenditure incurred on pure and applied research can be regarded as part of a continuing operation required to maintain a company's business and competitive position. In general, one particular period rather than another will not be expected to benefit and therefore it is appropriate that these costs should be written off as they are incurred. The development of new and improved products is, however, distinguishable from pure and applied research. Expenditure on such development is normally undertaken with a reasonable expectation of specific commercial success and of future benefits arising from the work, either from increased revenue and related profits or from reduced costs. On these grounds, it may be argued that such expenditure should be deferred to be matched against the future revenue.[22]

It is usual for the value of a business as a whole to differ from the value of its separate net assets. The difference . . . is described as goodwill. . . . In deciding whether a particular asset falls into the category of separable net assets, the test is whether that asset could be identified and sold separately without disposing of the business as a whole.[23]

Purchased goodwill . . . should normally be eliminated from the accounts immediately on acquisition against reserves. . . . Purchased goodwill . . . may be eliminated from the accounts by amortisation through the profit and loss account in arriving at profit or loss on ordinary activities on a systematic basis over its useful economic life.[24]

The first five statements indicate that long-term assets such as technology can be valued on an economic basis and depreciated on whatever basis seems appropriate. The sixth and seventh statements indicate that most IT applications can be treated as 'development' and therefore capitalized on the balance sheet and amortized through the income statement. The accounting standard on research and development goes on to describe uncertainties typical of development projects and advises that, where they exist, the expenditure should not be capitalized. However, if most of the uncertainties described were present in an IT project, most IT professionals and managers would not approve the application at project appraisal stage – *unless* it was formally regarded as an experimental or R & D IT project. The last two statements suggest that, when accounting for acquisitions, most systems would be regarded as goodwill and either written off against reserves or amortized through the income statement over their economic life. The technologies themselves are likely to be regarded as separate net assets and included as fixed assets on the balance sheet and depreciated.

The principal management conclusion about accounting for IT is this. In managing IT as a strategic resource, firms should ask whether current accounting treatment could possibly be creating uninformed attitudes or acting as a deterrent to investment and action. If so, they should work within the flexibilities allowed and adopt more appropriate accounting policies.

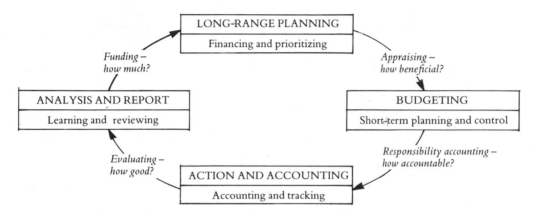

Figure 8.3 Paying for IT: a control model.

SUMMARY AND CONCLUSIONS

This chapter has suggested that the important aspects of management control of IT activities fall into four areas. Figure 8.3 portrays this classification within the traditional model of management control. It is couched in terms of paying for IT because this is how most management control concerns arise at the enterprise and corporate levels. The model suggests how the four control issues are interconnected and feed forwards and backwards on each other.

Hopefully, the overall control philosophy is driven by the mission for IT. Indeed, if an information management strategy, as discussed in Chapter 6, has been formulated, the mission or mandate should drive the management control of IT activities. Building on Parson's model of linkage strategies – called mandates in Chapter 6 – Table 8.13 suggests the different characteristics in control and controls involved. This model is not intended to be prescriptive. Management control is never so neat, tidy and integrated as that. Designing the management control of IT activities requires appreciation, understanding and analysis of each of the areas discussed in this chapter. The model in Table 8.13 merely suggests the relationship between management control and strategic mandate in two ways. The likely strategic management consequences of any particular management control practice can be judged by seeing what mandate heads the column in which the practice is found. Alternatively, the most characteristic management

Table 8.13 IT mandates and directions of management control

Mandate/ control issue	Centrally planned	Leading edge	Free market	Monopoly	Scarce resource	Necessary evil
Strategic grid	Strategic or turnaround	Turnaround or strategic	Turnaround or support	Factory or support	Support or factory	Support
Funding	Strategic planning	Discretionary directional spend	Revenue based	Committee review	Budget driven	*Ad hoc*
Appraising	Four-way framework	Informal justification	Users justify	Formal cost benefit analysis	Return on investment	Payback/ urgency
Responsibility accounting	Profit centre	Service centre	Profit centre	Cost centre	Cost centre	Cost centre
Evaluation	Strategic impact	Strategic change	Financial goals	User satisfaction	Resource productivity	Not noticed

control practices for each strategic mandate can be found by reading down the relevant column.

Overall, however, six conclusions can be drawn about the strategic management control of IT activities:

1. Spending levels on IT are a function of IS strategic direction and the number of positive net present value projects available.
2. IT should be managed as an investment, not an expense.
3. Economic appraisal of IT projects would be improved by use of multi-stage methodologies or the four-way framework. The wider three-dimensional cost benefit analysis matrix can then be applied.
4. Chargeout and responsibility accounting for IT are interrelated. The appropriate arrangements for any firm are likely to be influenced by the strategic importance of IT, the stages of technology assimilation, and the pattern of organizational control.
5. Measurement of performance in IT involves evaluation at three different levels. Many methods are available; most require careful and sensitive application.
6. Accounting for IT can give misinformed views about a firm's IT assets and some accounting practices may deter investment in IT. However, there is scope to choose more appropriate policies.

NOTES AND REFERENCES

1. See Nolan, Norton & Co., *Stage by Stage*, European issue, Spring 1985.
2. See Price Waterhouse, *Information Technology Review 1987/8*.
3. *Ibid.*
4. See Nolan, Norton & Co., *Stage by Stage*, 1985.
5. Despite popular claims and beliefs to the contrary, a CBI report in 1987 concluded that 'the city was not short-term' in its thinking and that 'communication' between industry and the city was the major area in need of improvement. See CBI, *Investing for Britain's Future*, Confederation of British Industry, London, 1987.
6. See the literature on advanced manufacturing technology, for example ACARD, *New Opportunities in Manufacturing: The Management of Technology*, Advisory Council for Applied Research and Development, HMSO, London, 1983, and Gold B., 'CAM' sets new results for production', *Harvard Business Review*, November–December 1982.

7. For a discussion of capital budgeting and alternative techniques see any major corporate finance textbook, for example Brealey R. and Myers S., *Principles of Corporate Finance*, McGraw-Hill, 1981.
8. See, for example, Kester W.C., 'Today's options for tomorrow's growth', *Harvard Business Review*, March-April 1984.
9. See Earl M.J., Feeny D.F., Lockett M. and Runge D.A., 'IT, competitive advantage and innovation: maxims for senior managers', Oxford Institute of Information Management research and discussion paper (RDP 88/2), Templeton College, Oxford, 1988.
10. See Ives B. and Vitale M., 'Competitive information systems: some organisational design considerations', in Earl M.J. (ed.), *The Information Systems Organisation of Tomorrow*. Oxford Institute of Information Management and PA Computers and Telecommunications, London, 1988.
11. See Earl *et al., op. cit.*
12. Brearley and Myers, *op. cit.*, p. 233.
13. See Brown C. and Blackler F., Current British practice in the evaluation of new information technologies', *ESRC Newsletter* (No. 58), September 1986.
14. A term used by Dittman and Ferris in their study of transfer pricing in general: Dittman D.A. and Ferris K.R., 'Profit centre – a satisfaction generating concept', *Accounting and Business Research* (No. 32), Autumn 1978.
15. See Butler Cox Foundation, 'Measuring the performance of the information systems function', Report No. 48, Butler Cox Foundation, December 1985.
16. Accounting Standards Committee, *Accounting for Depreciation*, ED37.
17. *Ibid.*
18. *Ibid.*
19. *Ibid.*
20. *Ibid.*
21. Accounting Standards Committee, *Accounting fo. Research and Development*, SSAP13.
22. *Ibid.*
23. Accounting Standards Committee, *Accounting for Goodwill*, SSAP22.
24. *Ibid.*

FURTHER READING

Allen B., 'Making information services pay its way', *Harvard Business Review*, January-February 1987.

Brearley R. and Myers S., *Principles of Corporate Finance*, McGraw-Hill, 1981.

Dittman D.A. and Ferris K.R., 'Profit centres – a satisfaction generating 'concept'. *Accounting and Business Research* (No. 32), Autumn 1978.

Earl, M.J., and Hopwood, A.G., 'From management information to information management', in H. Lucas, F. Land, T. Lincoln and K. Supper (eds), *The Information Systems Environment*, North-Holland, 1980.

Kaplan, R.S., 'Must CIM be justified by faith alone?' *Harvard Business Review*, March-April 1986.

McCosh, A.M., Rahman, M. and Earl, M.J., *Developing Managerial Information Systems*, Macmillan, 1981.

McFarlan, F.W., and McKenney, J.L., *Corporate Information Systems Management: The Issues Facing Senior Executives*, Dow Jones Irwin, 1983.

Meredith, J. R., and Hill, M.M., 'Justifying new manufacturing systems: a managerial approach', *Sloan Management Review*, Summer 1987.

Nolan, R.L., *Management Accounting and Control of Data Processing*, National Association of Accountants, 1977.

Parsons, G.L., 'Fitting information systems technology to the corporate needs: the linking strategy', Harvard Business School, teaching note 9–183–176, 1985.

Price Waterhouse, *Information Technology Review 1987/8*, Price Waterhouse, London, 1987.

Chapter 9

CHANGE STRATEGIES FOR STRATEGIC CHANGE

INTRODUCTION

In Chapter 1 it was suggested that the 1980s were seeing the realization of the information economy or post-industrial society where information processing activities and knowledge-based skills were becoming critical to most socio-economic endeavours. Further, it was asserted that IT within this context already was being exploited by corporations for strategic advantage. Finally, it was concluded that in this new IT era, information management was turning out to be quite different in many fundamental respects from the traditions that had grown up in the last twenty years of the DP era. This scenario is one in which the ability to make and manage *strategic change* will differentiate the leaders from the laggards.

As the 1980s begin to close, three general management trends are observable. First, the most conservative actors in this transition phase are often the IT professionals who have not caught up with this changing world. Conversely, it is often users and their managers who are pushing for technological advance and initiating change. Commonly, however, at senior management levels there is a visible technology gap – in the sense that the business, organizational and management implications of IT are not fully understood and that there is a lack of confidence in the arguments about either the strategic nature of IT or the ability of firms to harness it. So, collectively, these dynamics suggest that managing strategic change will continue to be difficult. Fortunately we are able to learn from those organizations who are successfully managing the transition.

However, a recurring theme of this book has been that not all organizations face an identical challenge. Their sector contexts differ, the competitive forces they combat vary, their histories are not alike, and they make different strategic choices. Thus it is imperative that each organization understands the nature of the strategic change it must make, works out the pace of change required, and adopts appropriate change strategies.

Organizations can begin by asking themselves at any point in time the checklist of planning, organization and control questions in Table 9.1. This helps assess and understand the degree of change in information management that is required to help

192

ensure that IT becomes a source of strategic advantage and not a strategic exposure. It is thus a useful checklist for discovering whether the transition is being made from the DP era to the IT era. But that is all. How to identify, make and manage the appropriate degree of strategic change are the concerns of the remainder of this chapter.

Table 9.1 Checklist for reviewing information management

Information management questions

Planning
1. Do your IT projects support the business objectives and strategies of your company?
2. Do you continuously examine what innovative opportunities IT can provide for strategic gain?
3. Are you adequately informed on the current and potential use of IT by competitive forces in your sector?
4. Do you have an adequate picture of the coverage and quality of your IT systems?
5. Are you confident that current technology policies and standards fit your business?
6. Are you content with how IT project priorities are set?

Organization
1. Are user ideas given due attention in planning and implementation?
2. Do your IT specialists understand your business and organizations?
3. Does the structure of your IT function fit your organization?
4. Are specialist-user relations constructive?
5. Do senior managers understand the potentials and implications of IT?
6. Are you developing the right IT specialists and users for the future?

Control
1. Are the responsibility and authority for IT direction, development and operations clear?
2. Is your expenditure on IT in appropriate areas and activities?
3. Are you confident that IT project proposals are properly appraised?
4. Do you know if the IT function is doing well or badly?
5. Is the IT function clear about goals, responsibilities and performance criteria?
6. How easy is it for brightsparks to succeed or risks to be taken?

The first section provides some frameworks for the strategic management of IT. Then the vital foundations of change, namely education and development, are examined. Keys to transforming the IT organization are proposed in the final section. This leads into a set of information management maxims which close the book.

STRATEGIC MANAGEMENT FRAMEWORKS

Both general managers and IT managers, if they accept that significant change is required in corporate information management, often demand to know what tangible, managerial actions are required. It is useful therefore to have a model by which different situations or postures can be compared. It also helps to understand how different businesses or sectors should respond. Finally, it could be valuable to have a model of the leadership required to manage the transition. This section develops three frameworks which address these issues.

Strategic grid extended

McFarlan and McKenney's strategic grid has been borrowed, interpreted and built upon in several chapters so far. We can now synthesize these thoughts by expanding

Table 9.2 Strategic management typology

	Strategic grid/ management responses	Support	Factory	Turnaround	Strategic
Management	IT planning mode	*Ad hoc*	Resource	Directional	Strategic
	Nature of IT organization	Back room	Department	Function	Complex
	IT control mode	Project	Budget	Programme	Mixed
	Technology policies	Eclectic	Conventional	Rethink	Architectural
Change strategies	IT spending patterns	Low	Average	Stepped	Compound
	IT executive	Specialist	Manager	Executive	Director
	Evaluation of IT	Exceptions	Audit	Visibility	Impact
	IT education	Self-taught	Professional	Management	Continuing

the management extrapolation of the grid introduced in Chapter 2 to include change strategies for each quadrant. Table 9.2 does this and is perhaps best understood by examining typical information management change strategies for firms in the turnaround quadrant. Here the degree of change required is highest.

Turnaround management therefore requires a directional emphasis in planning the use of IT. Focusing on major opportunities, threats and critical success factors is a typical posture for firms who discover that the strategic importance of IT in the future far exceeds that of the past. The IT function has to be re-structured, built up and given a new profile. The most important aspect of control is to sort out, prioritize and put focus into IT resource allocation, driving a few major projects very hard. Established technology policies have to be re-thought and new technologies and networks embraced. For some years maybe, IT expenditure grows in stepped amounts. The scale, importance and pace of all this turnaround activity requires the drive, experience and status of an executive level manager, perhaps director in title and reporting to a senior board member. In the turnaround period, the major concern of top management and perhaps the easiest way of evaluating performance is the difference in visibility of IT awareness and activity in the organization. Crucial to turning round the application and delivery of IT is investment in *management* education. Probably it is the first time that IT has been aggressively addressed by widespread management education in the firm.

The change strategies required in turnaround positions can be best understood by comparing like practices in the other quadrants. In support contexts, IT spending is low, the IT manager is likely to be very much a technical specialist, the organization only notices (evaluates) IT when something goes wrong and most managers are self-taught by experience or hobby on IT. In factory contexts, the expenditure on IT is likely to approximate average industry ratios, the IT executive is a strong departmental manager, performance audits are a valuable evaluation tool, and most information management education is technical in order to maintain high delivery performance. In strategic contexts, IT expenditure steadies after turnaround is achieved but grows at compound rates, the strategic importance of IT now requires the IT director to be on or near the board, evaluation of IT performance is more appropriately measured by the perceived impact on the business, and information management education by now is a normal and continuous process.

Finally, in complex organizations all four conditions can prevail. Thus it becomes important to recognize that the degree of change required and the appropriate change strategies will vary across business units. The same cautionary advice applies to use of the matrix in Table 9.3.

Sector management

In Chapters 2 and 3 it was suggested that there were differences in the potential, nature and management of IT according to *sector*. However the classification of sector was by information processing characteristic. Table 9.3 extrapolates these differences by suggesting the appropriate change strategies. This provides a complementary framework of analysis to the strategic management typology.

The delivery sector column perhaps demonstrates the greatest intensity of management response. Delivery sectors are those such as banking or airlines where IT has become the principal means of delivering or distributing the good or service, where computer-based transactions systems underpin business operations. The stimulus for strategic treatment of IT is that the sector infrastructure is IT–based and business threats and opportunities arise from how good individual firm IT infrastructure is and how well it is exploited. Without good infrastructure, the firm is exposed. IS strategy is an integral part of business and corporate strategy by definition and IT investment is continuous.

Table 9.3 Sector management typology

Management Sector		*Delivery*	*Dependent*	*Drive*	*Delayed*
Information management style	Planning linkage	Integral	Derived	IT-push	Default
	Organizational focus	Corporate	Business unit	Line	IT
	Control posture	Tight-loose	Loose-tight	Loose	Tight
	Technology	Architectural	Pragmatic	Enabling	*Ad hoc*
Change strategies	Strategic stimulus	Sector	Business	Technology	Nil
	Strategy mode	Infrastructure	Business-led	Opportunity-led	Reactive
	Organizational tendency	-led User	User	Specialist	Specialist
	IT direction	Board	SBU team	Line managers	IT manager
	IT investment	Continuous	Projects	Seed-corn	Cost conscious
	IT evaluation	Peers	Goals	Winners	Exception
	IT education	Pervasive	Management teams	Campaigns	Technical

A bank disclosed that 50 per cent of its capital expenditure recently had been on IT. The chief executive then declared that now this investment had been made, the challenge was to exploit it effectively. He was, of course, right. He was also wrong. Infrastructure in delivery sectors needs continuous renewal and enhancement.

Another bank in 1987 was concerned whether it could continue some of its operations because of the continued high levels of IT investment required. It felt it may have to either withdraw from some markets or seek strategic alliances. This was not faulty analysis of the funding question, but concern about the cost (profitability) structure – operational gearing not financial gearing. In other words, infrastructure is changing the economics of delivery sectors.

British Airways now measures its IT investment requirements in jumbo-jet equivalents. Renewal or enhancement of basic transaction systems often is a multi-million pound project. 'Everybody knows what a jumbo-jet is' and thus the scale of the infrastructure requirement can be better appreciated. The chairman of American Airlines confesses that he would prefer to own their reservation system than their fleet. This is an extreme, but strategic, view of the investment nature of IT infrastructure in delivery sectors.

Such is the scale, importance and interdependence of infrastructure in the delivery sector that the organizational arrangements for IT tend towards the specialist and central ends of the spectra. The board has to understand the strategic nature of IT and give guidance to, and verify assumptions about, the exploitation of technology. The most influential factor in performance evaluation is peer review (How do we compare in practice and benefits with our competitors?). Technology policies have to be architectural since misfit or exotic methods and standards are likely to limit connectivity, interfacing, development potential and efficiency. IT education needs to be pervasive since technology is at the core of the business.

Contrasts with the delivery sector are best seen in the investment, direction and evaluation rows. In dependent sectors where IS strategy is business-led, investment can be justified at the project level, direction must come from each business unit (plus corporately for corporate needs), and evaluation of IT can be based on whether it is supporting goal achievement. In drive sectors, where IS strategy is opportunity-led, seedcorn investment is needed to push initiatives, direction and drive comes from individual line managers, and evaluation of IT is influenced by whether any winning, competitive advantage or innovative applications have been generated. In delayed sectors, investment will be cost conscious and low in ratio terms, direction will be a function of how well the IT manager responds to requests, and evaluation will be on a management by exception basis.

Leadership model

An important row in the previous two tables was education. A research project by Earl *et al.* on information management education needs and practice discovered a recurring set of organizational dynamics once corporations recognized that IT was potentially a strategic resource. Figure 9.1 portrays these organizational dynamics in a stage model of the 'new age'.

Figure 9.1 suggests a prior stage where firms question or doubt the strategic importance of IT – the questionmark stage. When top management begins to realize that IT is important to the business and must be taken seriously, Earl *et al.* discerned a

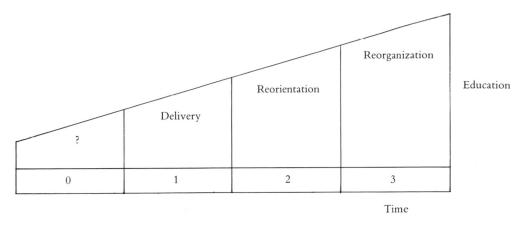

Figure 9.1 The new age.

set of actions that mark the onset of the 'delivery' stage. Typically there is a concern about the current performance of the IS/IT function and thus a top level desire that the basics are satisfied. This includes ensuring basic business systems are satisfactory, systems development projects are completed to specification and budget, IT operations are efficient, hardware and infrastructure policies are consistent, and users are satisfied with the service. Often this stage is initiated by replacing the DP manager (usual title) with an external recruit who has substantial professional computing experience as a DP manager, or with a computer manufacturer, and is perceived to have a good track record. The emphasis is on *delivery* and accordingly the new DP manager spends most of his time on matters internal to his department. His job is to restore credibility to the IT function and create confidence in user and top management that the function is supporting current needs and is run efficiently.

In the second stage, top management (or the director ultimately responsible for IT) changes the focus of attention. Now the priority is to exploit IT for competitive advantage and align IS investment with business strategy. It is in this *reorientation* stage that 'the business is to be put into computing'. The common reaction therefore is to appoint an IT executive or director over the DP manager. This new post is filled typically by an insider – a senior executive who has run a business or has been active at a senior level in business development, marketing or some such strategic activity. The incumbent has limited or long-ago experience of DP but is respected by general management and can formulate and prosecute strategies for change.

The stage two IT executive therefore spends – or seeks to spend – much of his time outside the function, trying to interpret business strategy, to raise user management awareness of new strategic opportunities afforded by IT, to create procedures and organizational devices which will ensure senior management commits to, and steers, IT, and to learn what other firms are doing. The chief executive may well promote IT but the substantive leadership and the initiation of actions to reorient the thinking about, and approach to, IT rest on the IT executive. Over time he tends to bring in strategy and technology consultants to advise, to recruit senior managers below him and to realize that top management, user management and some of his staff require education on IT in the new age.

The contrast between the delivery and reorientation phases is identified in Table 9.4. Eventually, the IT executive's task becomes simpler in one way and more complex in another. The company is largely reoriented *but* he has created high expectations, widespread awareness and a degree of local IT capability in different areas of the business. This marks the dawning of the *reorganization* phase.

In this third phase, the IT executive (by now IT director) is now concerned with managing the interfaces or relationships between this function and the rest of the organization. Some areas will be strategically dependent on IT whilst other business units look to IT more in a support role. Some departments will have significant IT capability, particularly with the advance of end-user computing. Indeed some functional and business executives will be driving IT and IS and themselves. At the same time, the IT executive may be thinking 'now I've done the reorientation job I should be moved back to a real business position, preferably very near the top'. Unfortunately, only he now understands the complexity of IT functional leadership and the ambiguities he has to ride. For here he is having to redesign the IT organization to relate to the different environments in the company. He has to know when to let user areas have more autonomy and when to intervene for the good of the whole. Issues of data management become more complex than ever before. And a situation has been created where user management want to direct and influence the use and, in some ways, the delivery of IT as well. Leadership of IT begins to pass from top management to line management. In stage three the IT director therefore is spending equal amounts of time inside the function, concerned with new delivery issues, and outside the function, liaising with line managers. His critical success factor is to build partnership between the IT department and the business lines and functions.

Table 9.4 Managing the new age

Phase/factor	Delivery 1	Reorientation 2	Reorganization 3
IT executive	External IT recruit	Inside business recruit	Same person
Management focus	Within IT/DP	Into the business	The interfaces
Priority concern	Credibility	Strategy	Partnership
Education needs	Skills	Awareness	Information management
CEO posture	Concerned	Visionary/champion	Support
Organizational leadership	The board	The function	The line
IT executive leadership	Reactive	Proactive	Interactive

There is one important 'misfit' in this pattern. Earl *et al.* encountered the occasional IT professional who lives through each of these stages and not only survives them but grows and advances with them. These 'misfits' anticipate each stage and lead their IT department accordingly.

The three stage model represents an evolutionary process of organizational *leadership* where top management exerts leadership in the delivery stage, the IT executive has to take over the leadership in the reorientation stage, and he begins to hand it over to line management in the reorganization stage. Thus as *leader* of the IT department, the IT manager is progressively reactive, proactive and interactive through the stages.

Crucial to this evolution is management education, as pictured in Figure 9.1. Its importance and extent increase with each stage. Education is necessary to cultivate, make and manage the change through the stages. In stage one it is sparse and mainly provided for DP personnel to improve their skills, techniques and delivery management.

In stage two education may comprise at least three forms. Top management is encouraged to go to executive briefings and similar events. User management may be provided with awareness courses on both the new technologies and the strategic opportunities and implications. Finally, the IT executive has to continually educate himself. He does this by frequent participation early on in IT manufacturers' events, attendance at an occasional course or conference, but largely by individual tuition. This is by three mechanisms: visiting other organizations; bringing in consultants; and eventually often building an ongoing relationship with one or two well-known experts who he meets from time to time – as one IT executive put it 'my guru'.

Education in the reorganization phase grows in importance. There is much more action-oriented and business- or function-specific education of business management. The IT staff are having to update themselves on the new IT age in technological, organizational and business terms. IT and IS may well be topics on the agendas of most management education and development activities in the company. In many ways, every manager by this stage is becoming an information manager.

The strategic management typology implies education is vital in the turnaround and strategic contexts. The sector management typology suggests education is important in different ways and intensities in all but the delayed sectors. The leadership model shows that investment in education increases with each stage. The next section therefore tackles management education and development in more detail.

MANAGEMENT EDUCATION AND DEVELOPMENT

Raising management's awareness and understanding of IT is frequently reported as a major issue by both IT-oriented studies and top management surveys. The conclusion is then swiftly drawn that more, better or higher level education is needed. It is difficult to argue against these exhortations. However the experience of information management education is more sobering. The following issues are typically raised by organizations who have embarked upon management education and development in this area:

1. We are not really sure of our needs.
2. Has anyone learnt how to educate senior managers on IT effectively?
3. How do we design education events which are relevant to our business?
4. How do you persuade top managers to give up time for education on IT?
5. Education and development of managers on IT seem to create more problems for, and unrealistic expectations of, the IT function.
6. Has any organization successfully introduced a programme to develop managers' IT capabilities over the longer term?

Given these doubts and anxieties, it is important to understand the rationale for management education and development on IT. Perhaps five major reasons stand out:

1. IT is capable of achieving strategic business impact, changing organizational functioning, improving business operations, or wasting large amounts of money. Therefore all levels of management must be aware of, and understand, this new era.
2. To exploit IT fully, substantial management, organizational and business change is required. Education is important in fostering awareness and understanding of change, facilitating acceptance of change, and implementing change effectively.
3. IT brings new possibilities, solutions and mechanisms. Therefore our skills and knowledge bases need updating.
4. IT is becoming pervasive in organizations and responsibility for some IT activities is being devolved to users and local units. Partnership between the specialist suppliers and the users is therefore necessary and is aided by joint education to build bridges and develop common understanding.
5. Capability in information management is beginning to distinguish successful from unsuccessful enterprises. Thus the development of all managers should include exposure to, and exploitation of, IT.

Education and development therefore become the warp and weft of building an organization's capability in IT and its management. Perhaps we now have more experience of education. Much of what follows is derived from the experiences of the Oxford Institute of Information Management in running educational programmes for large organizations.

Management education

Identifying information management education is a complex, often organization-specific, sometimes individual, matter. However a general inventory of needs can be proposed. For professionals and managers already in organizations (in-service education), four sets of requirements exist. As Figure 9.2 implies, these can be seen more as re-education programmes, namely the following:

1. Refocusing – the raising of executive management awareness and understanding of how important IT is for the business and exploring what needs to be managed differently.
2. Retooling – developing management or application skills and knowledge to follow up any new initiatives identified in refocusing.
3. Reskilling – educating and training the IT specialists on technology, management, and business skills for the IT era.
4. Reinforcing – building top management understanding, confidence and commitment to support the effects of the other re-education programmes.

All of these reasons for management education identified earlier were non-technical. Although it is still common to see and hear of 'educators' teaching senior managers how to program or give executives 'hands-on experience', these exercises are peripheral to the major concern. If senior managers want to use computers themselves, then they can be helped by proper tuition and support. If they do not want to, there is no reason why they should be forced into it. There are three more important responsibilities where re-education can help:

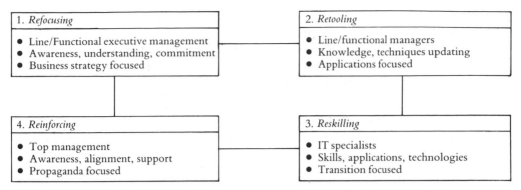

Figure 9.2 Information management re-education.

1. They need to know where and how IT can help *their* business performance, especially in gaining strategic advantage.
2. They need to know where they should be involved in managing IT activities and how in *their* organization.
3. They need to know as much as is necessary for *their* organization about information technology so that they can steer and approve IT policies.

In short, these three issues relate to the three levels of strategy addressed in this book: information systems, information management and information technology respectively. They form the agenda of refocusing programmes.

The knee-jerk reaction to these needs by many educational consultants and as many IT directors is to promote an educational programme for 'the board' or 'top management'. In the experience of the Oxford group, this is only half right. Certainly senior management is the place to start if these three areas are to be tackled sensibly – but *not* at the apex of the organization. The group's most successful refocusing programmes have been devised for executive management teams from divisional or SBU level, or sometimes at heads of functions level in centralized organizations. It is at this level that the competitive forces, product-market strategies and organizational capabilities are understood and 'felt'. Accordingly in a refocusing seminar a relevant, homogeneous, topical attack can be made on the strategic implications of IT, the strategic management of IT, and getting manageable segments of the organization behind it. This is the level at which to start in order to keep a business perspective and mobilize resources for change.

Refocusing therefore is most effective where it is organization-specific. Senior managers are only interested for the most part in *their* context and will be better stimulated to act if they can share with their own colleagues their concerns, visions and analyses and agree on a programme for action. Refocusing then is more effective if it addresses IT through tackling business, organizational and management questions; indeed the label 'refocusing' implies reassessing the enterprise in the IT era. We have found the motivation and interest highest when the management team feels it is threatened by some external innovation or an internal problem.

Thus as Figure 9.2 suggests, refocusing is concerned with enabling the management team to collectively improve its awareness of, understanding of, and commitment to

IT – but where the new focus is on business strategy. (The management team, of course, should include the IT executive.)

In this analysis, management teams become the generators of change. Reflecting on the Oxford experience, it has been noted elsewhere[1] that the three practical questions which refocusing events have to address are as follows:

1. Why is IT important and how important is it for our firm?
2. What strategic opportunities might we seek or gain from IT?
3. Given the answers to the above two questions, should we be managing IT differently?

These questions then give structure to a progressive process which can be looked at through the lenses of organizational development first articulated by Lewin.

The process behind question 1 is that of *unfreezing* current management attitudes and beliefs. The task is to open up new visions or horizons and to exploit current issues and discontents, the objective being to generate a healthy mix of interest and discomfort. The process behind the second question is *changing* managers' thinking, perhaps by discovering new emphases, threats or opportunities. The task is to develop the new visions and examine the discomforts, facilitating the group to embrace new goals, consider relevant strategies and adopt changed thinking. Finally, question 3 is about reassessing management practices to implement this new thinking – about *refreezing* again. The task here is to help the group agree what is required to put new ideas into action, provide realistic guidance, and forge common language and frameworks which will underpin further activity.

This organizational development perspective on refocusing is shown in Table 9.5. The last column suggests that the different frameworks for analysing IT and strategic advantage which were classified in Chapter 3 have a role here. The awareness class fits the unfreezing process, the opportunity class fits the changing stage, and the positioning class helps confirm ideas in the refreezing process.

Table 9.5 Refocusing: an organizational development perspective

Question	Development process	IT framework
IT importance	Unfreeze	Awareness
IT opportunities	Change	Opportunity
IT management	Freeze	Positioning

Retooling needs often are identified out of refocusing events and thus also tend to be organization-specific. Also the demands can be specialized and for a few managers only. Therefore retooling can be expensive in cost-volume terms. To ensure the value, there is no alternative but to find educators who really do know about, and have experience of, the specialist area. It is a mistake to believe that these different re-education requirements can be bought at a one-stop service establishment.

As Figure 9.2 indicates, retooling is concerned with equipping line and functional managers who become concerned to exploit or drive IT in specific or new areas. Some of the agenda may be imparting basic knowledge; often it is updating prior learning;

increasingly it is about understanding new techniques, applications and technologies. It is applications focused where the educators are not necessarily IT specialists but applications or business management experts.

> A manufacturing company commissioned a business school to provide programmes for its divisional management teams. In one of the programmes it became clear that IT was crucial in responding to strategic changes in that division's industry. A new set of retooling programmes was launched to update that division's management on the technology-induced changes in industry dynamics, to inform about specific technologies, to explain the rationale for, and motivate involvement in, a major IT application development, and to improve project management and implementation skills. Bids from specialist educators were sought for this initiative. Meanwhile in the company as a whole a set of retooling courses were made available in manufacturing systems and IT, an area identified in the refocusing events, and in IS strategy studies as starved of IT support. A specialist in manufacturing strategy was commissioned for this programme.

Reskilling is frequently overlooked. However, both refocusing and retooling tend to generate new demands on the IT function. Many IT specialists, though, have received their formal education in the DP era and have only been able to adapt to the new environment by *ad hoc* measures and accident. In Chapter 7, several new capability gaps were identified in IT departments. Education of line and functional managements only highlights them. They are both technological and non-technological. The Earl *et al.* study on education discovered that typically little technology education is provided for specialists; any other form is almost non-existent.

In theory, therefore, IT managers should ensure that they participate in refocusing and retooling events and discern the reskilling education their function requires. In general, as Figure 9.2 suggests, there are three needs: skills, applications and technologies. For example, once organizations embrace the new potentials of IT and adapt the organization of it, systems analysts, project leaders and systems managers need to be better educated in business and to improve their marketing, communication and social skills. Likewise if direction has turned towards a new applications area, applications knowledge is required. Most IT specialists learn about different business functions, applications and techniques when they have to and not before. Finally, IT specialists – like all specialists – need updating and continuous education on new technologies and methods in their profession. These three aspects of re-skilling are all required in making the transition from the DP era to the IT era.

Finally, there is *reinforcing* education. This is the top management requirement. Experience suggests that there are two opportune or appropriate times for these events. Either reinforcing comes after the other three initiatives or it is discovered to be necessary during and thus alongside refocusing. The aims are to develop and husband corporate support of IT and to build common understanding of the 'what, how and wherefore' between top management and executive management teams. So rather than start at this level, it seems preferable to use top management's scarce time to seek reinforcement of the new initiatives and engineer any support of, intervention in, or validation of strategies that have been worked out.

As Figure 9.2 implies, the spirit of reinforcing is propaganda. The events are political as much as rational, the objective being to 'get top management on your side' and to prod them to reinforce IT initiatives by their rhetoric as well as their actions.

Implicit in this prescription for re-education lie a number of factors critical for success. These should be made explicit.

1. Re-education should relate to action. Most managers favour active experimentation and concrete experience rather than reflective discourse and abstract connceptualization.[2] Thus linking refocusing to business strategy and designing follow-up actions through retooling, reskilling and reinforcing are important.
2. Re-education should be largely organization-specific. This helps satisfy the learning principle above and also is inevitable if re-education programmes are to address strategic threats and opportunities, deal with immediate management matters, lead to action, and recognize sector, timing and firm differences.
3. Different re-education needs should be addressed differently, by whichever educators are most relevant, and carefully designed to complement each other.
4. Re-education is valueless unless it is accompanied by, or relates to, other initiatives in the organization. Refocusing often generates an IS strategy study. Refocusing is often prompted by a change in organization structure. Retooling may need agreement to acquisition of new resources to follow. Strategy studies may require prior re-education.
5. Re-education should be continuous. If it were, it could be renamed education again! One reason why it is easy and acceptable to contrast the 'IT era' with the 'DP era' is that there is such an educational lag. On another dimension, the re-education model developed here implies classroom, formal mechanisms. It should be followed up by opportunity workshops, feasibility studies, systems prototyping and ongoing development programmes.
6. Re-education cannot be bought 'off the shelf'. Because it is largely organization-specific, the re-educators must invest in understanding the client and tailoring the programme. This involves understanding the business and its sector, meeting and acquainting with typical and participating managers, appreciating the unique and vital features of the organization, and being informed on the current state and heritage of the organization's IT and its management.
7. The IT director or senior IT management must be involved in setting up re-education programmes. These should help build partnership between the IT director, his function and the rest of the organization. He should vet, influence and take part in them – for if they fail, he will suffer by association or more directly!
8. It has been said by more than one company, that management education is 'counter-cultural'. It is always dangerous to override 'culture'. Thus it becomes important to work out how and when re-education programmes can succeed in each setting. In some cases the objective, of course, may be to promote cultural change; good intelligence about the organization is then essential and occasional conflicts may have to be tolerated or even designed.

The above eight imperatives suggest the ninth. Re-education can neither be done cheaply nor by amateurs. A well received programme will soon justify its cost in terms of multiplied benefits of understanding, commitment and involvement. Management education is a professional activity which *inter alia* requires experience, particularly in working with senior managers.

Management development

In Chapter 7, several capability gaps were identified where management development might provide a remedy. Unfortunately impediments commonly exist. First, management development is a long-term solution when short-term problems abound. Second, any one firm's management development programme can be subverted by the individuals' behaviour in supply-constrained labour markets. Then, many intended general managers resist the notion of experiencing IT activities. Finally, many exchange schemes between the IT function and line businesses become one-way movements – out of IT never to return!

However, not all these 'impediments' are as damaging as they sound. Furthermore, in some organizations (for example those in turnaround and strategic contexts or in delivery, dependent or drive sectors), 'the bullet has to be bitten'. Investment in information management capability is possibly more important than investment in the technology itself.

Table 9.6 Information management development domains

	User domain	Specialist domain
Doing domain	Hybrids	Professionals
Driving domain	Leaders	Impresarios

The management development challenge can be portrayed as in Table 9.6. The four classes of personnel represent the crucial human investment needs in the IT era.

'Hybrids' has become a contemporary description for people with strong technical skills and adequate business knowledge, or vice versa. The concept, for example, has been developed by Keen. In my classification, hybrids are people with technical skills able to work in user areas doing a line or functional job, but adept at developing and implementing IT application ideas. 'Leaders' are executives in user areas who can drive the exploitation of IT in their business and naturally champion, sponsor or support the ideas and experiments of the hybrids. 'Professionals' are the technicians on specialist career paths upon whom delivery of IT will often depend. They require all the experience of the traditional technologies and competence in the new ones. 'Impresarios' are the few executive level managers in the IT function whose task it is to either propel the organization into strategic consideration of IT or respond to user needs in a business-like manner or both. In large organizations, the IT director, many of the systems managers and the strategy manager are likely to have impresario characteristics.

The point of this classification is that the management development needs differ – and the nature of the impediments differs. For example, there has been much professional concern about hybrids because they may be seen as mavericks. Equally the importance of professionals has been backgrounded due to the promotion of 'strategic advantage' which tends to boost the profile of users and denigrate that of specialists. Yet management development programmes can be structured, with appropriate entry and exit points, to grow all four types.

Hybrids do need significant technical experience. Six months in a DP department is better than nothing, but not much better! The desired characteristics of a hybrid are described as follows:

1. Technological competence – a knowledge base which allows him to recognize an IT opportunity, scale its size and complexity, know what needs to be done, and perhaps prototype it.
2. Business confidence – experience and knowledge of the business area in which he is working, so that he can recognize an application opportunity, make the case for it, see how it fits into existing business operations and systems, and anticipate the implementation issues.
3. Organizational skills – understanding of the organization so that he knows who to call for support in the IT function, who should be enlisted in the user area, and when and how is the right time to initiate an idea; plus the social and political skills to make things happen and survive the ambiguities of his role.

This may seem like an impossible specification. However there may be trade-offs *except* that technological competence is an imperative. Technically ill-equipped hybrids cannot do, make too many mistakes, and get lost. Hybrids succeed by doing. It follows therefore that hybrids must receive some substantial training and experience in an IT department – two to three years minimum. They need a sound base which will propel them into action and carry them through, by updating, by doing, for some years. Many IT managers dislike the thought of losing technically competent people to users, given the scarcity of supply. However they become more alarmed when amateur hybrids make crucial mistakes or subvert technical policies because they lack good training. Perhaps, also, they should welcome the thought that properly trained hybrids become agents or ambassadors in the user areas and respect the IT function and maintain their connections.

Leaders only need adequate technical understanding. They cannot lead unless they know their business and have relevant organizational skills. The desired characteristics are described as follows:

1. Technological confidence – enough experience to be able to back the ideas or actions of a hybrid with confidence, help align investment in IT with the needs of his business, give direction to any IT activities in his business or functional unit, and work with senior IT executives.
2. Business competence – a knowledge and experience base of business and management so that he knows what is right in IT terms for his business, has seen what works (and does not) in businesses, and can construct IT visions for his business.
3. Organizational skills – be 'street wise' in organizational and political matters, as would be expected of any senior manager.

This too may seem a perfect ideal. However the specification stresses that for leaders IT can be an important matter, but only in its appropriate place. Their principal training and experience is in doing and running the business of the organization. Often they will have been 'fast-track' management trainees, having undergone experiential development in carefully selected jobs and situations. One of these placements therefore will be in the IT function – perhaps in a systems development role, often in a project manager or account executive position, occasionally as a tour of duty in a senior management job. In short, fast-track managers should spend a period in IT, for being groomed as a business leader in many sectors today needs secondment to IT, not a few days' 'induction' or total avoidance. At the same time, would-be leaders should grasp any opportunity to be involved in, manage or steer an IT project during their career progression.

Professionals need high competence in technology. Specialist departments do not survive without professional capability and firms in strategic contexts or delivery sectors soon value professionalism, if technological performance deteriorates. The desired characteristics are described as follows:

1. Technological expertise – a strong knowledge base and solid experience to be able to deliver applications reliably, assist in the formulation of sound technology policies, and cope with new technologies as they arrive.
2. Business awareness – enough appreciation of the organization's business to know how to make relevant technical choices and serve and work with users in specific application areas.
3. Organizational skills – where professionals are working in internal teams or interacting with users and their managers, the social skills which facilitate teamwork and partnership are essential.

This specification is clear. Technological competence is mandatory; other abilities are learnt and developed in anticipation of new assignments. It is thus important to remember that even in the age of devolution, competitive advantage, end-user computing and so on, career professionals are still required and are vital human assets of the business. For professionals, continuing education is essential in a rapidly changing technological environment. Most development is internal by experiencing different tasks in IT – not least to build up the mix of technology skills often noted in Chapter 7 to be lacking. However there is one external 'development' need which arises in the IT era: many IT professionals do not have a good 'feel' of their business, its people and operations. Given some experience 'in the field', they may start to remedy this deficiency and possibly suggest what, to them, seem obvious IT ideas whilst on secondment. Thus, some companies now ensure that all professionals spend, say, two or three days each year doing a different job in a line of functional department.

Impresarios are more difficult to specify, since they can be required at three levels of the IT department. At the first or second level below the IT director, they are often brought into the IT function from user areas for their business knowledge and organizational skills. For example, in the reorganization stage of the leadership model in Figure 9.1, account executive positions may be created requiring impresarios with a business leaning and good social skills. In the reorientation phase an IT director, systems manager, or strategy manager may be appointed from the senior ranks of a line business. In contrast, in strategic contexts within a delivery sector, the IT director must be strong on technology, intuitively sound in business, and effective in top management relationships. Thus the impresario role can differ in the balance amongst the three core abilities, but to be effective will require each of them. Thus the impresario needs the following qualities:

1. Technological ability to be credible and effective in the IT department.
2. Business ability to connect the IT department to business needs and direction.
3. Organizational ability to handle the complex relationships involved.

Given the different balances that may be required, some impresarios must have spent most of their managerial careers in user areas, whilst all impresarios will benefit from some experience out of IT. In other words, senior management positions in IT should not be seen as exclusively specialist in nature or the exclusive preserve of specialists.

These four types can partly share a common management development programme. For example, fast-track managers can spend some of their formative development period in the IT department. If they then become enthusiasts, they can be given a hybrid posting for a time. Eventually some of them could return as impresarios. Equally a frustrated professional could be posted to be a hybrid in an application area with which he is familiar. Some of these have gone on to become leaders. A leader could become an impresario in situations where the IT department itself needs turning round. Thus there are five management development lessons to be learnt here:

1. There is some flexibility available, with opportunities for rotation alongside set career paths.
2. Loss of a technologist 'to the business' can be a gain to the organization as a whole and eventually to the IT function.
3. Business managers, and their career planners, should see the IT department as a natural posting.
4. IT activities need to be incorporated into management development programmes and not treated as specialist islands or *culs-de-sac*.
5. Individual managers may themselves spot, cultivate or seize development opportunities in supplying or using IT.

Following the fifth lesson will go a long way towards 'normalizing' information management – an objective set in Chapter 1.

ORGANIZATIONAL TRANSFORMATION

The concept of normalizing information management, or treating information resources like other principal resources, in the formal and informal management processes of organizations, helped set the scene in Chapter 1. In subsequent chapters, we have seen how IT has been demonstrated to be potentially a strategic resource. IT applications cannot only support business strategies but also create strategic opportunities and options. Thus a major concern of this book has been how to strategically manage IT.

Chapters 3 to 6 were concerned with strategy formulation. This was seen to be a complex matter but too important to be left to the specialists. IS strategy was also seen to be much concerned with technological innovation. Chapter 7 dealt with the organization of IT activities. This was seen to be a complex matter but no longer the sole preserve of specialists. Indeed technological devolution was seen to be a key. Chapter 8 dealt with management control of IT activities. This was seen to be a complex matter and as much the responsibility of users as specialists. Treating IT as investment rather than expense underpinned this chapter, but funding, appraising, taking responsibility for, and evaluating it was seen to need widespread management involvement. Thus a characteristic of information management in the IT era is that IT is an organization-wide concern; an organization gets what it deserves.

Integrating IT and the organization

The study by Feeny *et al.* of the information systems function in complex organizations was reported in Chapter 7. The researchers noted that in organizations exploiting IT effectively, there was a high degree of integration between the specialist IT units and the rest of the organization. This would be predicted by the Lawrence and Lorsch theory of organizational design. It is perhaps in this sense that an organization gets what it deserves from IT.

The Feeny *et al.* study discovered eight characteristics which distinguished organizations with high integration from those with low integration. All these factors were present where integration was high; none was present where integration was low. They were:

1. Business unit management perceived that future exploitation of IT was of strategic importance.
2. An IT executive was established as part of the executive team or board for the business concerned.
3. There was ongoing education for business unit management in IT capability.
4. There was a top-down planning process for linking IS strategy to business needs.
5. The business mandate for IT was 'centrally planned plus some elements of leading edge' (to borrow from Parsons).
6. Some IT development resource was positioned within the business unit.
7. The introduction of, or experimentation with, new technologies took place at business unit level under business unit control.
8. There was a cost centre rather than profit centre orientation in controlling IT activities, with relatively unsophisticated chargeout procedures.

These factors come as no surprise to the reader, for they are consistent with messages throughout this book. However, they are directions quite uncharacteristic of the DP era and suggest that what is required to succeed in the IT era is an organizational transformation. The next and final subsection builds on these points and the collective research[3] underpinning this book to suggest eight maxims for managing this transformation.

Management maxims for the IT era

The following maxims codify management trends in organizations leading in the strategic exploitation of IT. Each maxim is briefly developed to show the implications for planning, organizing and controlling IT and information resources.

Encourage line management to take the lead
Innovation studies have shown that it is line managers who mostly have the ideas for

strategic use of IT and drive the applications. Equally, business unit management has been seen to be central to top-down IS strategy formulations. In business units with high integration between IT and the business, the IT executive is on the board working closely with the executive management team. Moreover, the specialist IT function is frequently strong on delivery but weak on direction. Finally, line managers are closer to competitive forces and perceive technological threats and opportunities more readily than IT functional managers or corporate management.

IT planning must therefore incorporate top-down methods within line units and the leaders of the line must drive and promote IT within a centrally planned (plus some leading edge) mandate. Organizationally, IT steering committees are obvious vehicles for line management leadership, but brightsparks and entrepreneurs (hybrids and leaders) must be able to prosper. In controlling IT activities, the aim is for line managers to argue the case for IT projects and thereby become the advocates in funding disputes. Line managers should take the lead in IT.

Uncouple strategic IT from IT strategy

Innovative, competitive advantage applications of IT come largely from inside-out processes of IS strategy formulation. Indeed most innovation avoids the rigours of formal planning and control. Conversely, use of IT to support rather than create strategic advantage is helped by top-down and bottom-up processes of IS strategy formulation. Thus methods for supporting business strategy by IT should be differentiated from the process of creating competitive advantage from IT.

Planning IS therefore clearly requires the multiple methodologies advocated in Chapter 4. Planning IT, discussed in Chapter 5, needs to have a goal of producing an architecture which not only fits identified business needs but facilitates use of, and experimentation with, technology. Organizationally, strategic IT can be enabled by introducing new technologies into business units and user hands. Control mechanisms accordingly should allow funding of technological experiments and initiation without the heavier justification for IS strategy-led projects or the deterrent accountability of chargeout. All these prescriptions seek to uncouple strategic IT from IT strategy.

Invest and build on IT infrastructure

Infrastructure is crucial in delivery sectors. A combination of hard and soft infrastructure is required to create the opportunity environment in drive sectors. Many competitive advantage IT applications evolve out of existing systems and infrastructure.

Thus in planning IT, architecture frameworks are required to balance control with flexibility in infrastructure development. In planning IS, bottom-up methods are valuable in examining the strategic potential of systems already in place. In organizing IT, infrastructure is the professional concern of the specialists and reserved powers will be needed at corporate and functional levels. In controlling IT activities, the funding of infrastructure can be a problem. Therefore, to move beyond 'act of faith' infrastructure investments, project appraisal, IS strategy formulation and IT strategy formulation must be interlocked. Successful enterprises invest in infrastructure and build on it.

Devolve IT activities to users where possible

Leadership of IT is already passing to line managers. Development of new technology applications seems more effective if delegated to users in the early stages of adoption. A substantially devolved set of activities is typical in turnaround and strategic contexts. Innovative application of IT is facilitated by high user involvement (and close customer involvement). Technologies are getting closer to end-users and becoming less mystifying.

The organizational policy question therefore is always 'why shouldn't IT activities be devolved to users?'. There may be very good reasons for limiting this movement – integration of systems, single stream businesses, core transaction systems protection, immature users etc. However devolution of direction, and of some development, is difficult to resist if high integration between IT and the business is the goal. In planning IS therefore it becomes equally important to ensure that corporate IS strategies are formulated – to address dependencies and look for synergies. In planning IT, architecture decisions become reserved powers for the IT function. The most important control message is that mechanisms should not conflict with the organizational control approach at large, but nevertheless err in favour of user responsibility and authority.

Build partnership between the IT function and users

Implicit in the previous maxim was devolution of some direction and development to users, but retention of much delivery in the IT function. The integration arguments of the previous sections are based on *both* specialists and users having responsibilities in IT. The reorganization stage of the leadership model in Figure 9.1 emphasizes the importance of relationships and interfaces between IT and the business. Partnership therefore seems crucial.

In Chapter 4 it was noted that major benefits of IS strategy formulation were improved specialist-user relationships and better understanding of the business and organization by IT professionals. Thus IS strategic planning is one way of forging partnership – indeed it needs it. Organizationally the IT function has to take explicit steps towards partnership. Typical moves include appointing account executives in the IT department, treating users as customers, and using marketing concepts to get close to them. Management control of IT activities for partnership involves sharing responsibility, much as implied in the profit centre or hybrid centre approach prescribed for turnaround or strategic contexts, decentralized organizations and stages three or four of technology assimilation.

Create a hi-tech culture

Gaining competitive advantage from IT has been seen to be an innovation problem. Patterns of success on this dimension have included presence of project champions, continuous and incremental application advancement, bridging expertise and experience gaps, avoiding mechanistic controls, and fostering risk and experimentation. These are all features of companies who successfully manage strategic change and hi-tech environments, as reported by Quinn, and Maidique and Hayes respectively. If a business is partially dependent on IT or is making a business out of information, such success factors seem doubly relevant.

So what can be learnt from hi-tech cultures? Planning of IS and IT must be 'hands-on' by senior management. It must also encourage continuous exploitation of IT and cope with continuous change and learning. It cannot be once-off. A hi-tech organization will develop, cultivate and encourage 'hybrids' and 'leaders' (or fanatics and entrepreneurs to quote Quinn). Management control procedures must not drive out risk and experimentation; resisting rigorous project appraisal and full chargeout for all IT developments is one key here.

Adopt loose-tight management

Consistent with a hi-tech culture are some of the lessons learnt in earlier chapters. 'Letting go some' from the formal planning, organizational and control approaches of the DP era is a clear message. In IT development projects, encourage prototyping to discover the detailed needs and unanticipated benefits behind the directional pointers suggested by strategy studies. Then appraise the project formally, but on a multi-dimensional or situational basis. Then use a tighter approach in post-implementation reviews. Devolve IT activities to users where possible, but invest in partnership and insist on reserved powers. Encourage inside-out approaches for strategic IT but condition the actors first by top-down and bottom-up methods *and* ensure new strategic IT applications are subsequently integrated into business strategies and their implementation.

It was Peters and Waterman who popularized the notion of tight-loose balances in management. In pursuing organizational transformation for IT, it seems that for some time at least, the emphasis should be on 'loose before tight'.

Tackle organizational development now

All of the above maxims have one thing in common. They cannot be achieved without substantial investment in management education and development. This is why these two topics have been central to the last chapter on strategies for change. A number of leading organizations are grasping this challenge by organizing tailor-made education programmes, by building in IT experience as part of career development plans, by experimenting with job rotation schemes between the IT function and line activities, and so on. Indeed, ongoing management education was one of the factors distinguishing high integration and low integration organizations.

Many of these leaders in the field are also discovering the impediments listed earlier in the chapter. However, the need is so great in companies dependent on IT that the price of education and development initiatives has to be paid – whether it is a market price, an opportunity cost, or a departmental loss. Perhaps this is indicative of an investment approach to IT. Others suggest that the organizational development problem will diminish when the next generation of managers emerges. For many organizations, however, the problem has to be tackled today – for the future is now.

The last clause was perhaps the only real exhortation or piece of evangelism in the book. It might be excused on the following grounds. To make the transition from the DP era to the IT era requires organizational transformation. However, organizations, in many senses, are only a collective of individuals.

A few IT directors, chief executives and line managers have been the heroes pioneering the management of IT for strategic advantage. The purpose of this book has been to build on their experiences and experiments in order to encourage and guide the information managers of today and tomorrow.

NOTES AND REFERENCES

1. See Earl M. J., 'IT and strategic advantage – a framework of frameworks', in Earl M. J. (ed.), *Information Management: The Strategic Dimension*. Oxford University Press, 1988.
2. See Kolb D. A., *Experiential Learning: Experience as the Source of Learning and Development*, Prentice Hall, Englewood Cliffs, 1984.
3. The research and education done at the Oxford Institute of Information Management.

FURTHER READING

Earl M. J., Feeny D. F., Hirschheim R. A. and Lockett M., 'Information technology executives' key education and development needs: a field study, Oxford Institute of Information Management research and discussion paper (RDP 86/10), Templeton College, Oxford, 1986.

Feeny D. F., Edwards B. and Earl M. J., 'Complex organisations and the information systems function – a research study', Oxford Institute of Information Management research and discussion paper (RDP 87/7), Templeton College, Oxford, 1987.

Keen P. G. W., *Competing in Time: Using Telecommunications for Competitive Advantage*, Ballinger, 1986.

Lawrence P. R. and Lorsch J. W., *Organisation and Environment: Managing Integration and Differentiation*, Boston Division of Research, Harvard Graduate School of Business Administration, 1967.

Lewin K., *Field Theory in Social Science: Selected Theoretical Papers*, Harper and Row, 1951.

Maidique M. A. and Hayes R. H., 'The art of high technology management, *Sloan Management Review*, Fall 1984.

McFarlan F. W. and McKenney J. L., *Corporate Information Systems Management: The Issues Facing Senior Executives*, Dow Jones Irwin, 1983.

Parsons G., 'Fitting information systems technology to the corporate needs: The linking strategy', Harvard Business School teaching note (9–183–176), 1985.

Peters T. J. and Waterman R. H., Jr., *In Search of Excellencee*, Harper and Row, 1982.

Quinn J. B., *Strategies for Change: Logical Incrementalism*, Dow Jones Irwin, 1980.

INDEX

215